FLIGHT MOST SECRET

Flight Most Secret

Air Missions for SOE and SIS

Gibb McCall

WILLIAM KIMBER · LONDON

First published in 1981 by
WILLIAM KIMBER & CO. LIMITED
Godolphin House, 22a Queen Anne's Gate,
London, SW1H 9AE

© Gibb McCall, 1981
ISBN 0-7183-0038-6

Photoset by Robcroft Ltd, London
and printed and bound in Great Britain by
The Garden City Press Limited
Letchworth, Hertfordshire SG6 1JS

Dedicated to the Men
Who Died in N-for-Nan
and
to others like them

All we have of freedom,
all we use or know—
This our fathers bought for us,
long and long ago.
RUDYARD KIPLING

Contents

Contents

List of Illustrations

Author's Note

Three men of a secret RAF squadron died when World War II was all but over as a result of two decisions made in Whitehall and the White House. One was strategic and perhaps accidental; the other tactical and deliberate.

It has been said that high strategy and low tactics go hand in hand. Never has this been more aptly illustrated than by the methods of implementing the war aims of the Allies as laid down after the Casablanca Conference of 1943.

President Roosevelt said then, almost as an afterthought, that the Allies would accept nothing less than Unconditional Surrender. Winston Churchill was astounded, but once the words were out there could be no turning back.

This clarion cry had the effect of boosting civilian morale at home and in the oppressed countries, but it horrified many senior Allied commanders. They realised that this determination to give no quarter would take the fight deep into Germany and prolong the war long after it could have been ended.

It could be argued with the long view of hindsight that this policy was a mistake, costly in lives and resources. Conceived at a time when fear and hatred of Nazism was at a height, Unconditional Surrender was a condition which Germany could never willingly accept.

Peace, yes. But not peace at any price. The ordinary German could be just as stiff upper lipped as the British; just as gung-ho as the Americans. They, too, would fight on the beaches, in the fields and in the streets.

Casablanca destroyed the last hope of bringing about the downfall of Hitler and his cronies by a negotiated political solution to end the war.

Consequently, by the late summer of 1944 it was apparent that if the Germans were to be forced to sue for peace-without-strings the conventional armies of the West would be forced to invade Germany. The Soviet juggernaut was already sweeping down from the steppes, intent on avenging the millions of dead in unmarked graves.

It was Total War, and to fight it the Allies would have to infiltrate more intelligence agents and saboteurs behind the enemy lines.

The Americans were ready and eager to get on with the job; the British less so. They were weary of war, but as the senior partners in matters of Intelligence they could not stand idly by while the 'upstart' Americans built up an independent spy network in what was traditionally their domain. And so the decision was taken to go.

The strategy of Casablanca dictated the tactics which were to destroy a tiny cog of the war machine: an obscure flight of light bombers which had never dropped a bomb in anger, but whose function had an importance far in excess of their numbers.

This is not an official history either of the special duties squadrons or of the agents they ferried to and from those missions in Germany and Nazi-dominated Europe.

But it is, perhaps, a page missing from the many good, bad and indifferent accounts of the secret war against Hitler; a story compiled from recently-declassified records, from unpublished files secreted in Foreign Office archives, from the recollections of a few aircrew survivors, and from the still sharply-remembered grief of the families of the dead who never really knew at the time just how important a contribution one relatively unknown unit of the RAF was making towards eventual victory.

In particular, it is a belated tribute to the men who died in the aircraft N-for-Nan, and to others like them who for a brief moment in history formed the tragic, ill-starred 'A' Flight of No 161 (Special Duties) Squadron – the Most Secret Flight of Hudsons.

Acknowledgements

More than a hundred people helped with the work involved in the research for this book, and for their efforts I thank them all.

There are others without whose help it could not have been started, like the RAF officers and their relatives who lived through the events and were unstinting of their time and experience.

In particular, Hugh Verity, the pick-up pilot whose help and personal account of Lysander operations are described in his book *We landed by moonlight*; Professor M.R.D. Foot for advice and the wealth of relevant material in his official history of the *SOE in France*; Len Ratcliff, the last of No 161 Squadron's wartime commanding officers; Syd Firth, the former Station Engineering Officer at the secret Tempsford air base; Lysander pilot Sir Robin Hooper, the former British Ambassador to Greece; Monsieur Gerard Livry-Level, the son of a French hero.

Others whose assistance was invaluable include the late Airey Neave, for encouragement and information about the escape lines; former tail-gunner J.F.Q. Brough, who used such a route to get home; the SOE agent Francis Cammaerts, now the Principal of Rolle College, Exmouth, who luckily did not need to.

For documents, letters, photographs and other papers from official sources, I am indebted to: Colonel E.G. Boxshall, of the Foreign Office; Colonel K. de Wulf, Military Attaché at the Belgian Embassy in London; F.F. Lambert, of the Public Records Office at Kew, who guided me through the labyrinth of recently declassified secret reports.

To Luxembourg I send my thanks to the villagers of Maulesmühle and Hupperdange, in particular to Madame Marguerite Daman-Uilbert; Pierre Eicher, the Principal Post Inspector at Clervaux; Michel Glod, the Communal Receiver there.

I must pay a special tribute to my unpaid interpreter, Christiane Martinez, of the Luxembourg Tourist Office, and to my patient translators of documents, Irena Jankowsky (German), Ann Jones, Malcolm Laycock and Christine Williams (French and Belgian).

And then there was Paula Wride, a constant source of wonder who made this book possible just by being there to soothe a fevered brow, calm a raging temper, and insist it would all come out right in the end.

Twenty-five Years After

They had died together on the first day of spring, entombed in a man-made fireball which fell out of a stormy, moonlit sky into a wooded hillside of the Ardennes.

Now, in a clearing marked by a crop of young trees, the crumpled wreckage of their aircraft lies there still as an official memorial, the path of its final, destructive flight marked by those trees much younger than the rest of the forest, trees which had started growing only after the scorched earth had recovered from the impact.

Now the forest is creeping back, gradually removing the scar made by man and his machine.

It is a beautiful summer day and the air on the hillside is heady with the fragrance of pine. A cool breeze, knowing no frontiers, blows in gently from Germany, across the crumbling emplacements, now overgrown with vine and scrub, of what once had been the impregnable Siegfried Line, ten miles to the east across the River Oûr.

For the small crowd gathered in the forest on this Saturday afternoon in the August of 1970 it is a time of remembrance. For the children among them it is a time to keep quiet, although they are not quite sure why.

But with the sensitivity rarely attributed by the old to the very young they speak only in whispers, awed by the sense of occasion.

The prayers for the dead have already been said by Monseigneur Jules Jost, the Colonel-Chaplain of the tiny Army of Luxembourg, and by his British counterpart, the Reverend David Miller. A sigh goes through the crowd as they murmur their amens, and there is a movement of shifting feet and shoulders as they wait expectantly for the first wreath to be laid on the six headstones grouped next to the grotesquely-twisted wreckage.

The aircraft is, or was, a Hudson light bomber, registration number FK 803, with the squadron code-sign N-for-Nan. It had flown eighty successful operational sorties over Germany and Occupied Europe during World War II, dropping agents and supplies by parachute, and enabling contact to be made with agents in the field by air-to-ground telephone. Four of these sorties had been daring pick-up operations in which the aircraft had actually been landed in enemy territory, virtually under the noses of the unsuspecting Germans.

N-for-Nan was, in fact, the aircraft which carried out the penultimate pick-up operation of the war by the RAF.

A Mark IIIA of the type manufactured by the American Lockheed Company of Burbank, California, it was among the last batch of eighty-three acquired by the RAF under the Lend-Lease scheme. Its life-span on active service was just seventeen months.

For much of that time it was flown by Terence Helfer, who took it out on one of his first operations when he joined the squadron whose activities even now are cloaked in secrecy. He was then twenty-three years old.

There were two other men on that early flight:

Air gunner Forrest Thompson, aged twenty-six, a cheerful New Zealander known as Tommy to his friends, who had crossed the world for the express purpose of killing Germans; and

Wireless operator Ray Escreet, then just twenty-one, who came from a small town in East Yorkshire and stuck pins into a wall map to keep score of his dangerous missions.

Five months later a navigator joined the squadron to make up the crew: Harry Johnson, aged thirty, a quietly-spoken scoutmaster from County Durham who hated killing in all its forms.

Their first successful operation together as a team was in N-for-Nan.

And all four were together on the last take-off made by the same aircraft from a top secret base in Bedfordshire. A few hours later the Hudson was ripped apart by machine-gun fire and plunged in flames into the forest above the village of Maulesmühle.

They were four men from widely different walks of life: an articled clerk in an accountant's office, a sheep farmer, a chemist, and a wholesaler of fruit and vegetables. Four men thrown together by the haphazard misfortunes of war, their destinies linked by an intricate piece of machinery which was to bring them safely back from all but their last mission.

The bodies of three of them lie in the shadow of the wreckage of N-for-Nan, buried side by side with the three secret agents who died with them.

The men from the village look uncomfortable in their dark suits; it had been a long walk uphill through the forest of Be'schent-Maulesmühle and their Sunday best had not been intended for such exertions under the hot August sun. Their womenfolk are fresh and cool in their bright, cotton print dresses and they give an almost festive air to what has become a pilgrimage to allow the villagers to pay homage to men they never knew.

They are by proxy wives and mothers, the fathers, the brothers, the sisters and all the loved ones of the men who lie buried here in graves marked by the aircraft which had carried them to their deaths.

Among the sprinkling of uniforms around the graveside there is the occasional glimpse of Royal Air Force blue, with bemedalled tunics matching the ribbons pinned above the left breast pockets of civilian suits.

The men in uniform had fought what has been described as a 'clean' war. The middle-aged civilians had been part of that 'dirty' war fought tooth and claw by the underground Resistance forces of Occupied Europe.

They had come together briefly at this graveside as a tribute to the fallen, and to give thanks that they themselves had lived to see the victory for which the others had died.

The ceremony had started earlier that day some three miles away at the parish church of Clervaux, a mediaeval town dominated by a feudal castle which had survived the ravages of pillage, time and weather since the twelfth century, only to be partly destroyed in the twentieth by the efforts of panzers and Allied armour during the so-called Battle of the Bulge.

After the *Clairon de la Résistance* had been sounded by bugler Johnny Schmidt, the weekend shopping crowds had been entertained by martial music played by the band of the 3rd Carabiniers, the Prince of Wales Dragoon Guards, flown in from their base which, with some irony, was in Germany. The selected guests had then left for a reception at the old château before leaving in a fleet of cars for Maulesmühle.

Among the dignitaries are Pierre Gregoire, President of the Luxembourg Chamber of Deputies; Count Selis de Longchamps, the Belgian Ambassador; Eugene Kossrov, the Soviet Ambassador. The British representative is a *chargé d'affaires* from the Luxembourg Embassy, and for France there is a counsellor to their own Ambassador.

They had left the cars in the village and set out on foot, leading a procession from the inn near the old railway station, along a mile of forest paths, winding up the hillside to a clearing near the top where the file had unwound to form an uncertain semi-circle around the wreckage.

The RAF officers and British civilians among them had flown the previous day into Findel Airport on the outskirts of the city of

Luxembourg. This time it had been in the comfort of a modern jet. And by day. Before, they had flown over that same countryside of wooded hills and valleys with only the light of the full moon for them to pick out signposts like ancient rock formations, distinctive châteaux and the silvery threads of the Moselle and its tributaries.

The two small boys serving at the makeshift altar twist awkwardly in their tight new suits. It is time for the speeches; the first by Pierre Werner, the Minister of State representing Her Royal Highness, the Grand Duchess Charlotte of Luxembourg. After the minister there is a hero of the Resistance, Major-General Albert Guérisse, a Belgian Army doctor who had organised the famous 'Pat' O'Leary escape and evasion line.

His network of 'safe' houses linked by escort couriers had taken six hundred people to safety in one year alone, most of them Allied airmen who had been shot down. For this, Guérisse had accumulated a total of thirty-two decorations, including the George Cross, and the scars of two years in Dachau and other concentration camps.

Never a man to waste words unnecessarily, he brings his address quickly to an end, and another wreath is laid with reverence by the commemorative headstone on which there is an inscription carved in English:

At this spot a British aircraft returning from a secret mission was shot down in flames by the Luftwaffe on March 21, 1945.

The French inscription is more specific, and reveals that the RAF plane had been brought down by an enemy aircraft. This contradicts contemporary newspaper accounts which reported that flak from German anti-aircraft batteries had set the Hudson on fire.

Tragically, there is a possibility that the men were victims of an American interceptor pilot who made a simple error of identification.

The villagers know the story by heart. The secret mission had been planned with the intention of parachuting three Belgian saboteurs into Nazi Germany. But it had been aborted over the industrial town of Erfurt because of bad weather, and the aircraft had been on the way back to home and safety when disaster struck in a burst of machine-gun fire.

The three Belgians, Lieutenant Guy Corbisier, from Antwerp; Lieutenant Léon de Winter, from Etterbeek; and Lieutenant Jean Morel, from Brussels, were the last Belgian agents to die in World War II.

They, too, are buried where they fell, their headstones facing those of the RAF officers, cradled between the bent and broken propellers of the twin-engine Hudson.

As the ceremony comes to an end, Monseigneur Jost hesitates, then makes the sign of the Cross. He turns, carefully picking his way past shards of jagged metal, and leads the way back down the forest path. Soon, the last voice dies away leaving only the sounds of the forest in that hauntingly lovely yet cruel scene.

The fact that the ceremony had been held at all is a tribute to the stubborn pride of the villagers of Maulesmühle. When a sort of peace came again to Europe, the civilians took over from the military to tidy things up. Part of the debris littering official records was the wreckage of a bomber and the bodies of the men who had died in it.

The Commonwealth War Graves Commission decided to have the bodies exhumed and removed to an official military cemetery at Hotton in Belgium. The villagers would have none of it. The elders conferred, then informed the young man from the Commission: 'These young men died for us, and now we must care for them.'

The authorities, with a flash of rare perception, respected their wishes and left well alone. The relatives were contacted and they, too, gave their permission for the bodies to remain where they had fallen.

As a compromise the names of the dead airmen were put on a special memorial tablet in the cemetery at Hotton, with a reference that the bodies were actually buried in an 'isolated' grave near Maulesmühle.

There they have remained, the six violent deaths marked every year by fresh wreaths and poppies to show the villagers have not forgotten.

One man will never forget. When the Hudson N-for-Nan took off from England on that night in 1945 for what was to be its last flight, there had been *seven* men on board – the three Belgian agents and a crew of four.

*

About 0045 hours, 21 March 1945: There was a blinding flash then suddenly it was quiet except for the sound of the wind in his ears as he came tumbling out of the sky, one hand groping for the metal D-ring of the ripcord, moving automatically with the reflex instinct of the need to survive. It was bitterly cold yet his hands and face burned with the intensity of the flames he had just escaped.

He turned slowly as he fell. How far to go? A falling body drops at . . . how many feet was it per second? And as he fell through the night air he knew he could not have long to live, and he wondered what had happened to the others.

There was a sharp crack above his head as his parachute snapped open, and as he drifted downwards he twisted in his still smouldering harness, searching vainly for a glimpse of the aircraft which only a few seconds ago – seconds lasting an eternity – had seemed so solid and safe.

But there was nothing. Just blackness. He was still looking when the ground came up and hit him . . .

. . . The night was becoming the new day and an RAF corporal checked his watch. They would not be coming back now. From the air the headquarters building looked like any of the other farmhouses scattered across the Bedfordshire countryside. But this particular farmhouse was a camouflage for the hub of clandestine operations reaching far out into Germany and all of what had once been the Nazi-occupied countries of Europe. The base itself was to be described later in a Government documentary film as 'one of the biggest secrets of the war'.

The corporal looked out for a last time at the brightening dawn, then turned to open the log book marked 'No 161 Squadron' and in red ink alongside the entry for the Hudson N-for-Nan he wrote: 'Failed to return – reported missing.'

There were two more entries to be made that morning, also in red ink, and a tired wing commander known as 'Ratty' to his men carefully prepared the text of a telegram. Copies would soon go out to the relatives of twelve men he had watched taking off in his squadron's Hudsons only a few hours earlier.

Only one of them was to come back from what was the bloodiest night in the Hudson Flight's brief but vital existence.

The war ended just six weeks later. Then came the peace and what was left of the squadron was disbanded. Its records were locked away in Air Ministry files marked 'MOST SECRET' and they were not to be seen for another generation.

It was as if the squadron had never existed.

PART ONE

The Rising of a Moon Squadron

Yon rising moon that looks for us again—
How oft hereafter will she wax and wane.
from *Rubaiyat* of Omar Khayyam

1

The Lockheed Hudsons were late arrivals to undercover work, although no strangers to battle. Built at Burbank in California, the early models were supplied to Coastal Command and were in action from the very beginning of hostilities. On 4 September 1939, a Hudson of No 224 Squadron became the first RAF aircraft to engage the Luftwaffe. The war was then less than twenty-four hours old.

A few weeks later a Hudson of No 220 Squadron became the first Coastal Command aircraft to score a 'kill' by destroying a clumsy Dornier flying boat over the North Sea.

In these, the early days of Hudson operations, this twin-engine light bomber was used primarily for maritime reconnaissance patrols, and for what might be described as an 'attacking-defensive' role. They protected coastal shipping and made regular forays against enemy convoys and minelayers.

With a top speed of nearly 250 mph and a ceiling of 25,000 feet, they were sturdy workhorses well able to take care of themselves against anything but the most advanced fighters the Luftwaffe had at that time.

During the first year of the war the ratio of losses to sorties was lighter than any other type of aircraft flying operationally with the RAF. But by the middle of 1942, improved German defences began taking their toll. At the same time, Flying Fortresses, Liberators and the deadly Lancasters began rolling off the production lines, all of them with ranges far in excess of the Mark I Hudson's flying distance of 1,700 miles. Several of the Coastal Command squadrons converted to the newer aircraft and the Hudsons were dispersed, some to the Middle East for operations over the Mediterranean, and others to a U-boat hunter-killer role and Air-Sea rescue work.

It seemed that the day of the Hudson in the north and west European theatre was to all intents and purposes over. But its real work was yet to come.

It was not until February in 1943 that the full potential of this remarkably versatile aircraft was realised, when a man who was to become an heroic legend in RAF folklore landed a Hudson in a small field in France, dropped off five secret agents, and took off safely ten minutes later with vital reports prepared by the French Resistance.

The Hudson airbus service for spies was about to go into business.

The groundwork had been laid back in 1940 when Winston Churchill became Prime Minister. Within days of taking office he called together his Chiefs of Staff and asked them bluntly if it were possible for Britain to continue the fight alone.

The reply came in a memorandum on 27 May: superiority in the air was to be the aim; Germany could only be put on the defensive by an unrelenting pounding of her industrial cities.

In the opinion of the war leaders, 'the only other method of bringing about the downfall of Germany is by stimulating the seeds of revolt within the conquered territories . . . '*

This was what Churchill wanted to hear, this was what appealed to his romantic, devious mind. But the British, unlike the emerging regimes of fascist and communist dictatorships between the wars, had no effective organisation for conducting subversive warfare. The nuts and bolts of British terrorism had yet to be put together.

Hugh Dalton, as Minister for Economic Warfare in the coalition Government, was given the job of setting up this organisation, which was to be known as the Special Operations Executive (SOE) and, unofficially, as 'The Cloak and Dagger Mob', 'The Racket', 'The Firm', or simply 'The Org' or 'Organisation'.

Dalton, like Churchill, knew a different kind of war would have to be waged before the defeated peoples of Europe could be set free: a war of stealth, of subterfuge; a war of treachery and intrigue, of murder and sabotage; a war in which small groups of resistance fighters would make mayhem their battle cry and take the killing grounds to wherever the enemy believed he was safe.

The task of SOE would be to build up these underground armies, to equip them and keep them supplied; to provide radio communications and control them from a central headquarters; to provide their leaders and train them in the skills of the professional assassin. Such an organisation could not be run by a typical Sandhurst product with a mind hidebound by a lifetime's training of doing things by the book. There *was* no book; or if there was, it was still being written.

The man chosen by Dalton to forge this weapon was Colin McVeagh Gubbins, a Scot serving with Intelligence, who had forecast in 1938 that the coming war with Germany would have to be fought with irregular forces. At a first, superficial glance, it would seem he was eminently unsuitable for the task of building from

*History of the Second World War; Grand Strategy, Vol II. Edited by J.R.M. Butler, (HMSO) 1957.

scratch a force of trained killers which had no parallel in the British tradition of going to war with a gun in one hand and a cricket bat in the other.

He was, to use that now antiquated phrase, 'a man of honour'. He truly believed that Britain had a duty to keep her word, no matter how dire the consequences. His upright figure, striding purposefully along Whitehall, always immaculately dressed with a red carnation at his buttonhole and carrying kidskin gloves, marked him indelibly as the epitome of the English gentleman. Even if he *was* a Scot.

It was perhaps inevitable that this man of high principles should have to fight his first battles against his own side. So far as the Establishment was concerned, SOE was an interloper, an upstart creaming off the country's brightest members of the Old-Boy-Old-School-Tie network for what were regarded at best as somewhat dubious exploits better suited to gangsters.

This opposition to its very existence was to hamper SOE's activities from the beginning; from the provision of supplies and the aircraft to fly them, right down to the allocation of offices in which to start weaving the threads of terrorism.

When it was formed in July 1940 – at a time when there was not a single agent in western Europe operating under London's control – it was given only a small block of offices at No 64 Baker Street, with a plaque over the door bearing the innocent inscription: 'Inter-services Research Bureau'.

By the spring of 1941, the basic staff work had been done and Gubbins with his team were now ready to get on with their job of masterminding the plan to organise, equip and lead the secret armies of resistance.

That was where the RAF came in. Or rather, did not come in with the alacrity one would have expected of a country at war. One staff officer, Bickham Sweet-Escott, recalls* how it was estimated in May 1941 that it would take 2,000 bomber sorties to equip 45,000 underground fighters. The total number of sorties being made by the RAF to western Europe at that time was no more than around 2,000 a month.

SOE, according to Sweet-Escott, would have been considered by the other services to be 'opening its mouth very wide' to have asked for such an allocation of aircraft.

When the Chiefs of Staff were informed of SOE's requirements

Baker Street Irregular, by Bickham Sweet-Escott (Methuen) 1965.

there were immediate and obstructive objections. Britain's only means of hitting back at the enemy in 1941 was by a bombing offensive which would carry the fight direct to the German heartland. There were no bombers to spare for such long-term projects envisaged by those shady characters in Baker Street.

In vain did Gubbins argue that one well-planned sabotage operation could do more at less cost than a raid by a hundred bombers.

His appeals fell on the deaf ears of the Chief of Air Staff, Air Chief Marshal Sir Charles Portal, prodded by his single-minded deputy, Air Vice-Marshal Arthur Harris.

Their motives can perhaps be traced back to a night in December of the previous year. Harris was on the roof of the Air Ministry, watching as a large part of the City of London went up in flames after an attack by the Luftwaffe. He called on Portal to join him and together they had a grandstand view of the devastation which could be caused by the apparently simple expedient of dropping bombs on a largely unprotected city.

As they watched, Harris turned to his chief and said in a phrase more memorable for its prophetic sincerity than for its originality: 'They are sowing the wind, and they will undoubtedly reap the whirlwind.'

This Dante's Inferno created by bombers made a deep impression on the man later to become controversial as 'Bomber' Harris. His other name was to be 'Butch', an affectionate term used by his loyal aircrews as an anglicised diminutive of the name the Germans gave him: *'Der Metzger'* – or 'The Butcher'.

He was a disciple of Lord Trenchard, the founding-father of the RAF who believed the bomber would always get through to its target. Harris was convinced that the Germans lost the previous war because they did not make sufficient use of what was then a new and deadly weapon – the U-boat.

He was determined that Britain should not make the same mistake. For him, the new weapon of World War II was the bomber, and it was his passionate belief that a constant pounding of enemy cities and industry could win the war alone.

In a way, Hiroshima and Nagasaki were to prove him right, but not in the way he anticipated.

When he was promoted to Air Marshal and given Bomber Command in February 1942, he whole-heartedly pursued a directive to 'bomb anything we can hit'. And so Area Bombing replaced the so-called precision raids in which only one in ten bombers was getting within five miles of targets in the strongly-defended industrial belt of the Ruhr.

Although he, personally, did not believe that the German morale could be broken by attacks on civilian populations – after all, he had seen how the resilient Londoners had joked their way through the Blitz – he felt sure that the indiscriminate plastering of industrial cities would eventually deprive the Germans of the means of carrying on the war.

Harris was a man with a powerful personality and has been described as a strong leader of men, a brilliant staff officer, and a ruthless commander.

It was this man, more than any on the other side of the English Channel, who was to hamper the activities of SOE. Official historians were later to portray the chief of Bomber Command as a man who

> made a habit of seeing only one side of a question and then exaggerating it. He had a tendency to confuse advice with interference, criticism with sabotage and evidence with propaganda.
> He resisted innovations and he was seldom open to persuasion.*

Controversy over the strategic bombing policy which Harris pressed home so vigorously raged for years after the war. Its merits or otherwise have no place here except to show how this dedication to pulverising what the top brass still called 'The Hun' played a major part in stunting the early growth of organised resistance in Occupied Europe.

Gubbins desperately needed aircraft and trained crews with specialised know-how for dropping agents and equipment. But both Portal and Harris argued that clandestine operations were hit or miss.

The former once told one of SOE's leading figures: 'Your work is a gamble which may give us a valuable dividend or may produce nothing . . . my bombing offensive is not a gamble. Its dividend is certain; it is a gilt-edged investment. I cannot divert aircraft from a certainty to a gamble which may be a goldmine or may be completely worthless.'

As late as November 1944 the warlords of the air were still jealously guarding their resources, even though by this time the two men disagreed on how to concentrate those resources. In a letter to

---

*Strategic Air Offensive Against Germany, 1939–1945, by Webster and Frankland (HMSO).

Portal, Harris objected bitterly to the demands being made on his bombers to attack targets as diversified as oil installations, U-boat pens, shipping, and ball-bearing factories.

His letter protested sourly: ' . . . and even the nearly defunct SOE has raised its bloody head and produced what I hope is now its final death rattle . . . '

This despite the fact that General Eisenhower, the Supreme Allied Commander, believed that the French Resistance, armed and trained by SOE operatives, had been worth fifteen infantry divisions during the first weeks of the Normandy invasion.

When Gubbins and his motley team were settling down to work in Baker Street they had to improvise with what was available. And all that *was* available for the first two years was one Special Duties Flight of four Lysanders, based initially at North Weald.

By February 1941, the flight had been reinforced by four Whitley bombers, which were by then considered too cumbersome for normal bombing operations. That was to be the pattern for much of SOE's existence. The only aircraft available would be those which Bomber Command could not use.

As Sweet-Escott puts it:* the Air Ministry had to be 'bullied' into making the aircraft available for secret operations.

> This step has been fought to the last ditch by Bomber Command . . . In the course of our discussions with them we had to make the fullest use of the argument that a hundred bombers can fail to hit their target, but one aircraft could drop a party of saboteurs who might make certain of it.

The best example of this dictum is the incredible story of how a team of SOE agents was parachuted into Norway to destroy the Norsk Hydro plant where heavy water was being produced for the German attempt to put together an atomic bomb. They succeeded where the RAF had said bombing was impossible, and where an attack by regular airborne troops had already failed.

Yet in 1943, in a Most Secret Note put before the other Chiefs of Staff, Portal wrote:

> As we cannot provide aircraft for the transport of arms and materials to resistance groups except at the direct cost of the bomber offensive, what is the exact price we are prepared to pay?
> . . . I feel that it would be a serious mistake to divert any more aircraft to supply resistance groups in Western Europe, which will only be of

*Op cit.

potential value next year, when these aircraft could be of *immediate and actual* value in accelerating the defeat of Germany by direct attack.*

It was in this atmosphere of misgivings that the Chiefs of Staff had decided in August 1941 to do something, anything, to comply with Churchill's almost forgotten edict to start setting Europe ablaze.

Ten obsolete Whitley bombers and three Halifaxes were allocated for special duties. Flight 1419 was dispersed, and the administrative covers were dusted off an old World War I bomber unit to form No 138 Squadron.

Six months later, on 14 February 1942, a St Valentine's Day love match was arranged when No 138 was joined by No 161, a squadron set up specifically for special duties.

And so a clandestine 'baby' was born, helped by the bickering, strident midwives of Bomber Command. Portal and his protege Harris had at last obeyed the order that was to lead to the beginning of the return to the mainland of Europe, and to the end of the dreams of conquest by the 'Thousand Year Reich'.

*

1800 hours, 20 March 1945: They were going out that night and there was less than an hour left. Time for another glance through well-thumbed letters and photographs, time for a quick meal and time perhaps for writing another of those short notes to be left in a convenient place. Just in case. It could always be torn up later.

Only 'Ratty' knew how many aircraft would be taking off that night with each crew briefed for a different mission. There were thirteen of them: five Hudsons and six Stirlings. Superstition played no part in SOE and Air Staff planning.

For the crew of N-for-Nan, as for the others, it was just another job. For the wireless operator it was his 47th operational sortie, although by now he had stopped numbering them in his log . . .

. . . Raymond Frankish Escreet would be immortalised one day as a model for a famous painting hung in the Imperial War Museum. But on 24 June 1942, there was no room in his life for art or beauty. It was the day of his first operation and he watched with elation as the bombs curved away beneath him and exploded with a mushrooming effect on the dockyards of St Nazaire.

He was seventeen years old when war was declared and impatient

*SOE in France, by M.R.D. Foot (HMSO) 1966.

to get into the thick of it. For nine long months he called every week at the RAF recruiting office in Hull, just to look at the posters and pray the war would not end before he could be part of it.

Since leaving school he had been working in his father's fruit and vegetable wholesale business in the Humberside city, twenty miles from the family home at Withernsea. Frank Escreet, a military medallist with the East Yorkshires in the first war, believed in starting his boy at the bottom.

After only a few weeks of fetching and carrying in the dispatch department, young Ray felt sorry he had ever left Hyman's College. Then came the war and his father told him tales of that other war with its long, slogging days in the trenches, and he resolved that when his time came he would do his fighting in the clean, blue skies.

His father, who had celebrated the Armistice in a hospital bed recovering from the effects of a shellburst which had torn four of his comrades apart, just smiled and told him the war would be over long before he reached the firing line. But behind the older man's banter lay a dread of the future.

Ray believed he could well be right. As the days were ticked off on the kitchen calendar, the war news sounded daily more ominous. Dunkirk fell. Then suddenly it was his birthday. He caught a bus into Hull and rode triumphantly out of Withernsea to present himself at rigid attention in front of the recruiting sergeant.

After basic training he qualified as a wireless operator and was posted to No 15 Squadron – 'Oxford's Own' – based at Wyton in Huntingdonshire, with three stripes on his arm and three 'Nickel' operations – dropping propaganda leaflets – to his credit.

Now, two years after pushing open the door of the recruiting office and three weeks after his birthday, he had carried out his first raid. He was jubilant as he watched the curiously artistic pattern of billowing explosions left behind by his and the other Stirlings in the bomber stream. At last he had put into practice the theories taught in those long months spent at training school.

Later he would note the event in his log book and on his next leave he would catch a train heading north to the bomb-blasted city near his home. There he would stick the first red flag into a *Daily Telegraph* World Map pinned to his bedroom wall and tell his parents: 'Now it's our turn. That's the first one for Hull.' There were to be many more. At twenty, Ray Escreet had come of age over St Nazaire.

The crew of N-for-Nan.
(*Left*) Flying Officer Forrest Harold 'Tommy' Thompson (gunner). (*Right*) Flight Lieutenant Terence Helfer (pilot).

(*Left*) Flying Officer Harry Johnson (navigator). (*Right*) Flying Officer Ray Escreet (wireless operator).

The Belgian agents who died in N-for-Nan: Lieutenant Jean Morel (in sidecar), Lieutenant Leon de Winter (pillion) and Lieutenant Guy Corbisier.

2

The operations of the secret squadrons were carried out at night, in the monthly period of the moon which guided the aircraft to targets reaching into Occupied Europe and, later, deep into the heart of Germany.

That they were ever formed at all is possibly due to the fact that the Westland Lysander was found to be virtually useless in the context of modern war for its original role as a reconnaissance and artillery spotter aircraft.

But it could land and take off, as its enthusiastic pilots would testify, on a pocket handkerchief. Or, more practically, on a small field. They were consequently offered to SOE as a sort of placebo. No one else had any use for them.

No 161 Squadron was equipped initially with seven Lysanders, some of them from the original Special Duties Flight at North Weald, and an assortment of aircraft which were considered by Bomber Command to be no longer capable of the punishing stresses of bombing operations. These were five Whitleys which had managed to survive the hazards of the early bombing raids and, oddly, two prototypes of the very excellent Wellington.

There was also a single Lockheed Hudson, a luxuriously furnished aircraft from the pre-war King's Flight, which had been used in peacetime for ferrying Royalty around Britain's air bases.

The two squadrons were actually based as a temporary expedient on the racecourse at Newmarket while the men at the top looked around without much enthusiasm, under constant pressure from Churchill, to find a more suitable airfield.

Officers posted to Newmarket were later to recall the experience with the nostalgia which mercifully casts a rosy glow over past hardships. One of them is Sydney Firth, an engineer who joined the RAF as an apprentice in 1922 at the age of fifteen. He remembers* being called into the headquarters office of a bomber station by his commanding officer, Wing-Commander Dermott Boyle, who was later to be knighted and become a Marshal of the RAF.

Boyle told him simply and without elaboration that he was to report to Newmarket and take up new duties.

* Personal interview.

'What duties?' he asked.

'I don't know,' replied the Wing-Commander with obvious exasperation. 'No one knows what those Johnnies at Newmarket are up to.'

Nor, it seemed, did 'those Johnnies'. When Firth arrived at the racecourse to take up his new posting, by then wearing the still unsoiled, sharply-creased uniform of a newly-commissioned pilot officer, he was welcomed by the adjutant sitting behind a ramshackle desk in a Nissen hut which served as an office.

'Thank goodness someone has turned up,' said Squadron-Leader Ronald Hockey. 'I've been running this place on my own and I'm still not sure what we're doing.'

It was about a year later that Hockey took off in an aircraft bearing his personal insignia of a hockey stick crossed with a trombone – he was a talented player on mess nights – on an operation to drop a team of SOE agents into Czechoslovakia.

Their mission was to assassinate SS-Obergruppenführer Reinhard Heydrich, the man who had drawn up the administrative procedure to be followed to carry out the 'Final Solution to the Jewish Problem'. This document led to the systematic mass murder of European Jews in the concentration camps of the East.

As one of Hitler's favourites and an architect of his policies, Heydrich had been sent to Czechoslovakia as the Reich Protector of the German-occupied sector known as Bohemia-Moravia.

He was to cauterize the growth of incipient rebellion against the Nazi regime. SOE planned to cauterize him first.

Fortunately for Squadron-Leader Hockey's peace of mind as he flew his silent and grim-faced passengers over the Erz mountain range, he was unaware of their deadly mission. Even if he had known, he could never have guessed at its bloody result.

As a reprisal for what Hitler called the cold-blooded murder of a Nordic hero, the Czech village of Lidice was razed to the ground, the adult population slaughtered, and a new page written in the Nazi catalogue of infamy.

A village in France was to suffer the same fate, this time as an *indirect* result of the activities of the SOE, when an SS division carried out reprisals to avenge the death of a popular officer killed by an unknown sniper.

There are several other incidents of a similar nature, but pilots like Ron Hockey rarely knew what their passengers were up to. They could only guess later at the parts they, personally, had played in what at the time were often world-shaking events.

For him, the flight to Czechoslovakia was just another job in the day to day business of getting on with the war; one of the necessary periods of danger sandwiched between the long hours spent on an RAF station waiting for orders to go out and risk life and limb yet again.

Another officer, John Nesbitt-Dufort, recalls* vividly how his first billet at Newmarket was in the racecourse grandstand. There was what he calls keen competition among the officers to secure a bed in the Royal retiring rooms, the only part of the building where they could be sure of hot and cold running water.

The aircrews were moved out eventually to Sefton Lodge, a training establishment near the centre of the town, where they were usually billeted over the stables in quarters which had been used by racehorse stablelads.

Meanwhile talks were going on at a very high level to find a base more suitable for secret operations. It was found at Tempsford, an emergency airfield just off the A1 trunk road running north from London through Bedfordshire, and adjacent to the main London to Edinburgh railway line.

Short of setting up a base in Hyde Park, the High Command could not have picked a more conspicuous place for what was intended to be a Most Secret jumping-off point for spies.

One of No 161 Squadron's pilots was to tell me many years later how incongruous it had been to see trains going by at regular intervals with passengers hanging out of the windows, waving to the ground crews as they went about their business of fuelling up a motley collection of odd-looking, out-of-date aircraft, which were obviously not suitable for either bombing missions or fighter defence operations.

Yet, strangely, the Germans never did try to interfere with the activities of the base although they knew from intelligence gleaned from captured agents forced to talk under torture that it was situated some thirty miles north of London.

Nor did they ever attempt what surely now would be the routine intelligence practice of putting a special watch on the base so that the spy-carriers could be intercepted or, better still, traced to their dropping and landing zones.

The move into Tempsford followed the usual service pattern of orderly chaos, transforming the sleepy village by doubling its population almost overnight. The villagers themselves did not quite know what to make of it all as the air crews and ground

* *Black Lysander*, by John Nesbitt-Dufort. (Jarrolds 1973).

personnel seemed very different to what they had been led to expect.

There was no bragging in the pubs about 'wizard prangs' and where so-and-so had 'gone for a Burton'. Careless talk about the squadrons' activities was very likely to cost lives and the men knew it. But not many months were to go by before the villagers guessed the squadrons were engaged on secret work and to their everlasting credit they never pressed the airmen for more information.

Even today the older people of the village are wary about saying what went on at the base which was once so much part of, yet apart from, their daily lives.

The settling down process did not take long, and so it was that by mid-1942 the special duties squadrons were ready to play a more positive part in the clandestine war of intrigue and skulduggery then being brought to a fine art by the SOE planners at Baker Street.

They were to play that part so well that in 1970 Colin Gubbins, who was by then a major-general with a knighthood, was to write as a foreword to the memoirs of a secret agent:*

> The build up of successful resistance in all occupied countries depended on two indispensable lifelines: developments in clandestine wireless telegraphy, and in supply by aircraft, whether of weapons or personnel. Without these material aids it would have been impossible to create and equip underground forces significant enough to affect the operations of regular forces . . .

Gubbins goes on to point out that during the war, in addition to the agents who were flown into the field to organise the Resistance, the special duties squadrons also delivered by air to France more than 10,000 tons of weapons, ammunition and other equipment. Similar, if not as many operations, were laid on for the rest of Occupied Europe.

Eisenhower, a man not given to flights of fancy or rhetoric, admitted shortly after the war that the activities of the French Resistance groups which had been supplied and equipped by the RAF had 'shortened the war by nine months'.

As the work of the special duties squadrons developed and expanded, it became the practice for No 138 Squadron, with its longer-range Halifaxes, to transport agents and equipment to a rendezvous and parachute them directly into the field. No 161 Squadron, with its Lysanders and, later, the Hudsons, tackled the

---

* *Xavier* by Richard Heslop. (Rupert Hart-Davis)

more hazardous and specialised tasks of landing agents in enemy territory, and picking up others who were either on the run from the Gestapo or who had been ordered back to Baker Street to be debriefed and given new assignments.

In this way several Very Important People indeed were snatched out to safety from under the noses of the Germans. Among them was General de Lattre de Tassigny, who was one day to return to France in triumph at the head of seven divisions of the French First Army, and to sign the German surrender document after the liberation of France.

No 138 Squadron has merited the occasional passing reference in the millions of words poured out in war histories and personal memoirs, and even in a few novels about the work of the Resistance. Oddly, No 161 Squadron has in the main been ignored, although its pick-up operations were unique and made a vital contribution to the work of the Baker Street Irregulars. For instance, what better boost could there be to the morale of underground fighters than to know the RAF was both willing and able to make direct contact with them?

Perhaps the explanation is that the squadron's activities were so wrapped in secrecy that few people knew at the time what was really going on, and it was not until thirty years after the war ended that its records were available to the public. And not all of them at that.

There are still some mysteries which must remain unsolved, at least for a few more years. For example, several pilots were awarded the Croix de Guerre by the French for their work with No 161. But in at least one case, that of a Hudson pilot, it has not been possible to find out why. He is not sure himself. Inquiries at the Public Records Office at Kew, quoting the Ministry of Defence reference number for his citation, can be fed through the computer which assimilates, digests, then spews out a reading which says sternly: 'Not to be opened until 1987.'

The squadron born in secrecy died secretively. Like SOE, it adopted very soon after its formation the unofficial watchword: 'Be secret, be silent, and above all, be careful.'

The man given the job of commanding the fledgling 161 and of organising its hush-hush move to Tempsford from the town of Newmarket, was Wing-Commander Edward Hedley Fielden, a courageous and highly popular officer with the most inappropriate nickname of 'Mouse'.

It had been given to him by Edward, Prince of Wales, when Fielden was serving as his personal pilot in the King's Flight in 1929.

The name stuck, and from that moment, even as an equerry to King George VI, he was known to everyone from Royal passengers down to the lowest 'erk' in the orderly rooms of the peacetime air force, as Mouse Fielden.

When the King visited the squadron for an informal presentation of medals – it had to be informal to maintain the squadron's secrecy – His Majesty was overheard to say during a break for tea and wads of sandwiches: 'What's this for, Mouse – stealing brandy from the Germans?'

It was a private joke between them. On one of his forays to France the Wing-Commander had been handed a bottle of the finest cognac by the Resistance men in the reception party. On his next visit to Buckingham Palace he had presented it to the King, much to the mortification of Churchill who heard about it later and felt peeved about not getting a bottle himself.

In many ways, this appointment to a highly secret job of a man so well known was not very good security. Often photographed, and often mentioned in the newspapers before the war, he was one of the few middle-ranking RAF officers known by sight and reputation to the Abwehr, the German military intelligence organisation.

It did not take long for them to latch on to the fact that his new command was to organise the transportation of passengers who were of a very different category to those of pre-war years: when the pomp and much-publicised Royal pageantry gave way to the stealthy flitting across Europe with lethal cargoes of assassins and the murderous tools of their trade.

Fielden was the first of three commanders of No 161 Squadron who would one day reach the highest echelons of the RAF. One became an Air Chief Marshal and Deputy Commander-in-Chief of Allied Forces in post-war Central Europe. The Mouse and one other successor rose to the rank of air vice-marshal.

Three others who commanded the squadron were killed in action, and *all* of them in this line of distinguished fliers risked death or capture by landing their aircraft on enemy-held soil. Command of a special duties squadron required special abilities, and carried hazards generally unknown to commanders of more orthodox units who had to spend much of their time flying desks in their headquarters.

The tradition of leadership-by-example was set in the very early days and was kept by station and squadron commanders with an almost suicidal zeal. There was a wing commander called Benham who was largely responsible for the administration of the base in the early part of 1942. It was while he was getting on with the paper work necessary for the smooth running of the two squadrons that he was called on to perform a service which could be said to be above and beyond the call of duty.

There was a top-level row blistering oak-panelled walls in Baker Street and Whitehall at the time, and the ramifications were burning up the hot lines in angry exchanges between London and Moscow.

It was at a time when the Red Army was fighting a desperate rearguard action. Stalin believed, like the French before him, that the perfidious British were prepared to fight to the death of the last Russian.

A party of Soviet agents had been languishing in the unaccustomed luxury of an hotel in the Marylebone neighbourhood, waiting to be dropped on a mission somewhere behind the German lines in central Europe.

The Russians were insisting that time was vital and hinted that the British were holding things up for their own devious ends. Sharp notes passed between the Foreign Office and the Ministry of Economic Warfare.

But the backroom planners of SOE were worried. It was a long flight, longer than any then attempted, over country about which there was very little information about the disposition of flak batteries, and where weather conditions were generally poor at that time of the year. The January moon period came and went without one night being considered suitable enough for a safe return flight to the target area. To make things more difficult, the special duties squadrons were still in the throes of moving to Tempsford.

The first nights of the February moon were no better. The weather had clamped down hard and any flying out of the station was reckoned to be out of the question. The Russians were furious. And adamant. Their soldiers were dying in their tens of thousands, and here were the British refusing to risk one aircraft!

The Soviet Ambassador in London insisted in vehement terms that the operation would have to be carried out, no matter how unsafe the conditions. Any delay, it was pointed out, would result in the cancellation of the mission until the following winter, because the dark hours of night would soon become too short for the flying distance involved.

Eventually an SOE staff officer was given a message handed down from ministerial level to the effect that the Foreign Office was insisting on the operation being given the go-ahead in the interests

of present and future Anglo-Soviet relations. He contacted
Tempsford by telephone. Wing-Commander Benham looked out
of his office window. The bad weather front blanketing southern
England was as bad as it had been ever since Christmas.

He pointed this out to the voice on the phone but was told, as
tactfully as possible, that the operation would have to be carried out
if humanly possible. Benham realised something really important
was afoot, as Baker Street always left the final decision on operations
to the Air Ministry and the men who would have to suffer any
consequences of things going wrong.

The buck was being passed down the chain of command.
Benham would have been well within his rights to have refused
because of the minimal chance of success. But as long as there *was* a
chance he knew it would have to be taken. He did the only thing
possible in the circumstances and agreed to lay the operation on –
as long as he could lead it.

He and his crew died somewhere over Czechoslovakia. As for the
Russians, they never quite believed that their agents had not been
quietly spirited away and disposed of by an SOE 'hit' team.

No 161 Squadron's first commanding officer was no less per-
severing in the ideal of leading from the front. But Mouse Fielden's
first job during the settling down period at Tempsford was to make
the base look as little used and decrepit as possible from the air.
Nissen huts and pre-fabricated blocks put up for living quarters and
offices were laid out in haphazard fashion around already existing
farm buildings.

There was none of the precision lay-out of regular pre-war bases,
all of them built to lavish standards between the wars at the expense
of research into aircraft design. Tempsford was for war service only,
and it had been handed over for special duties for the simple reason
that a high ridge of hills topped by the nearby village of Everton
made it too dangerous for use by a conventional bomber force.

The main runway was crossed diagonally by a secondary one,
and the adjacent farmland continued to be cultivated throughout
the war. From the air, to all but a low-level inspection, this base
which was the jumping-off point for terrorism in Europe was no
more than an innocent farm. In fact, it was to be known as Gibraltar
farm to both the villagers of Tempsford and nearby Sandy, and to
all the aircrews who were ever posted there.

It has been said by Sweet-Escott that the special duties squadrons
were given Tempsford as a base only because Bomber Command
could find no other use for it. Apart from the ridge which made

landing in bad weather a matter of skilled judgement or even better luck, that part of the countryside was prone to sudden and devastating blackouts caused by the descent of dense and frequent fog.

However, the Air Chiefs did not give in to SOE demands for a home of their own, with aircraft to operate from it, without imposing the condition that those same aircraft could also be used occasionally for bombing raids. Consequently, men who had been trained to a fine pitch with the objective of flying single aircraft through the night to make contact with a tiny pinpoint of light marking a rendezvous with the Resistance, occasionally found themselves part of a formation in an armada heading for the fury of combat over a pulverised German city.

The Thousand Bomber Raids planned by Bomber Harris, who had by then taken Portal's place as commander of the bombers, were as much intended to put heart into civilian morale on the Home Front as they were to pounding the heart out of the enemy. But to get the precious aircraft up to the magical number required for his 'Thousand Plan', he had to scrape the barrels of a hundred airfields around East Anglia.

Forty of his bombers failed to return from the first attack on Cologne in May 1942, and another 45 were damaged so badly that they had to be written off as beyond repair.

By the time of the second big raid on 1 June – the target for that night was Essen – he had only 956 aircraft left and he lost 31 of them against the defences of the industrial Ruhr. Inevitably, the biggest proportion of casualties was among the slower, older, and lower-flying aircraft in the formations.

Eventually there was a rush of brains to the head at staff level. The bombing duties demanded of the secret squadrons were swiftly discontinued and Tempsford was allowed to get on with its real and vital job of work.

It was realised, by even the most hawkish devotees of the bombing offensive, that it was a ridiculous waste to risk highly-trained aircrews in out-dated Whitleys. They had neither the range nor the bomb-carrying capacity of the Stirlings and Halifaxes, and by then the incomparable Lancasters were beginning to roar into the front line of the Air War.

There was another consideration overlooked by the Air Staff: most of the special duties aircrews had already achieved the near-impossible by surviving one tour of bombing operations, and therefore could be said to have already done their bit.

*1815 hours, 20 March 1945: They clambered out of the car at the southern
edge of the field where the Hudsons of 'A' Flight were parked. 'B' Flight's
Stirlings were out of sight on the far side of the base, but they could hear
engines turning over and they knew they would not be the only ones going out
that night.*

*In those moments of waiting the four men stood alone amid the bustle of
ground crews, an alien group as if from a race apart in their bulky flying
suits, the illusion heightened by their Mae West lifejackets and lumpy
parachutes.*

*Their aircraft would be the first to leave that night as they had a long way
to go, much longer and more hazardous than usual: a round trip of 1,200
miles – and 700 of them over Germany. Two attempts had already been
made by other crews in other aircraft earlier in the month, but each time the
pilots had aborted before reaching the target.*

*This time, it was hoped that N-for-Nan would be third time lucky. The
navigator, a man older than the others, had always believed more in God
than luck . . .*

. . . Henry Scurr Johnson qualified as an air observer at West
Freugh in Scotland when Ray Escreet was on his first raid over St
Nazaire. Unlike Escreet, he was 'below average' in aerial gunnery,
the training course revealed a flaw which reflected his character. His
was a gentle nature and he abhorred guns. He wanted, in the now
quaint parlance of that age, 'to do his bit for King and Country', but
he regretted the necessity of killing to do it.

After his failure as an air gunner he went on to pass his navigator's
course with a rating of 81 per cent, and so his career in the wartime
RAF was determined. Ironically, for a man who loathed killing, his
job as a navigator was to make sure the bomber and its cargo
reached the right target at the right time.

Johnson was older than the average airman, joining up in the
autumn of 1941, when he was twenty-eight years old. His younger
brother, Jim, had been invalided out of the RAF by then, after
surviving the shambles of the retreat to Dunkirk.

In those grim, early days, he had been working as a qualified
chemist, a member of the Pharmaceutical Society, managing a shop
in Sunderland and seemingly stuck for the duration in what was
then a reserved occupation. But as the casualties of the air war
mounted, the restrictions were dropped and he promptly volunteered. 'Someone in the family has got to be in uniform,' he told his
sister Edith.

He was the third child in a family of three boys and a girl, and he insisted they call him Harry rather than the despised Henry. He was born at Hetton-le-Hole and went on a scholarship to the Durham Johnston School on the bank of the River Weaver facing Durham Cathedral. The family moved to Sunderland when he was sixteen and busily taking part in the usual boyhood pursuits: playing football and tennis, and joining both the Sea and Boy Scouts.

He was a shy boy, too shy to have much to do with girls, and he grew into a serious young man with a reputation of being something of a dreamer. An avid reader, he could lose himself in a book, and he would spend hours alone by the main Newcastle to Durham railway line, collecting train numbers and imagining adventures on them at romantic destinations in Europe and beyond.

Further south, that same railway went past a village called Tempsford.

On 10 September 1942, he was promoted to flight sergeant and as the navigator of a Wellington he flew his first operational sortie over Dusseldorf. He was then twenty-nine, beginning to go bald, and was known affectionately to the young men around him as 'Pop'.

On a March evening of 1943 he was in a Wellington of No 199 Squadron attacking Essen from 12,000 feet. He saw the ground below flickering with pinpoints of brightness marking the 'creep-back' of incendiaries and high explosives dropped too soon by some of the aircraft in the preceding waves trying to zero in on the massive complex of the Krupp armaments factories. It was his first raid over the Ruhr – 'Happy Valley', as it was known to cynical, experienced crews. Johnson's Wellington lurched then lifted buoyantly as its single bomb dropped away into the night, a 4,000-lb blockbuster, also known as a 'cookie'.

With a shout crackling in his headset, 'Let's go, skipper,' the aircraft banked for home and he could see the full extent of the horror below, with patches of light flaring and growing larger in a chain-reaction, and as he watched he wondered how anything could possibly live through such devastation.

Less than an hour earlier the man who would one day be in the same crew for clandestine operations had flown over the same target, but with very different emotions. Ray Escreet's reaction as his Stirling dropped its load of high-explosives had been one of excited jubilation, and he was to record his feelings in his log book with the words: 'Krupps prang!'

For Johnson there was no sense of achievement. Just nausea.

After six months on ops he had become increasingly disturbed by the violence he was bringing by night to the faceless men, women and children below.

He was still only halfway through his first operational tour of duty.

3

A month after being formed at Newmarket, No 161 Squadron moved to the base which had been prepared with such great secrecy at Tempsford, and even today there is still some discrepancy about the number and types of aircraft it had available.

The two Wellingtons referred to in the previous chapter are recorded by Professor Foot in his official history of SOE's activities in France, and his source is a secret Air Ministry file. However, a brief history of the squadron's work, written just after the war and filed with the squadron records, makes no mention of Wellingtons. Instead, it is recorded that two Havocs were on station, 'equipped with special wireless apparatus, which enabled communications to be kept from air to ground with agents on the other side'.

The history goes on to record that 'this work became highly specialised and finally the Havocs were replaced by Hudsons in October 1943'.

One explanation could be that the Wellingtons were temporarily on loan from a bomber squadron, to be used exclusively for clandestine operations, but were returned to normal duties because of the horrific losses then being suffered by Bomber Command in 1942.

Wellingtons certainly played no part in the squadron's operations. The Havocs were American-built light bombers, originally designed as a passenger aircraft and named Douglas Boston. Its wartime nomenclature of 'Havoc' was presumably considered more suitable for a wartime role.

Like the Whitley and Wellington, it had two engines – 1,600 h.p. Wright Double Cyclone radials – and was capable of a little more than 300 mph with a 2,000-lb bomb load. Its range, however, was around only 1,000 miles and it is for this reason that its work as a radio listening post for agents in the field was transferred to the longer-range Hudsons in October 1943.

Another aircraft neglected by the historians is the Albemarle, which No 161 Squadron used as an experiment. Also a twin-engine job, made by Armstrong-Whitworth, it was intended originally for a role of bomber-reconnaissance, but it was found to be better suited as a special transport, carrying paratroops and towing gliders for airborne operations.

It was also used for general duties, ferrying mail and supplies to the Mediterranean theatre. It was faster than its sister aircraft, the Whitley, but had a lower service ceiling of only 18,000 feet, and a shorter range of 1,300 miles.

Crews from No 161 Squadron carried out specialised liaison work with the Albemarles from the Royal Navy base at St Eval in November 1942, but the results were considered by the squadron commander to be 'none too satisfactory' and the experiment was brought to an end the following March.

The fact that Foot does not mention the Havocs could be due to the possibility that they were used exclusively by the Secret Intelligence Service (SIS) for communications with their own agents, who operated independently of those with SOE. As indicated earlier, SOE was regarded with extreme suspicion by the older departments of British Intelligence.

SOE was engaged in organising resistance to the enemy, an activity which by its very nature would be bound to stir up a hornets' nest of German reaction which could well endanger SIS agents more concerned with keeping a low profile and gathering intelligence information.

It seems that inter-departmental jealousies and back-stabbings were as rife in wartime Whitehall as ever they were, and are, in the days of peace.

Even more disruptive was the hostility shown to SOE by the leader of the Free French in London, General Charles de Gaulle. A country section of SOE known as RF was set up to co-operate with the Gaullist intelligence service, *Bureau Central de Renseignements et d'Action* (BCRA), to organise resistance in the homeland using people sympathetic to the aims and ideals of de Gaulle.

But because not every Frenchman was a Gaullist – and in fact many hated everything he stood for, except his patriotism – an Independent French (F) section catered for all the other resisters: Communist and Christian, social-democrat and anarchist, patriot and *boche*-hater.

The General was suspicious of any direct British involvement in what he considered to be his concern and his concern alone. This all led to rivalries in the field for the limited number of supply drops which could be made, and sometimes to two groups of resisters operating in the same areas without one knowing of the other's existence.

It was an attempt to avoid any overlapping with other intelligence agencies that the Chiefs of Staff spelled out SOE's role in a directive just a few weeks after No 161 Squadron moved into Tempsford. They laid down that SOE should be primarily concerned with building up and equipping resistance organisations in readiness for the day when the Allies would return to Europe.

That being said, SOE was also able to turn in a considerable amount of information which was no part of their main brief. One organiser of a circuit (or *réseau*) operating in the dangerous prohibited zone around Le Havre returned to England after a Hudson pick-up operation in 1944 with intelligence about V-1 rockets which the Germans were preparing to launch from sites between the Somme and the Seine.

Nevertheless, for all the obvious benefits to be accrued from SOE operations, their work was to be plagued throughout the early days by the Air Chief's insistence on keeping up morale at home by plastering enemy cities at a time when the other armed services were necessarily unable to mount any offensive actions.

The result was that the secret squadron were deprived for many months of the aircraft they needed to carry out SOE's ambitious plans.

As Sweet-Escott points out*, the Chiefs of Staff wanted subversive operations to be carried out, but believed 'it would be unsound to sacrifice the effectiveness of our bombing efforts' by diverting aircraft from the raids.

He adds: 'They did not tell us to abandon our efforts to create subversion . . . they merely withheld from us the means of carrying it out.'

However, by mid-1942, the two squadrons at Tempsford had a total of around thirty aircraft for use by SOE, SIS and PWE – the Political Warfare Executive whose function it was to spread gloom and despondency among the enemy by propaganda.

The squadron's activities were dictated by the types of aircraft at their disposal.

No 138, with the long-range Halifaxes, was used for dropping agents and supplies deep into the far reaches of Europe, from Norway in an arc round to the Balkans. No 161, in addition to shorter-range drops with Whitleys and, later, Stirlings, carried out the pick-ups with Lysanders and Hudsons.

It can be said of the Lysanders that they became a legend in a very short lifetime, and the praises of this lively little high-wing monoplane have been sung by every agent who has been snatched to safety by them. Their chief advantage for operations behind

* *Op cit.*

enemy lines was their ability to take off and land on a strip of grass no more than 500 yards long.

Again, there are discrepancies in the records of their achievements, caused probably by inadequate documentation procedures in wartime. The squadron's 'Secret' file lists 266 sorties, of which 187 resulted in successful landings.

But Hugh Verity, a distinguished flight commander, puts the number of sorties at 279, of which 180 were successful.* According to his figures a total of 304 passengers – most, if not all of them, agents – were taken to France, and 410 were brought back to England. The homeward-bound passengers were a mixture of agents, aircrew evaders and escapers, French VIPs, and *réfracteurs* – who were people like Jews, on the run from the Germans.

This incredible effort was at the relatively inexpensive cost of 13 aircraft destroyed and 6 pilots killed, and the many tributes paid to the work of the Lysanders and the men who flew them are all fully justified.

Yet the Hudsons have been virtually ignored in war memoirs, although their work was no less important. Indeed, probably more so. The Hudson flight started operations two years after the Lysanders but still managed to fly a total of more than 300 sorties, of which 249 were successful.

Only 44 were pick-ups, with 36 successes. But because they were bigger aircraft they were able to take 139 agents into Europe and bring 221 passengers back without losing a single man or machine.

The other sorties were either parachute drops or patrols over the enemy coastline to establish air-to-ground communications with agents already in the field.

A total of 142 agents were dropped by parachute, but the cost was high: 10 aircraft lost and 36 aircrew killed, all in the final phase of the war. So although the Hudsons were the most versatile of the aircraft used by the two secret squadrons, a valuable year was to pass after No 161's formation before its full potential was realised.

It was to the Lysander that SOE first turned when it was found necessary in those early days to land agents directly in France rather than send them in by sea or parachute.

The first Allied aircraft to touch down safely in France after the Dunkirk evacuation was a Lysander flown by Flight Lieutenant Wally Farley. He went out empty and returned with Phillip Schneidau, an international hockey player, half-French, half-English, who had been on an exploratory mission for SIS.

* *We landed by moonlight* by Hugh Verity, (Ian Allan) 1979.

The Hudson pick-up pioneer Charles Pickard (*centre*) with his sheepdog Ming at Tangmere in 1943. Hugh Verity, who wrote the squadron 'bible' for pick-up procedures, is on his right. Also shown (*left to right*) are Lysander pilots Jimmy McCairns, Peter Vaughan-Fowler, and Bunny Rymills with his spaniel Henry.

An early visit to Tempsford by Marshal of the RAF Lord 'Boom' Trenchard (left), seen here with an Air Vice Marshal, a Group Captain, and 'Mouse' Fielden (right), who was then a Wing Commander.

SQUADRON
161 161
ROYAL AIR FORCE
LIBERATE

J.R.H.Heaton-Armstrong
Chester Herald
and Inspector of Royal
Air Force Badges.

ollege of Arms,
pril, 1944.

(*Left*) No 161 Squadron insignia:
the open fetlock symbolises the
breaking of the fetters shackling
Occupied Europe.

(*Below*) King George VI and
Queen Elizabeth inspect crews
of 161 and 138 Squadrons at
Tempsford on 9th November
1943.

It was as if the Lysander had been built specifically for the job. It was certainly not much use in its original role as a spotter aircraft. Powered by a single 890 hp Bristol Mercury radial engine, the Mark I model was said to be capable of 219 mph going flat out. The pilots found the top speed nearer 180 mph on operations, and it was happier cruising at about 165 mph. The long-range models fitted with an extra fuel tank could cover a round trip of about 1,150 miles.

Some models were equipped with three machine guns. These were very quickly stripped by the pilots as the little aircraft was no match for anything the Luftwaffe could put up against them except, perhaps, its near-equivalent, the Fieseler Storch.

It was nevertheless a beautiful little aircraft to fly, in spite of its rather clumsy appearance and its distinctive high wing which gave it the look in flight of an ungainly bird.

Five months were to pass before the second pick-up, carried out on 11 April 1941, by Flying Officer Gordon Scotter. He was awarded an immediate DFC for the exploit and went on to carry out his second pick-up a month later.

These three successes on behalf of SIS by what was no more than an experimental flight resulted in the reluctant acceptance by the Air Chiefs that a bigger effort should be made to support clandestine operations.

Consequently the flight was moved to Newmarket, given more aircraft, and expanded to form No 138 Squadron. A secluded corner of a fighter base at Tangmere, near Chichester, was allocated as a jumping-off point for Lysander operations, and in the late summer of 1941 the first agent was taken to France without the necessity of having to make a parachute drop.

This was the vital breakthrough in that it proved it was possible to ferry agents in and out speedily with up-to-date intelligence instead of having to rely on the arduous overland escape routes which were then being set up through the Pyrenees to Spain.

The first man to go in by this method was Major Gerry Morel, an SOE agent who was to become F Section's operations officer. An insurance broker, he had been a French Army liaison officer attached to a British regiment when he was captured in 1940. He contracted a serious illness and was allowed to leave a prisoner-of-war camp because the Germans believed he had little time left to live.

They miscalculated his dogged endurance. He made his way eventually into Spain, caught a freighter steaming to Brazil, and turned up in England by a circuitous route, arriving before very long at an office in Baker Street.

It was because of his previous illness and poor health generally that SOE headquarters decided it would be too risky to have him parachuted into France. Instead, arrangements were made for him to be flown direct to the rendezvous in an aircraft already earmarked for picking up another agent whose cover, in the idiom of the modern spy thriller, had been 'blown'.

It was a momentous decision. It was one thing to risk a pilot and an aircraft to pick up an agent in danger; it was quite another to take in an agent who, if caught, would be able to give the Germans brand-new information about SOE's work.

The pilot chosen for the operation was John Nesbitt-Dufort, a flight lieutenant known to all as 'Whippy', the nickname bestowed on him by an irate wing commander during a training exercise in the 'thirties'.

He was a regular officer, commissioned in 1930, and frustrated to find himself ensnared as a training school instructor at the outbreak of war, teaching the youngsters who went on to fight the Battle of Britain.

It had been while he was himself still learning the art or craft of aerial combat that he misjudged a camera-gun attack during an interception exercise. His fighter had screamed through two formations of Hawker Furies and Harts, dispersing them in a muddled panic all over the sky.

When he landed and taxied back to the hangar it was to find an ashen-faced commanding officer waiting for him with the furious question, 'Where the bloody hell did you think you were anyway? Whipsnade Zoo?'

He was stuck with the name 'Whippy' for the rest of his life. Another story has it that he once actually landed an aircraft at the zoo after running out of fuel, but while it is a better line to shoot, the former is more likely to be true.

Born of an English mother and a French father who went to the Western Front as a *poilu* in 1914 and was killed a few weeks later, Nesbitt-Dufort finally persuaded his superiors that his talents as a pilot were being wasted at a training school. He relished not at all the thought of being asked, 'What did you do in the war, daddy?' and having to reply in all honesty that he had taught others to do the flying and the fighting.

He did not anticipate that his eagerness to volunteer for more active service would lead him, because of his French connection, to the special duties squadron where the necessity for secrecy would require him to keep his lips sealed about his war until it was all over and his children grown up.

His first operation was laid on for 4 September 1941. It was a moonlight night and at an hour before midnight at 4,000 feet he spotted a pinpoint marker light which guided him over a lightly-defended stretch of the French coast.

Behind him in the passenger seat, Morel sat silent and showing no signs of being affected by the same butterflies then doing a mad dance in the pit of the pilot's stomach.

Meanwhile, at an hotel 200 miles inland, Major Jacques de Guélis was frantically hoping the Vichy French police would finish a spot check of identity papers and leave in time for him to pick up his bicycle and set off for the remote field where he had been told to expect a Lysander.

An hour went by. Nesbitt-Dufort and Morel peered anxiously out of the cockpit. By the moonlight they could see the flat, open countryside around Châteauroux and suddenly, exactly where they had expected to find it from aerial reconnaissance maps, was the field which had been selected for this historic return to French soil.

But where were the signal lights which by now should have been switched on by the agent on the ground?

At that particular moment, de Guélis was pedalling furiously along a country road. Overhead he could hear the characteristic drone of a Lysander's engine as the aircraft slowly circled the apparently deserted field.

Nesbitt-Dufort was just about to give up after deciding he could not keep stooging around forever without attracting the attention of prowling German nightfighters. Then he saw the lights flashing the correct coded signal. And as he made his approach his stomach muscles tightened as he realised the field was very small indeed, much smaller than those on which he had practised landings on the countryside around East Anglia.

However, in spite of all his doubts, he manoeuvred the 'Lizzie' into the line of approach and suddenly they were down and rolling to a halt. As the pilot sat back with a sigh of relief, Morel jumped out and hurried away into the shadows after a brief consultation, leaving de Guélis, a giant of a man, to scramble into the vacated passenger seat. He just had time to see Morel stoop to pick up a sack lying on the ground. It clinked. De Guélis realised to his intense chagrin that he had left behind two bottles of champagne and one of perfume, all unobtainable in wartime Britain.

He could only grind his teeth with annoyance as Nesbitt-Dufort opened the throttle to hurl the Lysander into the air, cutting through high-tension cables he had not noticed on the way down and slicing through the treetops at the far end of the field. The aircraft had been on the ground for no longer than four minutes.

That the operation was considered an unqualified success – in spite of the loss of de Guélis's black market bottles – was due entirely to luck. In his haste to reach the field in time the agent had picked the nearest one that was suitable. The field originally chosen for the suitability of its approach (and absence of cables and treetops) was further down the road.

Morel, incidentally, left the rendezvous safely and went on to do some useful recruiting and organising before he was betrayed and captured. Again he escaped and returned to England. By then his health had been completely ruined and he spent the rest of the war planning operations from Baker Street on a diet of biscuits and milk.

He was to return to France briefly, this time by a Hudson operation, for the unpleasant task of investigating an agent suspected of being a traitor. But more of that later.

Nesbitt-Dufort landed back in England after a flight lasting five hours and forty minutes, and de Guélis was whisked triumphantly to London by car for his de-briefing. He had been parachuted into France a month earlier to link up with agents organising the first *réseau* (circuit) to be set up by F-section. He returned with a vital progress report and a request for more arms, explosives and money.

The money, it needs to be said, was to be used for the day-to-day living expenses of agents, and for SOE's less well-known field activities of bribery, blackmail and extortion.¯

De Guélis was to survive all the hazards of the war, only to die tragically at the end of it, killed in a motor accident in Germany in 1946.

By the end of 1941, Nesbitt-Dufort had carried out two more pick-ups in France, and one was attempted by Flight Lieutenant 'Sticky' Murphy at Neufchâteau in Belgium. It was the first failure. He reached the correct rendezvous and although he could see a signal light it was not flashing the correct identification letter.

He decided to go down for a look, disobeying all orders and the dictates of commonsense on the grounds that he believed the agent to be in danger. He was. Down below the agent, a Belgian Air Force officer, was in a dilemma. He had set up the signal lights and was awaiting the arrival of the Lysander when a German patrol stumbled on the scene.

In the hue and cry that followed he managed to find a hiding place and he lay there, confident that the Lysander pilot would turn back when he failed to see an identification signal. To his horror the Lysander kept coming and there was nothing he could do to stop it, and as it swept low over the field it suddenly disappeared from sight and he knew by the sound of its idling engines that it had landed.

Murphy, meanwhile, was sitting in his cockpit nursing a revolver he had never used in anger when he saw a group of German soldiers burst out of a wood and run towards him. There was a burst of firing and as the flimsy aircraft shuddered under what seemed to be the impact of a series of hammer blows, he felt a sharp pain in his neck and he decided to make himself scarce. He returned to England with his Lizzie perforated by bullet holes and another in his neck where a round had passed clean through.

The agent he had tried to pick up, a Captain Jean Cassart, was captured a few days later, but managed to escape and eventually made his way to England.

Only one more pick-up was attempted by No 138 Squadron before the Lysanders were transferred to become the nucleus of the newly formed No 161 Squadron. The irrepressible Whippy Nesbitt-Dufort, by now promoted to squadron leader with a DSO for his three previous pick-ups, was the man chosen for the operation flown on 28 January 1942.

With one agent on board he had an uneventful outward journey and landed safely at Issoudun shortly after ten that night. The passenger disembarked and two others climbed on board for the return journey. Then the weather clamped down, a front of towering clouds the like of which Whippy had never in his life seen before.

His intercom broke down and his radio went out of action. Cut off from communications with both his passengers and his base, he decided to attempt to fly through the turbulence because he knew he did not have the ceiling to climb over it.

The game little monoplane was beaten and buffeted by the worst of the elements, and with the pilot grimly hanging on to the controls it was thrown all over the sky with the instruments gone haywire.

Fuel was running low and the Channel not even in sight when he made the inevitable decision to turn back in the general direction of France and put the aircraft down where best he could. By flying low he managed to take bearings and was able to make his way back almost to his starting point when he force-landed.

The agents, both of them decidedly green with air-sickness, thought they had reached England, but did not much care where they were just so long as they were back on land. When they recovered they were considerably chagrined to find they were still in France after all they had suffered.

After a night in a barn they set off for the nearest village and were able to contact local resistance leaders. Thirty long, boring days passed in hiding, living off the frugal rations which the family of a 'safe' house shared with them, until a message was delivered warning them to stand by for a pick-up operation.

They were taken to the chosen field, which Nesbitt-Dufort inspected and gave his approval, although he thought it considerably larger than really necessary. Soon the reception party heard an aircraft's engines, but it was not the distinctive sound of a Lysander. To his surprise, Nesbitt-Dufort realised that the plane silhouetted against the moonlit sky, swooping low just over the treetops at the edge of the field, was a twin-engined light bomber.

It was 'Gormless Gertie', a lumbering old Anson aircraft used for training flights and obsolete even at this early stage in the war. It really had no business flying over France at all, much less preparing to land. As it came to a halt a grinning head was thrust out of the cockpit window: it was Murphy, also now a squadron leader.

'I might have known it would be you, Sticky,' said Nesbitt-Dufort as he scrambled on board wondering why on earth they had sent this clapped-out aircraft instead of the trusty old Lysander.

But the Anson was equal to the task and they returned home safely; Murphy to continue on special duties, and Nesbitt-Dufort to be posted to a nightfighter squadron defending Glasgow. It was a routine and sensible precaution to post aircrew to sinecures after being shot down and evading capture, as they knew too much about resisters who had helped them.

This rescue by the Anson was to be the first in a new era of pick-up operations, but no one realised it at the time. Eleven months were to pass before another pick-up was attempted by a light bomber.

The main shortcomings of the Lysander were its slow speed and an endurance in the air of eight hours at the very most when fitted with extra fuel-carrying capacity.

In the best of flying conditions, with good weather, favourable winds and a direct route to the rendezvous without the need for diversions to avoid the formidable ground defences and nightfighter patrols, the Lizzie could be relied on for a range of no more than between 600 and 800 miles. From Tempsford, or even from Tangmere on the South Coast, this put much of southern and eastern France out of bounds.

The Lysander was also incapable of carrying more than three passengers in a tight squeeze, although on at least five memorable occasions, no less than four passengers managed to sardine themselves into the tiny compartment.

Nor could it be used for parachuting agents unless the pilot turned the aircraft upside down and allowed the luckless passenger to tumble out into the night. This would have been hardly the sort of method to recommend itself to any responsible staff officer, and any reports of agents exiting in this manner belong only to the pages of fiction. Parachutes *were* carried, but only to be used in emergencies.

So with these limitations placed on Lysander operations, No 161 Squadron had to make do with the five Armstrong-Whitworth Whitleys put at its disposal by Bomber Command.

Mouse Fielden had also managed to retain the Hudson he had once flown as the royal pilot in the pre-war King's Flight. But this regal air taxi which was eventually to provide a solution to the problems of range and passenger capacity was allowed to idle neglected and unwanted in the corner of a hangar at Tempsford.

The Whitley had been the first twin-engine, so-called 'heavy' bomber to be put into production for the RAF in 1937. Powered by Rolls Royce Merlins, it had a range of 1,500 miles and could carry a bomb load of 7,000lb. For bombs, substitute equipment containers, and SOE had an aircraft capable of dropping agents and supplies anywhere in western Europe.

But the aircraft was ponderous, unwieldy, and had a top speed of no more than 230 mph. As a bomber it had done all that could be expected of it in the early days of the war; those heady days when Bomber Command believed all you had to do was select a target to destroy it, when in fact most crews were unable to drop their bombs within a mile of it.

It was for the simple reason that they were becoming obsolete for bombing ops that SOE was able to get its hands on a precious few for special duties.

By November 1942 the Whitleys had been superseded by the Handley Page Halifax, the first four-engine heavy bomber to be diverted from the bombing offensive which Butch Harris was pursuing with all his energies. Even so, he would only allow five of them to be transferred to special duties at any one time, and only then after much pleading by influential friends of SOE in Whitehall.

The Halifaxes went into service when the Tempsford base was beginning to take on a more permanent appearance. Sydney Firth, the Station Engineer Officer, remembers* vividly the early days when he had to despatch messengers on bicycles to ask villagers to provide billets at short notice for airmen posted in to the base from all over the country.

By the time the huge Halifaxes arrived, the ground crews had been moved out of the cosy homes where they had been treated as family and had shaken down in Nissen huts around the perimeter of the field. The first few months of make-do-and-mend were coming to a close and Tempsford was settling down to tackle an ever-increasing workload.

The Halifaxes proved so effective in delivering supplies and parachuting agents that another twenty were allocated to the sister 138 Squadron six months later.

The reason was that by this time, in mid-1943, the famous Lancasters were rolling off production lines in large numbers, and Bomber Command was forced to concede that some of its less-effective aircraft would be more useful on special operations.

There *was* one little-known and, as far as I am aware, unrecorded occasion when three Lancasters were sent to Tempsford for special duties. The result was a disaster, according to John Affleck, one of the first Hudson pilots.† He remembers the Lancasters being flown into Tempsford by crews of the renowned No 617 Squadron – 'The Dambusters', whose exploits had become legendary even then.

They were tough, experienced, and had that swagger which marks men of an élite force. They were able to sport more medals per chest than even the much-decorated but unknown Tempsford crews. Affleck recalls with relish how they landed in impeccable formation, much to the fury of Mouse Fielden who did not much care for the beating of the big drum of bravado. Unless he was doing the beating for himself and his crews.

The three big bomber captains were carpeted and informed that the whole point of a secret base was that it should not draw attention to itself by formation flying.

Tragically, the Lancasters did not last long. On their first hush-hush operation, two of them were seen to go down in flames, and the third just made it back to base, the crew very much chastened by their experience. The experiment was promptly dropped.

* Personal interview.
† Personal interview.

It was consequently left to the Halifaxes to carry out the long-range work. The Mark I model had a capability of 1,885 miles and a useful speed of 280 mph. The aircraft's best attribute so far as the two secret squadrons were concerned was its carrying capacity of 13,000 lb, and until well into 1944 it was used for the unheralded and unromantic chore of ferrying SOE requirements deep into the heartlands of faraway occupied countries like Poland, Norway, Czechoslovakia and Yugoslavia.

This work was taken over eventually by an attachment of Stirlings from No 214 Squadron when Bomber Command decided that the Halifaxes would, after all, be required for the final blitz on Germany following the Normandy invasion.

The crews of the Stirlings were delighted. Whatever these special duties were, they could not be any worse than the bombing raids. Their aircraft were inferior in every important aspect to both the Lancaster and the Halifax. They flew lower at 20,000 feet and slower at a maximum of 260 mph, and as a result they had been taking heavier-than-tolerable casualties in the bombing offensive.

They were always the tail-end Charlies, lumbering targets for radar-linked flak batteries and by far an easier prey for Luftwaffe hunter-interceptors than the more heavily armed Lancasters.

Crews of other bombers can still remember, sometimes with shame, how they would cheer the news that Stirlings were to be flying with them on a particular op. They knew the Stirlings formed up below them would make juicier targets, and on the principle that a gun aimed at someone else is less likely to harm you, the natural stinct for self-preservation made the Stirlings a welcome reinforcement to any massed formation of bombers.

But it was to be the May of 1944 before the Stirlings reached Tempsford. By then much of the real work of planting agents and helping their activities to grow in occupied soil had already been done.

With the sole exception of the Lysander, all the aircraft used by No 161 Squadron were capable of dropping agents by parachute in close formation. In some cases the aircraft had to be specially adapted.

The Halifaxes had oblong trapdoors cut into the floor of the fuselage. The agents would attach their static lines securely inside the aircraft and await the dispatcher's signal to 'Go'. They would then jump rigidly to attention, feet together and arms pressed tightly to their sides, and plummet out into the night, leaving the static line to jerk the parachute canopy out of its container.

The Hudsons had an arrangement at the rear, rather like a water chute, on which the agent could slide away into space. Some liked going head first, just for the hell of it. Others, more sedately, would sit at the top of the chute, their equipment bags on their knees, and wait for the dispatcher to give them a gentle shove.

No matter how simple it sounds, the parachute was designed primarily as a piece of emergency equipment for the purpose of saving aircrew from a doomed machine, and only to be used as a last resort. The fact that so many agents were prepared to entrust their lives to this method of illegal entry to Occupied Europe speaks volumes for their courage and dedication.

The relief at making a safe landing had an additional spice for agents jumping into a moonlit field in the dead of night with the possibility of an armed enemy lurking in every shadow.

Nor was there much comfort in knowing accidents were rare. Imagine the feelings of agents arriving for jump training at Ringway – now Manchester International Airport – to learn on the grapevine that parachuting accidents were as low as five in every thousand jumps. Long odds, perhaps, but *who* were the five?

In spite of the hazards, the parachute was as good a way as any – and better than most – of putting agents into the field. Land routes took too long, and sea routes by either surface craft or submarines were suitable only for undefended coastal areas.

The air routes were quicker and had the advantage of deeper penetration. But they could still be dangerous: Six SOE agents were killed going in by parachute: one by being dropped so low that his 'chute did not have enough time to open fully; another by a bad landing; two because they had faulty parachutes or because they had not been packed properly; a fifth, tragically, because the static line which pulled the parachute automatically from the container when the agent jumped had not been hooked up to the inside of the aircraft.

There are no details available on the fate of the sixth victim, a Pole, except that he was properly dispatched from the aircraft, but was never seen alive again. And these were operations to France alone; many more were made to other parts of Europe.

The Lysander pilot, Nesbitt-Dufort, remembers* how one agent had dropped from a Whitley in which he was flying as second pilot. The man made a faulty exit and his parachute lines became entangled with the aircraft's tail. There was nothing the crew could

* *Op cit.*

do to help, and they had to watch helplessly as he was strangled, his body twisting and turning in the slipstream all the way back to base.

They had to land with the body still attached to the aircraft by the tattered shreds of parachute.

There are many other reports of agents landing badly, but suffering no more than sprains or bruises because of the terrain, or because they had been blown off course by a gust of wind, or because of any of the multitude of mishaps likely to overtake anyone jumping out of an aircraft. But in all the records and memoirs I have studied, there is no criticism of the work of No 161 Squadron's Hudsons.

The RAF, generally, had its critics from time to time. Flemming Muus, the organiser of an SOE *réseau* in Denmark, laid on reception parties for eighteen agents dropped in a four-month period during 1943. He complained bitterly in several signals to Baker Street about the way aircraft had approached the rendezvous to make their drops.*

One had flown too high at around 1,000 feet, and the descending parachutes could be seen for miles around. Another was so badly off course that one agent was dropped in a lake, losing his radio transmitter and nearly drowning in the process.

Francis Cammaerts, head of the *Jockey réseau* in south-eastern France, received his supplies from a base in Algiers, where the packing arrangements for supply containers are said to have been far less satisfactory than in Britain.†

He described the packing at the time as 'shocking' and in one report to London he protested bitterly about an operation in which parachutes had failed to open, causing one container to fall on a house, crushing the mother of a man in his reception party.

'. . . this bloody carelessness absolutely inexcusable,' he protested. 'You might as well drop bombs.'

But these criticisms must be put in the perspective of the overall picture. The RAF delivered about 1,800 agents to France alone, together with enough arms and ammunition to supply an underground army half a million strong. What *is* remarkable is that there have been so few complaints in post-war memoirs about the work of aircrews serving with the special duties squadrons.

Robert Boiteux, who was parachuted into France on the same operation which precipitated his partner, Bob Sheppard, onto the roof of a *gendarmerie* outhouse, was to recall the deeds of all dead

* *Inside SOE* by E.H. Cookridge (Arthur Barker) 1966.
† Foot, *op cit*.

Resistance fighters with a wistful regret that they had not lived to see the victory for which they had given their lives.

He goes on to say: 'I thought of the pilots who on every flight risked their lives in the slow, low-flying aircraft to bring in the arms.'*

Lieutenant Colonel Richard Heslop, one of the most effective and colourful agents, whose code-name *Xavier* is still a byword among the old *maquisards* in the mountainous region of the Ain and Haute-Savoie, was also to write of those days: 'I greatly admired the RAF; they always turned up when they said they would, and flew through dreadful conditions of weather and enemy defences to bring us our necessities.'†

Those necessities – the arms, explosives, money and other accoutrements of clandestine warfare – were every bit as important as the agents sent in to organise their distribution. According to the historian A.J.P. Taylor, the RAF dropped on SOE's behalf enough arms to France to equip an army of half a million men.** Much of it went astray, and a considerable amount fell into German hands, but enough got through in spite of all the hazards and the Resistance was equipped in time to affect the course of the war.

Eisenhower was generous enough to admit later in a note to Colin Gubbins, by then Director of SOE operations: 'The supply of agents and resistance groups in the field, moreover, could only have reached such proportions during the summer of 1944 through outstanding efficiency on the part of the supply and air liaison staffs.'††

Lines of communication between London and agents in the field were essential to the needs of organisations mushrooming in the dark corners of the New German Empire. In this work, too, the secret squadrons were able to play a vital part; without them the efforts of disorganised patriots would have been largely ineffectual.

Colonel Heslop's first mission to France was marred by the frustrations he suffered by not being able to contact headquarters directly. He was powerless without radio facilities. He returned to London, spelled out his requirements, then set off once more for France in the comparative luxury of a Hudson.

This time he was accompanied by a wireless operator, Dennis Johnson, who went to SOE on loan from its newly-formed

* *Watch for me by moonlight*, by Evelyn Le Chêne. (Eyre Methuen) 1973.
† Heslop. *op cit.*
** *The Second World War* by A.J.P. Taylor (Hamish Hamilton) 1975.
†† Foot. *op cit.*

American counterpart, the Office of Strategic Services (OSS). Where before he had been treated with some suspicion by the hard-bitten *maquisards* of the mountains, he was now welcomed as a saviour who had the power to bring down from the skies all the equipment they sorely lacked.

Wireless operators, or 'pianists' as they were called, gave circuit organisers the credibility they needed to win over the loyalty and trust of local leaders of underground units.

Several Hudsons of No 161 Squadron were also equipped with a special wireless which enabled agents to pass messages to aircraft flying in the near vicinity. These were known as 'Ascension' operations. A total of at least 103 of these missions were flown successfully by the Hudsons, 65 of them by crews flying N-for-Nan.

By using what was called an S-phone, SOE staff officers could be flown out from Tempsford to make direct voice contact with agents. This was a valuable addition to SOE's armoury. The leader of a circuit suspected of being blown by German penetration could be readily identified by what amounted to a simple telephone call.

But it was foolproof only if the agent had not been turned round and was co-operating with the enemy willingly or, as on at least one occasion, at gunpoint.

Another device used by the secret squadrons went by the name of 'Eureka' and 'Rebecca'. It was a variation of radar and was developed by the same team of research scientists which gave SOE the S-phone. Rebecca was a heavy piece of equipment which could be fitted into a Hudson while Eureka, which weighed about 100-lb, was parachuted in to Resistance leaders.

Eureka was in effect a beacon which transmitted a coded signal in response to a similar signal bleeped by Rebecca. These signals could be activated from a distance seventy miles apart to enable the aircraft to home in on the rendezvous.

Unfortunately many agents refused to use them. The official historian of the SOE in France says a large proportion of them were never seen or heard of again after being dropped with other supplies. The very good reason was that an agent would have considerable difficulty explaining away his presence should a patrol find him in a lonely field in the dead of night. His chances would drop to zero if he also had to explain away a hundredweight of complex radio equipment.

Good and speedy communications, and precision navigation by RAF crews were nevertheless keystones to the success of SOE operations. Gubbins, who had steered plans for clandestine warfare through the uneasy days of their inception, was to say later that 'without these links we would have been groping in the dark'.

And in a letter to Gubbins there came at the end of the war an unstinting accolade from Eisenhower: '. . . particular credit must be due to those responsible for communications with occupied territory.'*

He had good reason for his praise. At the time of the Normandy landings on 6 June 1944, there were in France alone some 150 secret radio sets operating behind German lines, activating the circuits and passing on the word from London to the thousands of resisters that the time had come to rise up and break the shackles of the Jackboot Occupation.

It was in anticipation of this event that No 161 Squadron had been given Royal approval a week before the invasion to adopt as its squadron crest the insignia of a Broken Shackle, or Fetlock, with the motto: 'LIBERATE'.

*

1830 hours, 20 March 1945: Somewhere out in the Atlantic a mass of cold air had come into conflict with warm air from the tropics and in the ensuing battle of the elements a depression had formed, and now a cold front stretched from Norway to Dover, moving steadily eastwards.

A second frontal system was following a few hours behind, and all along the route masses of cold air were burrowing into the warmth of air rising from the European land mass, and from their embrace were conceived the anvil-shaped thunderclouds of cumulo-nimbus towering higher than any Hudson could climb.

N-for-Nan would be flying into unsettled conditions which at the best would bring sudden showers; at the worst, thunderstorms of rain, hail and sleet. The pilot did not need to be a weatherman to read the signs.

He completed his routine checks for flaws on the exterior surfaces of the aircraft, then followed his crew and their three passengers inside . . .

. . . Terence Helfer was lucky just to be alive. His first operation was on the night of 2 September 1941. The target was Ostend, just fifty miles or so from the Kentish coast and only lightly defended. In time, such a sortie would come to be called a 'milk run', but for Helfer it had been as bad as anything he had been told by the line-shooters in the Mess.

---

* Foot, *op cit.*

They had been climbing over the coast after off-loading their bombs when a burst of flak caught them and turned their Wellington into a lumbering wreck which shuddered along the entire length of its sturdy frame with every spasmodic beat of one crippled engine.

He had been flying as second pilot to the squadron commander when the world seem to fall apart around him. The crew was ordered to jettison everything and anything not screwed down, and out through the hatches went all the loose equipment, the guns, and even the Elsan toilet.

Then, too low to bail out, the aircraft had gone completely out of control, dropping into the sea like a falling leaf.

One wing was ripped off by the impact, pulling the wireless operator into the water, still strapped in his seat. It was this, perhaps, that saved their lives. As the wing broke away from the fuselage it also pulled out the dinghy. It immediately inflated automatically right next to the surprised radio man.

While everyone else was still fumbling dazedly in the half-submerged wreckage, Sparks clambered into the dinghy and paddled around in the dark for two hours until everyone had been picked up.

The squadron commander had been particularly lucky. He was pulled to safety from the shattered cockpit, still unconscious, only minutes before the Wellington sank. Now all seven of them were wet and cold and hungry, but sufficiently in control of their fears to feel annoyed at having thrown away their emergency rations in their attempt to keep the aircraft in the air.

For Helfer, it was an unpromising start to operations: a baptism of fire and salt water. This was not the sort of flying he had dreamed about as a boy in his teens. Ever since watching an annual air display near his home at Hendon he had wanted to be a flier, but had not known how to go about it.

He was the son of a marquetry cutter and the grandson of a Frenchman who had brought the skills of his craft to Britain before the turn of the century. Granddad Helfer set up in business at Windsor where he came under Royal scrutiny, and before long he was commissioned to carve the beautiful *objets d'art* which Queen Victoria so delighted in giving to close friends.

In an earlier age the young Helfer would also have been taught the craft of his forebears, but his family knew better. A less leisurely era of mass production was coming, so he was packed off from Hendon on the Northern tube line every day to learn the skills of an articled clerk in a City accountant's office.

He hated it. When war broke out it came as something of a relief. It was his chance to learn to fly. He was not quite twenty when he first went solo in a Tiger Moth at the Elementary Training School at Cambridge.

By July 1941 he was learning to fly Wellingtons when he got lost on a navigational exercise across country. It was a shattering experience for a 'green' crew. Fuel was running low when at last they spotted the sanctuary of a strange airfield. They had no idea where they were and without waiting to ask for permission Helfer put the aircraft down in an emergency landing.

There were sighs of relief all round until a group of mechanics was heard approaching, jabbering excitedly in guttural accents.

'Skipper,' a strained voice shouted, 'take off. Quick! They're Jerries.'

They realised something was wrong when they became airborne again only to hear a testy voice from the control tower asking them in impeccable English what the devil they thought they were doing.

They were at East Wretham, a Norfolk airfield used as a base for a Czech squadron!

Two months later Helfer and his crew were posted to No 218 Squadron at Marham. After a few days learning their way around the station their names went up for that first operation which was so nearly their last.

Now they were down in the drink and wondering how long it would be before a rescue launch picked them up. They waited, and waited. Back at Marham telegrams were sent off to their next-of-kin. The odd glass was raised as a tribute in the Mess, but their faces were no more than a blur in most men's memories. They were new boys who had bought it on their first trip. *C'est la guerre*, they said, secretly glad it was someone else and not them. Only the squadron commander, known to them all, was really missed.

Four days after ditching, seven bedraggled and weary men walked ashore at Margate under the suspicious gaze of towns-people on the waterfront. They came in from the cold balancing on a sewer pipe reaching out into the sea. They left the dinghy where it was, to drift with the tide into the Thames estuary.

The war had begun in earnest for Terence Helfer.

4

High-ranking visitors to the Officers' Mess at Tempsford might raise their eyebrows, but otherwise they studiously ignored the set of footprints marking the erratic passage of a man who had apparently marched across the ceiling, defying both gravity and King's Regulations.

Not that there was much anyone could have done about it anyway. The footprints had been left there to mark the arrival of the new commanding officer, Wing Commander Percy Charles Pickard. One evening, flushed with the excesses of several hours at the bar, he had daubed his feet with coal dust, ordered several of his juniors to hold him upside down, and proceeded to tramp across the ceiling.

He had another stunt to entertain the mess and while away the off-duty hours spent waiting to resume operational flying duties in the period of the full moon. An imitation oak beam ran along the length of the bar, high enough for a man to suspend himself by his toes and inch his way from one end of the room to the other without touching the ground. If, perchance, a pint of beer or a large scotch had been left on the floor at the halfway mark, this was just another obstacle to overcome.

These, and other high jinks like touch rugby, were more than just a way young men could show off their physical prowess. They allowed them to let off steam which could build up to an explosive head in men who lived in constant touch with death and subdued fear, but whose upbringing demanded they should not show it.

Pickard took command of No 161 Squadron in October 1942, relieving Mouse Fielden, who was promoted to group captain and given overall command of the station. He was twenty-six years old when he arrived at Tempsford, and already a legend. He had less than two years left to live.

The youngest of a family of two boys and three girls, he was born in Sheffield and like any Yorkshire lad of spirit, he positively loathed his first name.

'It's a cissy's name,' he said, and kept it a secret from the other boys at school. Exactly when he adopted the abbreviated surname, 'Pick', is not known. But it was prophetic and was to stay with him for the rest of his life.

He joined the RAF in 1936 because he could not think of anything else to do, and because his high-spirited temperament was unsuited to the catering business run by his father and later swallowed by the Mecca organisation.

Pickard wanted adventure, and although the peace-time RAF with its petty disciplines and military-style bull is not particularly memorable for venturesome enterprise, he was able to sublimate his quest for excitement in his love of flying. And he certainly *could* fly, regularly earning an 'above average' rating from instructors who had learned their trade in the stringbag days of World War I.

This flying instinct was eventually to lead him to realise the potential of the Lockheed Hudson as a ferry bus for spies, and to earn him the distinction of becoming the first airman in the war to be awarded three Distinguished Service Orders.

He was truly a hero in the Biggles mould, straight from the Empire-building pages of the *Boys' Own Paper*. Sir Basil Embry, a close friend who was to become an air chief marshal, has referred to him as 'one of the great airmen of the war' and 'a shining example of British manhood'.

Wherever he was posted he carried with him that indefinable aura of a born leader, albeit one who was not too remote to have a drink with the boys. Several drinks, in fact. He was not a man for moderation in anything.

A hard-swearing, hard-drinking man, his favourite expression to cope with any unexpected emergency or disaster – or even a broken shoelace – was: 'There's always a bloody something.'

He was a man of strength and independence of will which could well have affected adversely a career in the peacetime RAF. He did not take kindly to authority unless it was his own, and he believed regulations had been devised for circumventing. In short, he was not the type of officer material likely to go far up the promotion ladder.

Then came the war and his type came into their own. War histories are studded with the exploits of men who went into battle seemingly oblivious to danger, and Pickard came out of the same mould. It did not make him universally popular; many men considered him a braggart. But he was respected because he matched words with deeds and got things done at a time when Britain needed men of action.

Only a few intimate friends knew his bravado masked the fears and doubts suffered by other men. His was a true courage and his drinking was no more than part of his pose as a devil-may-care hellraiser. On his return trips from sorties into France he occasionally made navigational errors – as everyone did – which brought him out over the Channel Islands instead of the more direct route over Cabourg.

His explanation was always the same: his compass had been affected by the metal whisky flask he stashed away in the top of a flying boot.

He became a national hero at a time when fighter pilots like the legless Douglas Bader were grabbing the headlines and the glory, and before bomber pilots were made fashionable by the dambusting feats of Guy Gibson.

Bomber Command decided early in 1941 that there was a propaganda war to be fought and won in order to get the best in men and materials. The top brains of the British film industry were conscripted to make the bombers more glamorous by filming their work and using real crews instead of actors.

Pickard was a casting director's dream. He stood six feet four inches, with the fair hair and rugged good looks of a blond Nordic god. He was a Yorkshireman with the inevitable pipe always clenched between his teeth, and his love of animals and dogs in particular made him almost too good to be true. He was type-cast for the leading role.

And that was how he became known to the British public, playing the part of Squadron Leader Dixon, flying F-for-Freddie in the now historic film, *Target for Tonight*.

A month later, in May 1941, he was posted to command No 9 Squadron and was very soon back in the thick of real-life action, leading the first operational sweep in the search for the German warship, *Prinz Eugen*. With one DSO and a DFC to his credit by then, he could have been forgiven for taking a desk job, especially in the August of that year when he completed more than two tours of duty with a total of 65 night operations.

But his greatest exploits were still to come. At a time when No 161 Squadron was forming up at Tempsford, Pickard was over on the other side of the country, commanding No 51 Squadron and preparing his Whitley bomber crews for a daring, Top Secret mission.

At this particular point in Britain's fight for survival, the technological war was in its infancy. A form of radar existed on both sides of the Channel, but neither the British nor the Germans knew exactly how advanced was the equipment used by the other. The boffins suspected the worst, but their warnings generally went unheeded by their respective High Commands.

From radar stations on the coast of France and the Low Countries the Germans could 'watch' the bombers forming up over East Anglia, gathering together like some angry cloud on their screens.

By a complex network of linked defences the ground controllers were able to send interceptors up in good time to harry the oncoming stream of bombers, land them for refuelling, and send them back into the fight.

The British had to discover how this radar worked in order to design effective counter-measures. The opportunity came when an aerial photo turned up what appeared to be a radio installation set on a cliff top not far from the Normandy coastal village of Bruneval. What subsequently became known as the Bruneval Raid, although on a tiny scale and with few casualties, now has its niche in military annals because of its success in terms of scientific and propaganda value.

It was a job calling for split-second timing, and Wing Commander Pickard was the man chosen to lead the twelve Whitleys carrying the raiding party. That the operation was an unqualified success was in some measure due to the efforts of the aircrews, although Pickard himself missed his own target for that particular night.

Shortly before take-off from an airfield at Thruxton, near Andover, he strolled nonchalantly among the soldiers waiting to emplane; a reassuring figure, apparently without a care in the world and puffing away at an unlit pipe.

But he had no reassuring words for their commander, Major John Frost. With characteristic bluntness he said as the men were climbing aboard the aircraft: 'I feel like a bloody murderer.'*

He was nearly and tragically right. He had successfully led the Whitleys to the target when they were caught by flak from coastal defences which according to all reports should not have been there. Most of the aircraft reached the dropping zone in time and dispatched their paratroopers accurately, but Pickard and the aircraft behind him had taken the brunt of the barrage and dropped their men too far south of Bruneval village.

As luck would have it, these men were able to join the battle later, just in time to cover the withdrawal to the beach where the Royal Navy was waiting to embark the raiding party with their precious pieces of German radar equipment.

Pickard received a bar to his DSO for this exploit. Major Frost,

* *The Bruneval Raid* by George Millar, (Bodley Head) 1974.

who led the fighting on the ground and was later to distinguish himself at Arnhem, was awarded a Military Cross.

Another highly secret instrument of the scientists' craft was used in the raid. A Rebecca was placed in one of the naval landing craft, to home in on the portable Eureka carried by one of the Royal Engineers in the assault party.

Pickard did not know it at the time, but he was soon to become very familiar with this navigational aid.

This, then, was the man chosen to lead No 161 Squadron at a critical point in the war. Before taking command of the squadron, he first had a period of acclimatisation with its sister unit, No 138 Squadron. He arrived at Tempsford in time to fly as a passenger in one of the first Whitley operations from the base.

His pilot was the amateur trombonist Ron Hockey, who was later to command No 138. Hockey is remembered by Tempsford men for a practical joke he played when a party of agents were being ushered on board an aircraft bound for France. Out of the twilight an apparition emerged, from the direction of the camouflaged barn where an SOE officer gave agents their final check-out.

The ground crew watched in awe as the sinister figure came closer, looking like a spy from a film melodrama: a huge beard, villainous-looking slouch hat, a flowing black cloak. The stranger was about to clamber in the crew compartment when one of the gaping airmen grabbed him by the arm.

'This way for France, chum,' he said, pointing to the passenger hatchway while still shaking his head with bemused disbelief.

'Not likely, laddie,' replied Hockey, whipping off his false beard to reveal a huge grin.

Pickard, as No 161's CO, brought his own brand of zaniness to the activities of off-duty aircrews. But on duty he was a martinet. After settling his wife, Dorothy, and their shaggy old English sheepdog, Ming, into a house within sight of the main runway, he set about perfecting the techniques of Lysander pick-up operations.

In the eight months of the squadron's existence before he took command, ten operations had been carried out successfully, putting ten agents into France and bringing fifteen out by Lysander. Under Pickard's leadership, the Lysanders completed eleven operations in the remaining three winter months of 1942, taking out fourteen agents, and bringing back twenty.

The squadron's obsolete Whitleys were phased out during this period, and replaced by five of the faster Halifaxes with their greater payload capacity. No 161 was getting into its stride, but Pickard was not a man simply to preserve the status quo.

There was more to be done and he knew it, and his attention was drawn increasingly to the blackboard in his operations room where he could see at a glance the daily changes in the strengths of his available aircraft and crews.

One item on the duty roster remained constant: the Lockheed Hudson O-for-Oboe of the King's Flight. It had been brought to Tempsford by his predecessor, Mouse Fielden, but without a role to play except possibly as a transport, it had been stuck away in a hangar, unwanted and rarely used.

Aircraft were still at a premium at Tempsford and to Pickard it seemed a pity to waste one. Air Vice-Marshal Harris was still stubbornly refusing to give the secret squadrons any more than their basic requirements, so dedicated was he to pursuing his plan to bomb Germany flat.

But Pickard had his own plan. The potential for using twin-engine bombers in a pick-up role had always been there; it was just that no one had done anything about it. One successful flight had already been carried out by Sticky Murphy in an Anson before Pickard was posted to Tempsford, but for some inexplicable reason the idea was not developed. It was perhaps felt that the Lysanders were adequate for the job, and so they were in a limited sense.

Now, with hindsight, it is glaringly obvious that an aircraft with a longer range than a Lysander, and with a greater carrying capacity, would have been of inestimable value to the hard-pressed resistance movements.

One of the problems facing SOE was the occasional need to rescue agents and resisters who were on the run from the Gestapo or Vichy police. By the end of 1942 several escape routes had been brought under the aegis of an SOE unit known as DF-section and the business of escape and evasion was becoming highly organised. But the routes involved long, tortuous and extremely risky journeys through France, followed by the perils of crossing the Pyrenees into neutral and unsympathetic Spain.

The escape lines were linked by safe houses made available by ordinary men and women who risked execution if caught, or an even more horrible death in a concentration camp. Numerous escape lines had spread tentacles all over Occupied Europe in 1940 without any prompting from London. They were set up by patriots unwilling to accept the harsh facts of life as a conquered people. This way was their only way of hitting back at an enemy who may have been able to crush governments and armies by the blitzkrieg, but not entirely the spirit of the people.

They sprang up initially by random chance. Parties of troops cut off from their units after Dunkirk and St Valéry would be given food and shelter, and passed on to a friend or relative in another town or village. In this way they would work their way by road and rail towards Marseilles or the Pyrenees.

Smuggling was a tradition, almost a way of life, in the villages around the frontier. And only a few years earlier lines of communication had been set up across the mountains by Republicans fleeing the Franco regime after their defeat in the Spanish Civil War.

The routes became better organised when London realised their value and set up a department, MI9, to study and improve escape and evasion techniques. One of the better known and more effective was the *Pat* or *Pat O'Leary* line organised by Albert Guérisse, the Belgian army doctor who, twenty-five years after the end of the war, was to stand on a hillside in the Ardennes to pay his tribute to the crew of a No 161 Squadron Hudson.

The escape routes took on an even more important significance when the aerial bombardment of Germany began gathering momentum. The increasing number of bombers used in the raids, and the improved German defences, meant the loss of more valuable and highly-trained aircrews.

It would be pertinent to ask in these more materialistic days if the end product of saving these shot down airmen justified the means used to get them home. Was it really worth risking so many lives of civilians?

And the lives of skilled agents put into the field to help them? The answer must be an unqualified Yes! It was essential to get the trained personnel back into action; aircraft could be replaced but there was not an unending supply of men of suitable calibre to fly them.

But more important was the psychological value of the escape routes. The morale factor in war is vital. A much quoted Napoleonic maxim is that morale is three times more decisive than material.

To send airmen out night after night on what they knew could be one-way tickets could have sapped the fibre of even the most resolute. If they knew there were friends on the other side who could lead them to safety, the fear of being shot out of the sky did not hold quite so many terrors.

The escape lines were like parachutes: you hoped you would never have to use them, but you were glad to know they were there.

Then there was the psychological boost where it really counted –

in the occupied countries. Ordinary men and women may balk at taking an active part in resistance. After all, it *is* no easy thing to slit a man's throat, even if he *is* the enemy.

But they could be made to feel they were playing some part in the war by taking Allied airmen into their homes and looking after them until more active resisters called to escort them down the line. People who would have been apathetic, dispirited or just resigned to the Occupation, were given a sense of belonging to a brotherhood.

It was this desire of ordinary people to strike some sort of bloodless blow against the invader which led to the escape routes springing up in such a haphazard fashion like a network of veins, often leading nowhere, across the face of Europe. It was not until the spring of 1942 that a semblance of order was imposed to sort out the confusion.

The routes were brought under the ministerial umbrella of MI9, and one of its best-known organisers was a young man who, as a subaltern with a searchlight battery, had been wounded and captured in the retreat to Dunkirk. After a series of adventures which make the exploits of fictitious heroes look like bedtime stories, Airey Neave was eventually incarcerated in the supposedly impregnable fortress of Colditz.

He escaped against all the odds and made what was known as a 'home run', returning to England with the help of the *Pat* line in 1942. But *his* war, like Charles Pickard's and Terence Helfer's and others who had survived the early years, was just beginning.

His task in MI9 was to organise the evasion lines for hundreds of Allied personnel, from France, Belgium and Holland, and to plan for the safety of the hundreds of Allied airmen still in hiding after the Normandy landings. When the war ended he was twenty-nine years old. His bitter-sweet revenge for his hardships in captivity came when he was called on to serve the war crimes indictments on Goering, Ribbentrop, Keitel and other high-ranking Nazis who were put on trial at Nuremberg.

Many years later, by then a Member of Parliament, he was to tell me that the importance of the escape lines was not so much that they guided so many men and women to safety, but that they existed at all. They were a guarantee, he said, that Britain would keep on fighting and would one day return to France in force.

Soon afterwards, in 1979, this man who had fought the evils of fascist tyranny was himself murdered by Irish terrorists, in the name of *their* 'freedom'.

The growth of the escape lines made Pickard aware of the need to have a bigger and faster aircraft for clandestine operations. There was also an incident a month after he had taken command of No 161. He had successfully landed an agent in a field near Rouen and was on his way home when his Lysander was attacked by a pair of German fighters.

Although his aircraft was in theory no match for the faster enemy, Pickard was a superlative pilot and used every aerobatic advantage of his more manoeuvreable Lizzie to keep out of trouble.

But it was an unequal duel which should only have had one result. Luckily he found a cloudbank in time. When he had started out on his flight he had been carrying 215 gallons of fuel in a specially-fitted long-range tank; more than enough to get him to Rouen and back.

However, the evasive tactics he had been forced to use to outwit the fighters had burned up his reserves and he landed with only five gallons left.

It was with this escape still fresh in his mind that he set about celebrating the birth of his son, Nicholas, on New Year's Day, 1943. He went about it with the same dedication he gave to flying, and his celebrations took the form of hanging upside down from the mess rafters.

This time he failed to make it to the other side and landed in a crumpled heap on the floor, much to the laughter and applause of his fellow officers.

As they helped him to his feet, he gingerly explored various parts of his body and made the inevitable comment: 'There's always a bloody something.'

He had broken his thumb!

A few weeks later he was in the air again, still with his wrist in plaster, when he flew a Lysander to a field in Issoudun, some seventy miles due south of Orleans. He landed one agent and returned with two passengers, again running short of fuel and having to make an emergency landing in Cornwall.

His relieved passengers thankfully signed their names on his plaster cast – and that was how he discovered he had brought back René Massigli, the former French Ambassador to Turkey.

After these two narrow escapes, Pickard again considered the possibility of using a longer-range aircraft. The Hudson O-for-Oboe seemed ideal for the purpose. On 1 February he and Squadron Leader Hugh Verity, commander of the Lysander flight, took the aircraft up on a flight lasting an hour and a quarter. They put the bomber through all the possible permutations to test and familiarise themselves with its flying characteristics.

All that was left to do was put it through a permutation that was not in the book . . .

The date was fixed for 13 February, not exactly an auspicious date for the first attempt to land a Hudson in enemy-held territory, but Pickard cared little for superstition.

There had been considerable discussion at No 3 Group (Bomber Command) headquarters about the wisdom of allowing an officer of Pickard's specialised knowledge of secret operations to risk falling into German hands. The tried and trusty Lysander was one thing; a Hudson was quite another.

Could it really be done? There was only one way to find out and Pickard was adamant that he should be the man to try it.

It was not just bravado or glory-seeking. It was in many ways just plain commonsense. Pickard believed himself to be the best flier on the station, and if anyone could bring a Hudson down safely on an unknown field with nothing but the moon and torchlights to guide him, then he was the man.

He looked on it as just another Lysander operation, with the difference that he would need around a thousand yards – double the distance needed for a Lysander – to be sure of a safe landing and take-off.

The field had been carefully chosen by an agent who understood and had been trained in the techniques of night landings. On the day of the operation two coded signals were broadcast by the BBC to alert the reception party. Operation Sirene Berenice was on.

It was half-past eight on that Saturday when O-for-Oboe was trundled out of the hangar at Tempsford, the roar of its twin, 1,200 horsepower engines drowning the sounds of revelry in the nearby Mess. Five figures in civilian clothing emerged from the barn called 'Gibraltar farm' where they had been inspected to ensure they carried nothing incriminating, like English cigarettes or money, which would expose their cover stories if they should be captured on the other side.

Pickard watched from the cockpit as the agents were ushered on board by his Canadian navigator, Pilot Officer Dickie Taylor, and his gunner, Flying Officer Henry Figg. Then he opened the throttle and the first secret Hudson operation was under way.

An hour later he picked out the French coast at the entrance to the Seine estuary at Cabourg, and set a course east of the Loire to Nevers. After that he followed the river line south to Digoin and there, over on the port side, he picked out a pinpoint of light flashing the correct identification signal.

As an experiment – or just 'to see what happened,' as he put it later in his report – he replied by flashing an incorrect signal. All the lights below immediately went out. He then gave the correct identification and the lights came on again.

Convinced all was well, he made his approach and came in smoothly in an aircraft that flew like a bird in the air, but was notorious as a clumsy duck on the ground. Then he was down and eating up the yards, slowing in time to turn in an arc around the last torchlight marker and jerk to a halt facing the way he had come in.

The five agents clambered out, several bundles of mail were thrown through the hatch for delivery to SOE headquarters, and a few muttered greetings were exchanged. Ten minutes after touch-down the Hudson was once again airborne, landing at Tempsford just six hours after taking off on the pioneering operation.

It had been 'a piece of cake'. A week later Pickard took O-for-Oboe* up again to land one agent and pick up six homeward-bound passengers in an operation which lasted only seven minutes on the ground.

Three days later, on the night of 24 February, he made his third and last pick-up in a Hudson for that month. It was an operation which so nearly ended in disaster. Pickard himself laconically described the operation as 'a lucky escape' and it was to signpost the main drawback in using a six-ton aircraft for pick-ups.

The story is told in the squadron records and is worth setting out in full, if only to compare its matter-of-fact brevity with the colourful account which was later to be written by an agent who saw it all happen as a spectator in a frightening and often ludicrous drama.

The operation was code-named 'Pampas'. In addition to Taylor and Figg, Pickard decided to take along a third crew man to supervise the passengers. A flight lieutenant called Putt was borrowed from No 138 Squadron, and asked to volunteer. It was to be a fortunate choice.

It was nearly half-past ten at night when Pickard took off, crossing the Channel west of Tangmere and reaching the French coast over the usual pinpoint near Cabourg. Taylor then advised an alteration

---

* When the Americans entered the air war late in 1942 it was decided to use their phonetic alphabet to avoid confusion. I have done so throughout, with the exceptions of F-for-Freddie and T-for-Tommy, codenames which are famous in RAF lore. However, some British crews stuck to the old phonetic alphabet, hence the use in some war histories of O-for-Orange and H-for-Harry, instead of 'Oboe' and 'How'.

in course over the Loire as a thick bank of fog was obscuring the ground and preventing any possibility of picking up identifiable ground features.

The fog persisted until they reached Le Creusot where they were able to verify their position and set course for the reception area. In spite of more fog patches along the route, the Hudson was in sight of the field at 0130 hours. But an alarming two more hours were to go by before Pickard was able to make his final approach. His report takes up the story:

> . . . owing to conditions and fog, landing extremely difficult and about twenty attempts were made before getting it right, and then this was made somewhat heavily to the side of the flarepath at 1330. And then at the end of the path, became bogged.
>
> With the assistance of some of the onlookers [the aircraft] was dug out in approximately half an hour. But on taxi-ing for about quarter of a mile, the aircraft became bogged again. About half the village had now turned out and with the help of some of the more intelligent, the aircraft finally was extricated although at one point hope was almost given up.
>
> In this connection, Flight Lieutenant Putt is to be commended for the coolness and energy he displayed, and the manner in which he organised the labour. It is very difficult to get any sense out of the French as to distances, and could not locate original flarepath, so went back as far as possible, after having embarked passengers from position, and then took off.
>
> This was only just made, and wing tip and leading edges were damaged with contact by trees, which put 'George' out of action. On becoming airborne at 1530 hours it was thought that one or two cars could be seen approaching. Set course for base and crossed French coast north of Le Havre at 0703 hours. Dawn breaking so asked for flight protection, but none forthcoming. Eventually reached base 0800 hours.
>
> A very striking note in the operation is the fact of remaining unmolested by the Germans, as the fact of first making so many circuits before landing must have caused some attention.

The phraseology may not be in the best traditions of English word structure, but this report which Pickard so hurriedly scribbled down must surely have a niche in the annals of understatement. In its way, it is a masterpiece.

The 'George' referred to was the automatic pilot system, the only casualty of an incredible operation in which ten agents were landed in France, and another ten people brought out for debriefing in London. It would have taken a Lysander three, or more probably four trips to ferry the same number, with the risk of discovery and capture tripled or quadrupled as a consequence. On the debit side, a Lysander weighing no more than two tons fully loaded would probably not have got into such difficulties on the ground.

By sheer chance this operation was watched from the shadows by a British agent, the renowned Peter Churchill, who had intended using the same field for a Lysander operation during the same February moon period.

His account of this incident* bears little resemblance to the report written by Pick Pickard, but it goes a considerable way towards explaining why it took two hours and twenty attempts to put the Hudson down in an operation which was so nearly a monumental foul-up.

Churchill's first mission to France had ended on 14 February 1942, the day the No 161 Squadron had been formed. Before the year was out he was back in France and making arrangements in December to have five French generals picked up and flown to London. Churchill himself could not understand why on earth London wanted them because they were quite obviously 'mothball' soldiers, and of World War I vintage at that.†

However, there was a series of mishaps or misunderstandings, and the expected pick-up aircraft failed to arrive on the scheduled date. It was while awaiting a new date that he witnessed the incident recounted by Pickard on his third Hudson pick-up.

Churchill had been hoping to get his generals away on two Lysanders, and had chosen a field at Tournus, twenty miles north of Macon. After the initial failure a second attempt was planned.

Everything had been laid on except the actual time and date when he found to his horror that the field had been piled high with mounds of bricks.

He thought about it for a time, pondering the possibilities: was it a routine security precaution to make potential landing grounds unsafe for aircraft? Or had the Germans been tipped off that this particular field was scheduled for an imminent operation? The first alternative was the more likely, because if the Germans knew about the operation they would surely have laid an ambush instead of making the field unfit for use.

He kept a wary eye on the situation. One night, as he was cycling along a road bordering the field, accompanied by one of the local

* *Duel of Wits* by Peter Churchill (Hodder and Stoughton) 1953.
† So called because many late arrivals to the Resistance were ex-army officers whose uniforms had been stored in mothballs after the fall of France.

Resistance men, they heard an astonishing hubbub . . . astonishing because of what was going on, why it was being done, and the noisy racket being made.

They dismounted and crept nearer, until from a vantage point behind a hedge they confirmed what they found hard to believe: the din was being caused by what was unmistakably a reception party for a pick-up operation.

There were men rushing about all over the field, shouting and gesticulating as if they were at a football match instead of organising an operation in which secrecy, or the lack of it, could mean the difference between life and death.

What had happened was that another *réseau* had planned a pick-up by sheer coincidence on the same field as Churchill. It was by no means unusual for an SOE circuit to be operating parallel to one run by Gaullists without the leaders knowing of each other's existence.

Churchill was in a quandary. He could announce his presence and offer to help. Or he could sit tight and let them get on with it. Two considerations helped him make up his mind: first, there was the likelihood that the excitable resisters now scurrying around the moonlit field would not take too kindly to an intruder stepping out of the shadows with a tall story about being a British officer; second, to reveal himself would expose his cover and jeopardise the security of his own circuit.

Churchill, while undoubtedly a man of courage, was never regarded by his contemporaries as a particularly security-conscious operator. But on this occasion he put caution first and stayed discreetly where he was to watch proceedings from a safe distance.

After about half an hour he and his companion heard the drone of an aircraft engine, but still the field was nothing like ready for landing. The reception team worked frantically to clear a strip through the bricks. Churchill had reckoned on taking three hours to move enough bricks to make the field fit to land a Lysander. But the aircraft by now circling patiently overhead sounded much bigger, and he realised with a thrill of horror that it was a light bomber.

It would need a clear landing run of anything from a kilometre to 1,600 metres.

Peter Churchill, like his famous namesake, was a romantic for whom special operations were something of a lark, an adventure which gave spice to living. Many of his reports to London were sent in a Damon Runyonesque style: verbose, first person singular, present tense Americanese. Which, while a source of amusement to SOE staff and deciphering clerks, did little to convey the dangers and urgency of his work.

In his description* of this operation he sometimes slips into another *genre*, referring to himself in the third person, by his code-name, *Michel*:

> The bomber circled the field patiently; the pilot could have no notion of what was waiting for him but, like all these pilots, he would stay as long as the petrol held out. All along the hedge dozens of people were watching the strange moonlit scene. *Michel* fancied that in view of all the uproar it would have been surprising indeed if anyone within radius of miles could still be sleeping.
>
> The drama about to be enacted was already giving *Michel* the creeps. This operation was pure murder. For forty full minutes the hectic heaving of bricks continued unabated.
>
> Occasionally a howl of anguish pierced the deafening roar from the Hudson's low circling, as a brick went astray, striking a hapless worker on its dangerous flight . . .

The events described by Churchill made the operation seem very much a French farce, whereas in fact it was an extremely dangerous undertaking with death as the penalty for error. However, a stretch of the field was cleared eventually, torches were switched on to mark the makeshift runway, and the signal was given to bring Pickard down.

Churchill watched as O-for-Oboe floated over the top of a hedge bordering the field. It touched down neatly between the two parallel rows of men holding torches. As it did so, one of them immediately disappeared in an avalanche of mud which squelched up like the bow wave of a torpedo boat as the aircraft careered down the field.

It reached the end and turned, and as it came to a halt its wheels sank to the axles in a quagmire. It is not difficult to imagine the scene, nor Pickard's language when he realised what had happened.

An eerie hush descended on the field, broken by the sound of the engine ticking over. Ten passengers scurried out of the aircraft and another ten clambered inside, exchanging not a word with the incoming agents. Two minutes after landing the Hudson's engines were opened to full throttle for take-off. Nothing happened.

A second attempt was made, but again the aircraft refused to budge. It was wedged firmly in its bed of mud.

* Churchill, *op cit.*

Again the silence, and as the watchers fidgeted from a distance, the aircraft door opened once again. Ten figures trooped out, and placed themselves around the wheel and a wing on one side. They were joined on the other side by the men who had just landed.

Pickard revved the engines, but still the Hudson refused to move. This time the cabin door opened and out stepped one of the crew. Churchill believed it to be the pilot, but it was more likely Flight Lieutenant Putt whose efforts in this emergency were later to be commended by Pickard.

As the agent watched, still in his hiding place, his heart warmed to his compatriots of the RAF when he heard the subdued reception party addressed in schoolboy French, flavoured by a strong English accent: 'Who is the chief of this band of savages?' asked the exasperated officer.

A young Frenchman stepped forward to be told in no uncertain terms that not only had the Hudson been brought down in what appeared to be a brickyard, but also in what was quite definitely a swamp. It is not known how much of this tirade was understood, but there was a general shuffling of feet and embarrassed explanations, all to the accompaniment of gesticulating sign language.

Eventually a farm hand turned up, leading two powerful plough horses. They were speedily yoked to the Hudson, and with everyone pushing and pulling it was finally dragged on to dry ground.

The ten outgoing passengers climbed aboard once more, and this time the aircraft was able to take off. But not without one more incident. The field was so inadequate for a light bomber that it took to the air only at the last moment. It appeared to Churchill to graze the trees at the far end of the runway – a fact later confirmed by Pickard in squadron records – and carry away branches caught in the retracting undercarriage.

Churchill recalls that he heard many years later a story of how the Hudson had passed over German flak defences 'looking so like a lame duck, carrying a large twig to build its nest, that the gaping Germans let him pass and he landed safely on his own aerodrome.'

That, however, is what the aircrews would have called 'shooting a line'. Although Churchill survived the war after capture, he never appeared to take it too seriously. Francis Cammaerts, the agent mentioned earlier for his criticism of an inaccurate supply drop, told me in a pub not far from their old Baker Street headquarters that he often seemed to regard his work with the Resistance as rather a jolly jape.

'Poor Peter,' he said. 'He never quite grew up. If he had been more security-minded he may never have been captured in the way he was.'

But for all his romanticism and schoolboyish ways, Peter Churchill has been described by SOE's official historian as a man who was undoubtedly a skilled agent, with several successes to his credit in the early days of operations.

As he watched Pickard's Hudson tearing itself free of the swampy ground at Tournus, no one would find fault with his sentiments as he pulled a hip flask from his coat pocket to drink a health to the then unknown pilot with the words, whispered in the night air: 'To a Victoria Cross – for succeeding in accomplishing the impossible.'

He was so nearly right. It was not to be a VC for Pickard, however, but a second bar to his DSO, and with it the citation: 'By his outstanding leadership, exceptional ability and fine fighting qualities, he has contributed in a large measure to the high standard of morale of the squadron he commands.'

Percy Charles 'Pick-up' Pickard had shown the way to solve SOE's problem of getting large numbers of people in and out of the field in just one operation.

But he, and a few others like him, were the cream of the RAF, men who had flown in the peace-time air force and who had a natural love and knack of flying in their blood.

The demands which were to be made on the squadron when Germany was in her final, agonised death throes, were to prove fatal to many of the less well-trained 'War Service Only' aircrews who were to come after them.

*

1848 hours, 20 March 1945: The Cyclone radials howled like furies as the rich mixture of fuel pumped through the copper arteries, and with a lurch N-for-Nan left the runway. The wheels came up with a bump into their housings as the aircraft crossed low over the main L.M.S. railway line, and the pilot banked to head east.

They passed over the village of Everton perched on the ridge overlooking the base, and in the fading light the crew would be just able to make out people moving around the High Street.

Behind there was the dark shape marking Bedford, with only a small scattering of lights although blackout restrictions had been lifted for several weeks now.

The gunner's wife was down there somewhere, at her mother's home. She

*was pregnant now and it was beginning to show. Still a few months to go
and already they had picked out a name. They both knew it was going to be a
girl . . .*

. . . Forrest Harold Thompson, or 'Tommy' to his friends, knew
why he was fighting: to kill Germans. It was as simple as that. He
had come all the way from New Zealand to do it. He and his brother
Onslow had been working on the family sheep farm in the tiny
township of Waipiro Bay when the news came over the radio that
Britain and the Empire were at war.

They had immediately volunteered for the RAF and put in for
pilot training. Onslow had made it and very soon was awarded a
medal. Tommy had 'washed out' in training, but *his* medal was not
long in coming.

On 18 March 1943 he was on his way home from a sortie over
Nuremburg with No 218 Squadron, the unit named after the Gold
Coast which had adopted it. A pilot called Helfer had joined the
same squadron eighteen months earlier, but they had never met
and another year was to pass before they would fly together.

As the fires marking Nuremberg faded into the distance, 25-year-
old Thompson was keeping a sharp look-out for the night-fighters
which were expected soon to be harrying the returning stream of
Stirlings. Not that there was much of a stream left. The bombers
were scattered all over the sky. Casualties for this month were to be
worse than anything experienced by Bomber Command since the
bloody summer of the year before.

His Stirling had come through the Nuremberg raid unscathed,
and the engines were filling the cramped compartment of his rear
turret with a constant backwash of sound, the vibration rattling the
perspex canopy and blurring his vision.

They had told him he could never be a fighter pilot because of his
size. Six feet tall and yet the RAF made him a rear gunner and
wedged him in a tiny turret!

Suddenly an enemy airfield swam into view immediately below.
For some inexplicable reason the Luftwaffe had ignored blackout
regulations and had left the flare path and barrack buildings clearly
outlined.

Knowing the bomb racks were empty, Thompson swivelled his
quad-mounted .303-calibre machine guns and squinted down the
sights, and watched his tracers spew out in a descending arc, hitting
the target just as he had scored a bull's eye on a searchlight battery
only a month before.

This time the result was equally spectacular. Every light below was extinguished, and his pilot confirmed that fires could be seen blazing in several sections of the Luftwaffe base. It was Thompson's eighteenth operational sortie. Long ago he had made it clear that he did not intend to return from an op without using up at least some of his ammunition.

He was to continue his private war the following month when he shot up trains in marshalling yards near Sedan. One of them, perhaps more, was seen to disintegrate in a cloud of smoke and steam.

He was a flight sergeant at the time, still a little envious of brother Onslow's status as a fighter pilot. But his aggression led at last to his own award of the Distinguished Flying Medal. His commanding officer wrote on the recommendation: 'He has always displayed coolness and spirit of a high order, and set a splendid example . . .'

His station commander added: 'A very keen and competent air gunner whose determination, resource and coolness in difficult circumstances have been a helpful factor in the success of the large number of sorties in which he has taken part.'

A woman in her late middle age had kissed her two sons goodbye in the doorway of a farmhouse in Waipiro Bay. 'Look after yourselves,' she told them as they left home for the first time. 'Behave yourselves and don't do anything silly when you're over there.'

She had good reason to be proud of her boys. The whole township turned out to cheer when they left.

A year after Tommy's award he was commissioned and posted to Tempsford for special operations. Onslow was killed flying a Mosquito.

PART TWO

The Waxing . . .

Look for me by moonlight,
Watch for me by moonlight,
I'll come to thee by moonlight,
Though hell should bar the way.
                    ALFRED NOYES.

5

Ming raised her head and growled softly when the stranger walked into the living room. Dorothy Pickard noticed and thought it odd, but not important. Her husband's dog was usually friendly to the point of fawning over anyone brought into the home.

The year 1942 was coming to an end and Pickard still had to make his first Hudson pick-up on the night he brought the Frenchman home to meet his wife. Ming promptly left the room and is on record as refusing to go anywhere near Henri Déricourt on subsequent visits.*

As it turned out, she was no bad judge of character; better certainly than many of the RAF officers who were to come to know this very able but mysterious organiser of pick-up operations in France.

The dog's faculty for scenting danger was first noticed by Dorothy Pickard back in 1940 when she had been aroused one night by Ming's whining and restless behaviour. Pickard was flying Wellingtons at the time with No 99 Squadron and was out on a sortie that very night. Dorothy switched on the bedside lamp and checked the time. It was twenty minutes past three in the morning. She considered ringing the station, then thought better of it.

Pickard, meanwhile, was in a dinghy in the North Sea. He had been forced to ditch with a malfunctioning starboard engine after being hit by flak in a raid over the Ruhr. Fourteen hours later he and his crew were picked up safely.

At home, Ming appeared to relax, took her first bite to eat since the previous day, and settled down for a nap. Pickard arrived home later that evening with profuse apologies, like any wayward commuter, for being a little late for dinner. He explained that the 'bloody something' on that occasion had been his Wellington running out of air. He held up his wrist watch as proof. It had smashed on impact with the water. Dorothy looked closer and saw that the hands had stopped at twenty minutes past three.

But the unusual behaviour of the big English sheepdog when a guest called for dinner nearly three years later failed to sound any alarm bells, although her hostility was noticed and mentally filed away.

* *Wings of Night*, by Alexander Hamilton. (William Kimber) 1977.

Very little was known about Henri Déricourt in the Tempsford mess, but he was destined to become a key member of SOE's organisation in France as head of the *Farrier* circuit. He had been sent to Tempsford for instruction on how to organise receptions for Lysanders, and as the Air Movements Officer based in Paris, he was to arrange more pick-ups than any other SOE operator.

He was also a German double agent who was in constant touch with the Germans, and is believed to have been paid £20,000 by them as the price put on the heads of four agents captured shortly after their arrival in France; one by a Lysander, the others by a Hudson.

To call him a traitor would be too simple an expedient for what was an incredibly complex jig-saw in the secret war fought by the Allied and German intelligence agencies, both against each other *and* against rival departments in their own multi-faceted organisations.

The squabbles, however, between SOE and Bomber Command, and with other Allied agencies, were serious at times but were no more than bickering compared with the ferocious antipathy which festered between their enemy counterparts in Paris and Berlin.

Some clarification is needed here about that most dreaded of all organisations: the Gestapo, or Geheime Staatspolizei. Literally, Secret State Police, it was actually only one branch of the SS, or Schutzstaffel, the Nazi Party security machine controlled by Heinrich Himmler. The work of the Gestapo overlapped in places with that of the SD, or Sicherheitsdienst (Security Service), which was also part of the SS.

These Nazi-inspired organisations often came into direct conflict with the Abwehr, the intelligence service of the Armed Forces, or Wehrmacht, which was commanded by Admiral Wilhelm Canaris.

The conflict became so bitter during the period of German reverses in 1944 that Himmler finally managed to discredit the Abwehr and have Canaris dismissed. By the spring of that year the entire apparatus of military intelligence had been swallowed by the SS and Canaris himself was eventually sent to a concentration camp for his indirect complicity in the abortive July bomb plot against Hitler. He was executed in 1945 a few weeks before the Allies liberated the camp.

It was as a future accomplice of the SD that Déricourt became a firm friend of Pickard and his pilots, and of agents like Francis Cammaerts. There is some evidence that his dual allegiance was not unknown to those in the highest reaches of British Intelligence, although the full extent to which he co-operated with the Germans may never be known.

His only true loyalties were to himself, and to his petite blonde wife whom he loved dearly. Although it is now believed he sent some agents to grisly deaths at the hands of the SD –perhaps not deliberately – nothing has ever been proved conclusively. There is no doubt, however, that he made an outstanding contribution to the work of SOE and the Allied cause.

He arrived in Britain on 8 September 1942, a day before his 33rd birthday, after making contact with British Intelligence in Syria the year before.

He was an airline pilot and a stunt flier before the war, and was flying transports for the French Air Force until France surrendered. He went back to civil aviation and was resting overnight in Aleppo when Allied troops marched in. He promptly offered his services to the British. But first, he said, he had to return to France to tidy up loose ends.

As soon as he returned home to Paris, he married his girl friend, gave her a large sum of money to keep her going during his absence, and set her up in a home in what was later seen to be a suspicious locality. He then contacted the embryo *Pat* escape line and was whisked to London.

In several quarters he was considered a security risk because of the possibility that he had been contacted by German Intelligence either in Syria or Paris. But SOE staff officers kept insisting he was 'clean' and finally persuaded Whitehall to give him a chance to prove his loyalty.

Déricourt had strenuously resisted the blandishments of the Free French. He insisted he would only work for the British because he could not stomach de Gaulle and his politics. He was, it seemed, a tailor-made godsend for F Section: an experienced pilot with 4,000 flying hours, he knew intimately what France looked like from the air, and he could be expected to assess as well as any RAF pilot exactly what sort of field would be suitable for clandestine landings.

On the debit side was the fact that he was a well-known figure in France and consequently would be unable to blend anonymously into his environment – a prerequisite of any agent. Déricourt's solution was as uncomplicated as any good plan should be: he simply went back home and lived openly with his bride.

The revelation after the war that the next-door neighbour to their town flat in the Rue Pergolèse was an Abwehr sergeant would seem to be no more than a coincidence. This same sergeant, Hugo Bleicher, became renowned for counter-espionage coups which led to the smashing of several of SOE's circuits, and to the arrests of Peter Churchill and Odette Sansom.

But Bleicher has always insisted he was never in contact with Déricourt. This can be explained by the fact that the Frenchman was working with the SD, whose chiefs jealously shielded their invaluable contact from the inquisitive Abwehr.

To this day Déricourt remains a mystery man. Contemporary accounts of his trial after the war credit him with being the son of a well-connnected family, not too far removed from the *aristos* of nobility. He never actually said he was of noble blood. Nor did he ever deny it.

In fact, he was born below stairs in the servants' quarters of a well-to-do family's country home.

After his first meeting at Tempsford with Pickard and the rest of No 161 Squadron's officers, he made his first parachute jump into France not far from Orleans in January 1943 and promptly began making arrangements for agents and supplies to be air-lifted for the ill-fated *Prosper* circuit operating around the environs of Paris.

His first mission was to arrange a landing ground near Poitiers for a double Lysander operation on 17 March. Four agents were taken in; another four were sent back to London. Everything went smoothly and the reception was considered a masterpiece of efficiency. The only snag was a misfortune which nearly overtook Flying Officer Peter Vaughan-Fowler when he discovered flames belching from his exhaust after touchdown. He braked hard, jumped out of the aircraft, and smothered the flames with his lifejacket before they could spread.

In the moon period of the following month Déricourt brought in two more Lysanders on a landing ground he had reconnoitred in the meadows of the Loire, near Amboise.

One agent left for London and four were put down in France. It was then that the first germs of suspicion began to fester. One of the incoming agents was Henri Frager, and he distrusted Déricourt from the first night they met.

Frager had been operating earlier in France as staff officer to a flamboyant former painter, André Girard, who had grandiose plans for recruiting a secret army of 250,000 fighting Frenchmen. Girard had persuaded SOE in the very early days that his plans were both feasible and necessary if there was ever to be a successful popular uprising against the Germans.

The alacrity with which SOE accepted his heady schemes can be excused on the grounds that they were made at a time when there was very little organised resistance in France, and because Baker Street desperately needed something to show for the demands then being made for an allocation of special duties aircraft in the face of Bomber Command's obduracy.

Girard's organisation, known as *Carte*, appealed to the more orthodox minds in London because of its military nature and aspirations. But it never had a chance of being effective, and was a constant security risk to agents like Peter Churchill who were sent in to organise supply drops and communications.

Frager, a hard-headed activist, was opposed to Girard's head-in-the-clouds romanticism and had gone to London in March 1943 to voice his doubts about *Carte* at headquarters. Girard was already in London. He had been taken out of France on one of the first three Hudson operations, possibly the third one which had been so chaotically organised.

Girard and Frager argued their respective cases, but the result was never in doubt. By then it had become clear in London that a loosely-knit organisation the size of *Carte* was too unwieldy, too insecure, and was likely to have been penetrated in several places.

Girard failed to convince London that his so-called secret army was anything but a disorganised rabble, and he left eventually for the less dangerous circuit of America's lecture halls where he gave a series of talks on undercover operations in war-torn Europe.

So much for his security.

Frager went back to France in April by the double Lysander operation laid on by Déricourt. His job was to supervise the dismantling of *Carte* and the setting up of smaller circuits with more limited, but more definite objectives. Déricourt was at the field to meet him and together they cycled twenty miles from Amboise to Tours, where accommodation had been made ready for Frager in a schoolhouse.

Next morning, as he was tucking into a frugal French breakfast, the agent was horrified to find the Gestapo calling at the school to carry out what they called, in the argot of the police forces the world over, 'routine inquiries'.

Frager, keeping well out of the way, was not convinced. He believed Déricourt had tried to betray him and vowed to report his suspicions back to London as soon as he could make contact. Ironically, his fears on this occasion were unfounded. The Gestapo had called at the school merely to inspect the children's text books.

It was part of the German educational programme designed to ensure that future generations of French men and women were not being brought up on a classroom diet hostile to the Third Reich.

A week after Frager's arrival and narrow escape, Déricourt was recalled to London, leaving on 22 April in a Lysander flown by Hugh Verity. He took with him a bottle of perfume, then obtainable in England only by having the right connections in the black market, as a present for Dorothy Pickard.

He spent two weeks discussing operations at staff level in London, and pick-up methods with Pickard and Verity at Tempsford.

He had been recalled partly at the instigation of the latter, who considered there had been an error of judgement during a pick-up operation in which a pilot had flown his Lysander into a small tree. Both man and machine survived to make the return trip, but Verity decided that Déricourt was becoming over-confident after his initial successes. As an experienced pilot he should have realised the danger of placing landing lights too near an obstruction like a tree.

As commander of the Lysander flight, Verity took scrupulous care to ensure that his pilots' lives were not put in jeopardy unnecessarily. To make a dangerous job as safe as possible he compiled an instruction manual for pick-ups which he expected his pilots and the reception ground agents to follow to the letter.

So Déricourt was brought back, as Verity put it later, to be 'torn off a strip'.*

Déricourt himself claimed afterwards that it was during this period that he was instructed by a department of British Intelligence – but not SOE – to make contact with the Germans on his return to France.†

But according to Professor Foot in his very comprehensive history *SOE in France*, there is nothing in the files of any British service to confirm the validity of this claim. Not that it is likely there would be.

The fact remains that when he parachuted back into France on 5 May, it was not very long before he made contact with the SD. He provided them with information about the times and places of several pick-up operations, and with photo-copies of mail and reports being sent back to London by agents in the Paris area.

Whether this was on the instructions and with the connivance of British Intelligence – but again, without the knowledge of SOE – or

* Verity. *op cit.*
† *Double Agent?*, by Jean Overton-Fuller. (Pan) 1961.

whether it was the result of a deal he had done with the Germans, will most likely never be known. Certainly, with a wife he loved as a potential hostage, he was in a tricky situation once the Germans tumbled to what he was up to.

So while Henri Frager's suspicions of him were well justified, Déricourt almost certainly played no part in the break-up of the *Carte* organisation. This had been penetrated well before he arrived in France early in 1943 to set up his own *Farrier* network of safe landing grounds and air-drop reception areas. And the penetration had been made by the Abwehr, not by the SD.

Again, it was probably just by blind chance that his next-door neighbour in Paris was to become the mastermind of several successful Abwehr operations against SOE. A man of burning ambition, Hugo Bleicher was destined never to rise above the rank of sergeant in spite of several brilliant coups. That he was able to smash *Carte* at a time when Déricourt had just arrived in France to begin operations was just one of those quirks of fate.

The organisation had been penetrated late in 1942, but Bleicher bided his time, making painstaking inquiries with a policeman's thoroughness. He began to draw the net tighter when Frager was in London with Peter Churchill to raise the issue of Girard's leadership.

While they were still away Bleicher made contact with Odette Sansom, Churchill's courier, who had been left behind to attend to the day-to-day running of the organisation. She had been betrayed by a captured agent, but Bleicher took care not to move too soon. He was after bigger fish, not realising that Odette herself would have been no mean catch.

With a charm which belied his unremarkable looks, he introduced himself to her by the pseudonym 'Henri', and posed as a colonel acting as a spokesman for high-ranking Army officers who wanted to do away with Hitler and make a separate peace with the Western Allies.

Mrs Sansom, a woman of astonishing courage who had left her three daughters in England to fight for her native France, was suspicious of this 'Colonel Henri', but appreciated that London would have to be told about him and his offer.

As she had more than half expected, the message came back to break off all contact immediately and go to ground. What she did not know at the time was that Churchill, who was later to become her second husband, was ordered not to get in touch with *her* on his return to France. She had become compromised.

Unfortunately for both of them, she was among the reception party when he came back by parachute, lustily and unwisely singing the 'Marseillaise' on his way down on a night in April 1943. Together they made for St Jorioz where she had booked him a room at an hotel. It was then that Bleicher moved in to lop off the heads of the organisation.

Both survived the war; Churchill possibly because the Germans believed for a time that he was a distant relative of Winston and could therefore be used as a hostage; Odette because of luck and in spite of brutal tortures and the horrors of Ravensbrück.

Bleicher himself was never responsible for ill-treating any agents he captured. His interrogation methods followed more orthodox police lines, and on many occasions they were more successful than the brutalities practised by Gestapo thugs who claimed his prisoners after he had finished with them.

His name is inextricably linked with those agents whose lives so often depended on the courage and abilities of the men who flew the Lysanders and Hudsons. He has been described, oddly, as a man with 'a little fire smouldering in his loins' to account for his prolific sex life.* Although why he should be singled out as any different to other men with the same opportunities is not readily apparent.

Like hundreds of thousands of people with ambition in the Germany of the 'thirties he joined the Nazi Party to further his career as export manager for a Hamburg firm. Suddenly it was 1939. He was 40 years old, balding, married to a hard-working *Hausfrau* called Lucie, with a ten-year-old son and a job with little excitement and a small pension at the end of it.

His call-up and early promotion to sergeant in the Geheime Feldpolizei (Field Security Police of the Wehrmacht) augured well for a long-dead ambition: to become an officer in the new élite of the Third Reich.

For Hugo Bleicher, as for many other men all over the world, the outbreak of war opened a door to a second chance of life with limitless opportunities: men like Déricourt . . . Peter Churchill . . . Charles Pickard . . . and others with appetites for danger and the Calculated Risk.

His activities first came to the attention of SOE shortly after the destruction of one of the first circuits.

The first agent parachuted into France is generally acknowledged to be Georges Bégué, a wireless operator who was dropped

* *Odette* by Jerrard Tickell. (Chapman and Hall) 1949; reprint: Kaye and Ward, 1973.

just north of Châteauroux on 5 May 1941. Within a few days he was joined by Pierre de Vomécourt, one of three sons of an aristocratic French family.

His mission was to set up a circuit known as *Autogiro*, and to persuade influential Frenchmen that the British could and would give them every support by supplying arms and stores. After three months he was joined by de Guélis, who spent a few weeks assessing the requirements for underground warfare before returning to London by the Lysander in which Nesbitt-Dufort made the first touchdown on French soil with an incoming agent.

De Vomécourt was obviously not aware that by then the first big intelligence network set up in France had already been penetrated. Known as *Interallie*, the circuit was based on Paris. It had grown out of the despair of Poles cut off from their homeland, and of patriotic Frenchmen and women who would have no dealings with the armistice negotiated by Pétain and administered by the puppet Government at Vichy.

By an unlucky chance an Abwehr officer investigating a tip-off called at the Cherbourg office and asked the sergeant on duty to help. It was Hugo Bleicher. The tip-off led to an arrest, then another and another until the entire organisation had been rolled up.

It looked like the end of the line for a gutsy little French nurse called Mathilde Carré, one of the leaders. But she was not the stuff of which martyrs are made. Within twenty-four hours of her capture she had forsaken her Polish lover, the man who had built *Interallie*, to become a double agent and mistress of the Abwehr sergeant with 'a little fire smouldering in his loins'.

It was into this maelstrom of treachery that de Vomécourt was unsuspectingly launched when his radio man Bégué was arrested. Now desperately in need of a wireless link, he decided to make contact with *Interallie*, an organisation which he knew to be transmitting intelligence to London.

Through one of his fringe contacts he was put in touch with Mme Carré, who went under what was to become the very apt code-name of *La Chatte* – the Cat – with all that animal's instinct for self-preservation.

By the time he had managed to arrange a meeting in the closing days of 1941, she was already operating as a very important pawn in the game being played by the Abwehr. She had assisted the Germans by naming *Interallie* agents, and was collaborating in a plan designed to convince London that all was well and that more supplies and agents were needed to be sent in by air.

This was the first major skirmish in the 'Secret Radio War' in which the Allied transmitter was 'turned round' to send German-inspired misinformation designed to confuse and mislead British Intelligence.

De Vomécourt had his second meeting with her in February 1942, at a cafe in Paris, with the full knowledge and blessing of Bleicher. His first request was to ask her to have a message sent to London explaining that Bégué had been arrested and to send him another radio man.

He also needed more money to start rebuilding his collapsed circuit. Mme Carré passed the message on and Bleicher, delighted, agreed that it should be sent. Fortunately, SOE did not have a trained wireless operator immediately available, but the money was sent by way of a foreign diplomat for a neutral country.

The arrival of the money assuaged some of de Vomécourt's early doubts about the wisdom of working through another circuit. But soon those suspicions were fanned alive again when *La Chatte* handed him a message purportedly received from London, advising him that a Lysander was being sent to pick him up and take him back to headquarters.

The message was genuine. But it was given to him too late for him to reach the field where the pick-up had been planned. Bleicher had no intention of allowing such a well-connected, British-trained agent to slip through his fingers.

Other snippets of information finally convinced de Vomécourt that *Interallie* had been smashed, that the radio was being worked by the Germans, and that Mathilde Carré was a traitor. It was then that he concocted a daring plan to escape by using his knowledge of her double dealings.

Always a woman with an eye for men, she was not unattracted by this aristocratic man of the world and she agreed immediately to go along with his scheme, no doubt for reasons of her own but not unconnected with her love of intrigue.

He found it a simple task to convince her – and she in turn convinced Bleicher – that she should return with him to England. Bleicher's motive was obvious: if his ever-loving Mathilde could get inside SOE headquarters, it would be a feather in his cap which would surely lead to his much-coveted elevation to officer status.

The arrangements were made by the 'turned round' radio. London laid on a high-speed naval launch and Bleicher told his girl friend to go with de Vomécourt to a rendezvous on the Channel coast. After a number of abortive attempts, they finally got away on

26 February in an operation supervised by an SOE staff officer, Major Nicholas Bodington, and watched from a nearby hiding place by the Abwehr sergeant.

The escape had all the elements of Noël Coward at his most mischievous. Here was a British agent slipping out of France in an operation instigated by the Germans – and taking with him his enemy's woman.

As soon as they were back in London, de Vomécourt lost no time in denouncing her, and waltzing Mathilde never got her chance of dancing the delicate steps of a Mata Hari in the corridors of Baker Street. Instead, she was put under house arrest for the duration and tried after the war for collaborating with the enemy.

She was found guilty of betraying thirty-five people – about one-third of the actual number she was believed to have delivered to Bleicher. Her death sentence was commuted to life imprisonment, and she was released in 1954.

While his manipulation of the *Interallie* radio can be said to be Bleicher's first important success in counter-espionage, de Vomécourt's escape and subsequent collapse of the radio bluff can be said to be his first failure, and one from which he never fully recovered.

However as he had many triumphs still to come, it is strange indeed that he remained a sergeant until the end of the war.

His next important successes came a year later with the smashing of *Carte* and the arrests of Peter Churchill and Odette. This was at a time when his neighbour in Paris, Déricourt, was enjoying the occasional hospitality of pilots in the Tempsford mess.

Bleicher was to say later he knew Déricourt was a secret agent, but that he had been warned by his superiors to steer clear of him because he was working with the SD and was consequently an untouchable so far as the Abwehr was concerned.

Déricourt parachuted back into France for a second time on 5 May 1943, and within a week he had arranged a reception for two Lysanders on a field at Touraine, near Azay-sur-Cher. The aircraft were flown by Hugh Verity and Flying Officer Frank Rymills, known to all as 'Bunny'.

Their passengers included two women: Mme Julienne Besnard, who was to become Déricourt's courier for the eleven months before she was whisked back to England; and Vera Leigh, a remarkable woman of forty who designed dress fashions in peace-time and became a crack shot during weapon training.

She was sent into the field as a courier to *Inventor*, a circuit working alongside Henri Frager's *Donkeyman*. She was to be executed in revolting circumstances at Natzweiler concentration camp shortly after the Normandy landings.

Also on that flight to join *Inventor* were Sidney Jones, a 41-year-old cosmetic salesman who had the job of training raw Resistance recruits in the use of firearms and explosives; and Marcel Clech, his wireless operator.

One of the passengers on the homeward trip was one of F Section's best agents, Major Francis Suttill, who had built the huge *Prosper* network just south of Paris after the collapse of *Autogiro*. He returned to France two weeks later after being briefed to prepare for an invasion, just in case it should be launched later that year. It wasn't. But before the year was out his network had been destroyed and he was enduring months of brutal torture before his death at the hands of the Gestapo.

Again the spectre of treachery arises to haunt the survivors. Suttill and Déricourt knew each other, and the latter used *Prosper*'s wireless to finalise arrangements for the early pick-up operations.

In June 1943, Déricourt supervised yet another double Lysander operation not far from Angers. Three more women marked for death clambered out of the aircraft flown by Rymills and Flying Officer Jimmy McCairns: Diana Rowden, who was to be executed at Natzweiler; Noor Inayat Khan, murdered at Dachau; Cecily Lefort, who died or was killed at Ravensbrück.

Was Déricourt responsible? The connection is there, but there is no way of knowing for sure.

All three of these tragic women lasted for several months on operations in the field before being captured separately as a result of a combination of different circumstances. All that is known about their arrival in France is that Déricourt put them on bicycles and accompanied them to the railway station at Angers where he saw them apparently safely on their way to their destinations.

Noor Inayat Khan, who incidentally was a great-great-great granddaughter of Tippoo Sultan, the Tiger of Mysore and the last Mogul Emperor of southern India, headed for Paris. Her biographer believes she was *not* betrayed by Déricourt, although by that time it is now known that he was co-operating with the SD.[*]

Noor – her name means 'Light of Womanhood' – worked for four months, sending radio messages for the *Prosper* circuit at a time when it was being blown wide open by the Germans.

[*] *Noor-un-Nisa Inayat Khan (Madeleine)*, by Jean Overton-Fuller (East-West Publications) 1971.

Diana Rowden was seriously compromised by the arrest of her immediate chief a month after her arrival, but she continued to carry out useful work as a courier in south-east France, along the Swiss and Italian frontiers, before her arrest towards the end of the year.

Cecily Lefort was sent in as a courier to the new *Jockey* circuit then being set up by Francis Cammaerts.

She was arrested while staying at a house which Cammaerts had warned her against using, so she was clearly not a victim of Déricourt's double dealings. Déricourt himself went back to London on 20 July for one night only, for reasons which have never been made public. It was at a time when growing suspicions about his activities were being voiced in several quarters.

Nevertheless he was allowed to return to France. He travelled in Verity's Lysander and was welcomed at Châteauroux by a reception party organised by a Resistance group with which he had no previous dealings. He immediately made himself scarce, travelling across more than 100 miles of country, unmolested by German patrols and police checkpoints, to plan his first Hudson operation at Angers the very next night. This itself was a masterpiece of organisation.

Meanwhile, the feeling at Tempsford in that first half of 1943 was that Déricourt was a jolly good fellow who knew what he was doing. As far as the pilots were concerned, it was comforting to know that he would be in charge of a reception because as an experienced pilot he would never try to bring them down in conditions, for example, which faced Pickard on his third Hudson operation.

The tree incident was put down to a mistake caused by over confidence, and was considered unlikely to be repeated after the reprimand given to him by Verity.

On the ground, the mechanics and maintenance men were under the eagle eye of the Station Engineering Officer, Syd Firth, a pre-war regular who joined the RAF as a fifteen-year-old apprentice in 1922 and finished the war as a squadron-leader. A strict disciplinarian, he was intolerant of shoddy work. In the year since the beginning of operations at Tempsford he had taken the ground crews by the scruff of their communal neck and welded them into a team which took pride in keeping the aircraft in flying condition. With so few aircraft at the squadron's disposal it is to the ground crews' credit that so few missions had to be scrubbed because of mechanical defects.

He always emphasised at ground crew briefings that it was essential for every aircraft to be in tip-top condition. Resistance fighters were risking their lives just to lay on receptions, and if the aircraft failed to turn up their lives would have been put in jeopardy for nothing.

'Old Syd', as the youngsters of the air crews called him – he was only thirty-six – was always in Air Traffic Control for take-off.

If anything sounded wrong he would make the decision to halt the flight for a snap inspection. He would always take a look at the engines himself, and the sight of him forever clambering up ladders to peer into an aircraft's innards always gave the pilots a reassuring surge of confidence.

The maintenance failure rate at Tempsford was kept to the bare minimum because of a practice from which he never deviated. He always insisted that the 'War Service Only' fitters were supervised by regulars who had been through the rigorous pre-war apprentice scheme.

He also made it his business to threaten new arrivals at the station with dire consequences if they were ever caught gossiping about the squadron's activities. He told them their phone calls would be tapped and their letters opened; and he would then dismiss them, grimly satisfied by their boggling stares that at least he had given them something to think about.

The squadron was now settling down a routine, enlivened by the moon period of operations, with few of the makeshift improvisations of the early days. The pilots were tough and most of them were experienced in the dangers of bombing operations with other squadrons; the ground crews were the best in the business.

But in the New Year of 1944 many of these young veterans would leave for other duties, to be replaced by new crews who would have the same dedication, but who tragically would lack the same training and experience against an enemy whose defences were growing stronger.

*

1930 hours, 20 March 1945: They were out across the sea when there was a staccato crackle of gunfire, ending abruptly, and once more there was the familiar throbbing of the engines as the Hudson powered on through the night towards the now peaceful coast which had once been so hostile.

The wireless operator relaxed. It was just Tommy testing the guns he loved so much. Since joining the secret squadron he had never had the chance of using them on the ground targets he used to shoot up.

They were considering volunteering for the Pathfinders before the war ended. It would mean more action. Tommy was older and married, but they had a lot in common. Both had been flight sergeants on bombing operations, and both had been awarded the DFM . . .

. . . He hurried out of the hotel, almost at a run, with his parents close behind, and looked up and down the Strand for a taxi. Up in Yorkshire taxis were like telegrams: only to be used for emergencies like weddings and funerals. But today was different, a very important day in June 1943. It would not be right to keep the King waiting.

He raised an arm, and as the battered wartime cab pulled into the kerb, an impish smile broke across his face when the driver lowered his window and asked where they were going.

'Buckingham Palace, please,' he replied, and the cabbie nodded. He had seen it all before. As the taxi clattered round Trafalgar Square, passing under Admiralty Arch to head up the Mall, Janet Escreet thought with secret relief about that map stuck on the wall back at home in Withernsea.

It now had 28 pins marking bombing raids; 28 signposts, each one signifying a dangerous moment in her son's life; each one pointing to this day and this event at the Palace.

The last one had been stuck into the spot marking the 'pranged' city of Essen just a few weeks earlier. Ray Escreet's tour of duty with No 15 Squadron's Stirlings had now expired. He had beaten odds which historians were to calculate later gave only ten in every hundred of the early bomber crews an expectation of surviving a full tour.

He had parted company with his old crew at the squadron's base at Bourn. There had been Flight Sergeant O'Diggins, the first of them to be awarded a DFM after that raid on Hamburg in July 1942. They had been shot up by flak on the way home and the port outer engine was out of action when they were jumped by a Messerschmitt 110.

A second German fighter had joined the battle. He still had the newspaper clipping which gave a brief account of the engagement: 'Sergeant Diggins coolly directed his pilot in evasive tactics, and by skilful use of his guns he caused the port engine of the fighter to burst into flames.'

It had been their twelfth op, all of them with Pilot Officer Meredith, and their closest brush with death since the first sortie when the undercarriage had collapsed on landing.

They had been forced to make an emergency landing at Coltishall, coming down fast and lop-sided, piling up on the runway and slithering to a halt with a screech of tortured metal which even now he could hear in his eardrums. He had escaped with no more than a graze on his cheek. All he had told his worried mother was that he had bumped into a doorway in the blackout.

Then there had been his close friend Freddie, a French-Canadian sergeant who had spent his weekend leaves at Escreet's home because he had nowhere else to go. Janet Escreet had started knitting him a warm, woolly balaklava to match the one she had done for her own son.

One day he told her there was no point in finishing it. 'Freddie won't be needing it now,' was all he had been able to tell her.

She had not asked any questions. There was no need to.

All that was behind him and now he was settling into the rut of routine flights with the Base Maintenance Unit at Mildenhall. He helped his mother out of the taxi while his father got out the other side to pay the fare.

Once inside the Palace they were ushered along corridors and shown into a long room, resplendent with red and gold-upholstered chairs, and with matching décor.

Escreet was then escorted out of the room to join a group of young men; most of them in air force blue, a few in khaki and naval uniforms, some with wounds still in bandages, and on crutches or in wheelchairs.

His parents, with others of their age, looked around and wondered about the clocks, more than a dozen of them and all keeping the correct time. In spite of the solemnity of the moment, Janet Escreet found it hard to repress a giggle when she thought about the Palace servant whose job it was to look after them.

What was he called? The Royal Winder-upper? The Palace Time-keeper? Strains of orchestral music filtered through from what she later discovered was the Throne Room.

Ray, meanwhile, had been paired off with another airman, the two of them part of a human centipede which shuffled slowly forward. Then suddenly he was standing before a dais covered in red velvet, and a man in the uniform of a Marshal of the RAF was saying something in a gentle voice which could not quite hide a slight stutter.

He could not catch the words, but there was no mistaking the warmth, and at that moment when he felt dizzy with pride, he felt he really would be prepared to risk his life for this man who was his

King. The medal was pinned to his tunic for 'skill, devotion to duty and a great keenness to participate in operations.'

It was a beautiful day in June and Ray Escreet had just celebrated his 21st birthday.

6

The door of the Mess swung open and the big man strode towards the bar. He was with a senior officer from the staff at the Air Ministry. Eyes followed their progress curiously. Something odd here. The big man had a deep suntan and the lived-in face of middle age, yet the rings of rank on his sleeve showed him to be a mere flight lieutenant. Not many junior officers were accorded the privilege of a top brass escort when they arrived to take up a posting at Tempsford.

Charles Pickard was at the bar with station commander Mouse Fielden. They had been expecting the newcomer and knew a little about him; enough to have their own imaginations whetted about this formidable Frenchman.

Philippe Livry should never have been in the RAF at all. He was a colonel of Artillery, a Chevalier of the Legion of Honour, with a Croix de Guerre, several citations, and the scar of a wound to show for his exploits in World War I. At the outbreak of Hitler's War he had rejoined his old regiment and was wounded again, this time seriously enough to give him a permanent limp, while on duty in the Maginot Line.

He had escaped to England by the simple expedient of catching a first-class sleeper to Lisbon and he arrived in London with the express intention of getting back into the fight with *les sales Bôches* as soon as possible. RF section of SOE wanted him, but he would have no dealings with Gaullists, and in any case he had no desire to fight the war from behind a desk in London.

As the RAF appeared to be doing all the real fighting in 1941, he made up his mind to join the war in the air. There was only one snag: he was far too old. But that handicap was soon overcome, once again, by simple measures. He marched purposefully into a recruiting office near Euston station to sign on as an ordinary aircraftman after telling an inventive story about his age. It says much for his commanding personality that he was able to overawe the recruiting officer into accepting what must obviously have been a transparently blatant lie.

He arrived at Tempsford shortly before his 45th birthday after a vigilant officer in Air Intelligence had the wit to realise his talents could be better utilised as a navigator on clandestine missions over

the familiar countryside of his native country than as an 'erk'
polishing brasses on a base Somewhere Else in England.

Livry was actually a *nom de guerre*. His real name was Level, but he
took a pseudonym to protect his wife and children who were still
living at the family home not far from Caen. As far as the Vichy
authorities were concerned he, and other Frenchmen like him,
were breaking the law by continuing hostilities against Germany.
He later adopted the pseudonym officially and the family is now
known by the name Livry-Level.

This, then, was the man Pickard and Fielden watched walking
towards the crowded Mess bar on that day in February. Tall, nearly
as tall as Pickard, with a powerful physique a little overweight at
around 15-stone, and with a magnificent, military-style moustache
which made the wispy efforts on the upper lips of young men
around him seem gossamer imitations.

Livry paused at the door and looked around the large rectangular
room. In the centre there was a brick fireplace giving off a warm
glow. Through the smoky atmosphere he could see scattered
groups of officers, some chatting, some playing cards or reading,
others dozing in comfortable armchairs. In one corner, apart from
the British, a sprinkling of Poles chatted and gesticulated in an
animated manner which set them apart from the others.

The hubbub of conversation died a little as he walked on towards
the bar where the two senior officers were waiting to be introduced.
After meeting Fielden, he turned towards Pickard. The two big men
eyed each other then shook hands, both perhaps putting a little
more into it than was really necessary. Pickard winced. He had
forgotten his broken thumb had not quite recovered from the
damage it had suffered in the New Year's Eve revelry in the Mess.

After that unpromising start Livry went on to explain to his new
squadron commander that he had fought the first war in the
trenches and the second from a rampart in the Maginot Line. His
experience of night flying was limited to some fifty hours or so – and
all of it over the sea.

'That's not important,' Pickard replied with what seemed to Livry
to be a supreme optimism. 'Flying by night can be extremely
pleasant – you can't see the obstacles.'*

For all his seniority in the French Army, Livry was given no
special privileges with No 161 Squadron, and his quarters were as
sparse as those of any other lowly flight lieutenant: a small room,

* *Missions dans la RAF*, by Colonel Philippe Livry-Level. (Ozanne) 1951.

about 14 feet by 8 feet, with just enough room for a single bed, two armchairs and a dressing table.

Accustomed as he was to the luxuries of a flat in a fashionable *arrondissement* of Paris, and with an eighteenth-century château called Audrieu as his country home, Livry did the only thing possible to improve his home comforts at Tempsford by switching on his portable electric fire on that very first winter's night.

Against all the regulations he left it on day and night until the following July.

Apart from the English winter, he also had to suffer another extreme hardship: English cooking, à la RAF mess hall style. He looked on it as the type of food which the Germans gave to prisoners-of-war.

It took a week before he could settle down to life on the station; possibly because on his own admission he was not a conversationalist – or 'chatterbox' as he called it – and possibly because he was so much older than most of the other men.

His first operational sortie was a failure, and for him it was a disaster. He had been so determined to prove to his young comrades that youth did not have a monopoly on courage or ability in war. He had been assigned to the squadron's flight of five Halifax bombers, whose job was to parachute agents and supplies deep into Europe. Each of the aircraft carried a row of nappies painted on the fuselage to indicate successful missions, in the same way that fighter pilots marked their 'kills' with swastikas. A dirty nappy meant a 'washed out' mission.

After the briefing for his first foray over enemy territory, Livry spent hours planning the route. The target was a field in Brittany, where they were to drop twelve containers packed with supplies for a Resistance *réseau*. They survived a light flak barrage on the way across the French coast, but were blown off course by a north wind. Livry failed to compensate for it. A little later they were picked up by searchlights around an airfield and once more came under fire from anti-aircraft guns.

A shell exploded along one side of the fuselage, and there was a loud bang near one of the wings.

'It's finished, it's all over,' thought Livry, more in surprise than fear.

But it was by no means all over. Again the aircraft got through, but by this time it was too late to think of searching for the rendezvous and the pilot returned home, leaving Livry burning with a feeling of shame. After a safe touchdown the middle-aged navigator, now feeling much older than his years, confessed to Fielden, his contemporary, that he felt he had no aptitude for night flying.

The station commander told him not to worry about his first 'dirty nappy' sortie, that he had done no more than make all the usual mistakes on coming under fire, and that he would eventually learn how to cope with it.

Fielden was right. Within a month the Frenchman had recovered his *sang-froid* by guiding his pilot right up to the outskirts of Paris, where they dropped two agents complete with bicycles. He was so cheered by this success that he wanted the pilot to return via Caen so that he could look down on Audrieu, the château where his wife and children lay sleeping.

He also wanted another tilt at those searchlights and anti-aircraft defences which had so thoroughly surprised him by their venom on that first mission. But this had to wait for another year, until he joined a Mosquito squadron with Pickard.

A few years later he wrote:* 'It was always difficult to pass those searchlights south of Caen without remembering the fear of that first mission.'

It was not until he was homeward bound from another mission, and peeled away from the formation on a private, low-level raid to shoot them up, that he managed 'to take care of that old debt'.

While Livry was settling down to the tempo of life at Tempsford, the Hudson pick-up operations were still very much in their infancy. After the success of the first three by Pickard, the following month passed without any attempted landings.

Livry concentrated on learning the ropes of night navigation with the Halifax flight, and spent his off-duty hours trying to keep his vow to cycle 30 kilometres a day to exercise the leg which was still troubling him nearly three years after he had been wounded during the Allies' precipitate retreat through France.

He was no longer the new boy of the squadron as a newly-commissioned pilot officer had just been posted in as a replacement: John Affleck, who had completed 23 bombing sorties with No 77 (Scottish) Squadron – one sortie for every year of his life at that point. Affleck was not too unhappy when he was told he was being taken out of the firing line before he had finished the usual tour of 30 operations.

In common with many aircrew, he had acquired a veneer of fatalism which accepted that survival was a matter of chance.

* Livry-Level, *op cit.*

Consequently he was quite willing to accept the chance of a quieter
life-style with No 24 Operational Training Unit and the rural
delights of the base at Honeybourne in the Vale of Evesham.

Still a flight sergeant at the time, he very soon picked up a
reputation, as he was to tell me later, for being 'a bit of a bolshie'. He
had scant respect for authority when it took the form of non-flying
wing commanders and above who owed their rank to the fact that
they were administrative career officers of the pre-war RAF.

Of course, even in the wartime RAF, Affleck could not beat the
system. His private feud with authority came to a head after a night
training flight with a crew of raw recruits in a Whitley.

He remembers it as vividly as if it were yesterday: 'One of the
engines conked out and although it was only a training flight we
were carrying a full load of bombs. I couldn't just jettison them any
old where, so I told the crew to bail out and set a course on
automatic which would take the aircraft out to sea.

'I was just about to leave myself when I found the pupil-navigator
still in the fuselage and paralysed with fright. He'd actually pulled
his ripcord *before* jumping out, and kept pulling until yards and
yards of useless silk lay in folds around his feet. It was quite a
problem.'

It was out of the question simply to jump and leave the navigator
to sort out the problem alone. So Affleck went back to the cockpit,
took charge of the controls once more, and managed to nurse the
bomber back to Honeybourne where he piled it up on the runway.
Luckily, the bombs failed to detonate, otherwise he would not have
lived long enough to become one of the key men in No 161
Squadron's Hudson pick-up team.

After helping the badly scared navigator out of the remains of
their Whitley, he was ordered to appear before his commanding
officer to explain why he had endangered his life and everyone
else's by bringing back a crippled bomber filled with high explosive.

The explanation did little to satisfy his superior. But as he had
done nothing he could really be criticised for, the CO decided that
the navigator should be court-martialled instead. Which would
have been an ideal solution to a problem constructed by a red-tape
mind but for the fact that Affleck calmly announced that he was the
only witness and that he had no intention of giving evidence.

At that point, as the Americans would have said, something really
did hit the fan. Affleck was made to realise that flight sergeants were
in no position to say what they would and would not do, and he was
posted to what was known as the 'Bad Boys Course' at Brighton.

There, miscreants spent their time drilling on the parade ground and working off their surplus bloody-mindedness under the unforgiving eyes of the RAF's physical training instructors.

These establishments were known officially as Aircrew Refresher Centres – there were others at Bournemouth and Sheffield – and were about one degree removed from an army 'glasshouse', the difference being that the inmates were not under arrest or confined to barracks.

It was there that Affleck met Dickie Richards, a flight sergeant with boisterous high spirits who was to become his navigator at Tempsford.

After Brighton he returned to Honeybourne to find little had changed. He regarded the training programme as disastrous and pointed to the number of deaths and injuries in accidents as evidence that the 'green' crews were not being given adequate instruction.

His doubts were well justified. Figures produced after the war showed that 5,327 aircrew were killed and 3,113 injured in training accidents. The record of the Operational Training Units was appalling and one unofficial historian estimates that some courses lost as many as a quarter of their trainees before graduation.* The OTU's were anything but a rest cure, as the tour-expired crews were to discover when they were posted to instruct recruits in clapped-out aircraft.

While the inadequacies of the training programme were obvious to the young veterans, there was a war on and they had no option but to get on with the job of passing on to the newcomers all they had learned in the skies above Germany.

But John Affleck was not content to let it rest at that. When the Air Officer Commanding the programme visited No 24 OTU on an inspection tour, the Scotsman told him exactly what he thought.

Then came the bombshell: he learned he had been awarded the Air Force Medal (AFM). That more or less sealed his fate. When a sergeant crosses swords with an air vice-marshal and rubs salt in the wounds by winning a medal, there can only be one outcome. One or the other would have to go.

Affleck went. He was told he was being returned to Main Force bombing duties to complete his tour of 30 operations. Luckily, a squadron leader called Bob Hodges, who was later to become an air chief marshal, came to the rescue. They had become friendly after a chance meeting, but all that Affleck knew of him was that he was

* *Bomber Command* by Max Hastings (Michael Joseph) 1979.

flying with a somewhat furtive and secretive outfit somewhere in Bedfordshire.

Hodges offered him a job with a promise of all the excitement he could handle without the dangerous monotony of bombing operations. He accepted and arrived at Tempsford in March 1943 in time to be part of the squadron élite under Pickard, whom he iconoclastically came to regard as a glamour boy trying to live up to his film role as a war hero.

March . . . a time of relative calm, with no operations laid on for the Hudsons and only six for the Lysanders. It was as if the squadron were holding its breath, waiting and gathering strength for the demands which were to be made on it in the months to come.

It was a time for writing letters and catching up on lost sleep, and for celebrating the simple joys of merely being alive, in pubs like the Wheatsheaf opposite the village church, and the Dick Turpin just a short walk away on the main road to London. One of the attractions there, apart from the warm beer, was a famous tail gunner with the 8th United States Air Force, which had bases nearby. His name: Clark Gable.

Early vegetables were beginning to appear in the fields around Gibraltar farm, and the contingent of two hundred or so young girls of the WAAF held what they called a 'Gala Dance with Tea' to commemorate the first anniversary of their arrival at Tempsford, and lectures were held for all Other Ranks only on the dangers of VD. The officers obviously knew all about it.

It was spring and love was in the air in this all too brief a breathing space.

That unreal month of March soon came to an end and the chill wind of war began to blow once more across the bleak fields of Tempsford. People in high places were beginning to realise the importance of air operations in building up the restless underground armies of resistance.

The Secretary of State for Air, Sir Archibald Sinclair, arrived at the base, full of curiosity, for an official but highly secret visit. He returned to London full of enthusiasm for the work being done, and somewhere, in some office in Whitehall, the signal was given for the full go-ahead.

The squadron responded with maximum effort. The exceptionally good weather for April enabled the crews to carry out a record number of 32 operations with the Halifaxes, fifteen with the Lysanders, and two with the solitary O-for-Oboe Hudson.

Both were carried out by Pickard with his inseparable friend and navigator, Flying Officer Alan Broadley, who had been with him since their first operations with the Wellingtons of No 99 Squadron back in April 1940.

Now, exactly three years later, they landed two agents at Pont de Vaux. There was some confusion and a lot of excited chatter by the reception party when Pickard touched down to find eleven people waiting to be taken back to London when he had expected only four.

Eventually he compromised by taking back eight. Three unfortunates had to be left behind because on this particular operation two senior officers had made the trip unofficially just to see how the Hudson handled on its fourth pick-up.

Any other pilot would have received a monumental rocket in the ear or somewhere for taking non-essential sightseers. But Pickard was the CO and as such a law unto himself. The journey of Wing Commander Brooks may not have been entirely necessary, but the other passenger was Wing Commander Guy Lockhart. As one of the original Lysander pilots, by then working in Air Intelligence as a liaison officer for clandestine flights, he could perhaps be excused.

So with these odds stacked against him, the landing ground organiser, Paul Rivière, made no formal complaint. Rivière, who worked for the Gaullist RF-section of SOE, was second only to Déricourt in the number of pick-ups he organised, and was in fact responsible for getting more people in and out of France than any other SOE agent.

Three nights later Pickard carried out his last Hudson operation, landing at la Plaine de Chamet after some initial difficulty in locating the landing lights, and taking off twenty minutes later with eight Frenchmen.

Curiously, the reception is recorded as being organised by *Michel*, which was the code-name for Peter Churchill. But he had actually been arrested on his own return to France by parachute two days earlier. Incidentally, the dispatcher who had helped him out into the night with a gentle tap just as he was beginning his rendering of the 'Marseillaise' was none other than Flight Lieutenant Philippe Livry.

Unlike Pickard and many of his other young officers, Livry was deeply concerned about the political implications of the war. While they thought no further than just getting on with it, he looked ahead to how his beloved France would be changed by it.

A realist, he knew things would never be the same again. He told

Hugh Verity* that France had always been good to him in that he was born with position and privilege. He was much better off than most Frenchmen and therefore felt he owed more to his country. That was why he was fighting for it when many of his age were content to play less active and certainly less dangerous roles.

Although he was anti-communist by both upbringing and instinct, he never allowed his personal antipathy to influence his actions.

He once suggested to John Affleck, a wicked grin spreading across his seamed face, that they should fly their Halifax to a region of Brittany where he knew of a huge quarry, and drop into it the four known communist agents who were at that moment sitting huddled together near the exit hatch in the floor of the fuselage.

It was not, of course, a serious suggestion. Like many thousands of Frenchmen he was prepared to abandon ideological differences for the duration to erase the stigma of the French capitulation and the German occupation. Setting the troubled house of France in order could come later.

The end of the April moon period brought changes to Tempsford. For Pickard, the war appeared to be over. He was grounded, very much against his wishes, after completing exactly one hundred operational sorties with four squadrons.

But first, there was an incident in the Mess which I am assured had no bearing on his departure from Tempsford.

It was one of those nights when the crews had been stood down from operations because of the weather and Pickard was at the bar killing time and large whiskies.

It was getting late when Fielden arrived glowing with satisfaction and obvious pride, and sporting a brand-new decoration on his already much bemedalled tunic. He was now a Commander of the Royal Victorian Order, a stepping stone along his way to an eventual knighthood.

Pickard, who had a DSO and bar, with a DFC and a second bar to the DSO in the pipeline for his Hudson operations, was the first to spot the new decoration. With a howl of feigned rage, he clutched at his own medal ribbons, ripped them from his tunic, and threw them into the fireplace.

Fielden was not very amused, but it was no more than coincidence that the news of Pickard's posting came through not very long afterwards. He was promoted to group captain and sent to command the RAF station at Lissett, up in East Yorkshire.

* Verity, *op cit.*

For a man like Pickard it seemed an inconspicuous end to what had been a distinguished and exciting career. He was going out in a blaze of anonymity. The aircraft at his disposal were to be the slow, ugly Ventura bombers, which the pilots called 'the Flying Pig' and which he himself condemned for having all the flying characteristics of a suitcase and the elegance of a turnip.* Like the Hudsons, they were built by Lockheed and were in fact an advanced version. But by that stage in the war they were virtually useless for bombing operations.

He took one look around his new command, then told his wife not to bother looking for a new home at Lissett, but to stay where she was at Tempsford. He had no intention of seeing out the rest of the war mothering newly-qualified pilots in obsolete aircraft.

'I've had more excitement chasing rabbits and washing nappies,' he wrote in a letter home, conveniently ignoring the fact that he had never washed a nappy in his life.

From that moment on he devoted all his considerable energies to persuading his superiors that he should be posted to a more active unit. He fully intended to get back where the action was no matter what obstacles were put in his path by well-intentioned and highly-placed friends who believed he had already done more than his bit for victory.

Pickard's job at Tempsford was taken over by one of his keenest disciples: Squadron Leader Lewis Macdonald Hodges, known to all as 'Bob' and a man who was to have all the honours of his country thrust on him. His appointment to command No 161 Squadron was one of the first steps of a career which was to reach its climax in 1973 when he became Deputy Commander-in-Chief of all Allied forces in Central Europe.

When he rescued John Affleck from the petty disciplines of a non-combat unit he had already been earmarked for distinction as commander of the squadron's flight of Halifaxes when it was detached to an advanced base at Kinloss in Scotland at the beginning of 1943. He was then not quite twenty-four years old.

His job was to lead them on a mission ranging 1,000 miles to Norway, but the ideal weather conditions deemed necessary for the operation failed to materialise and it was aborted. Hodges returned to Tempsford in time to join the congratulations for the success Pickard had just achieved by completing the first three pick-ups in a Hudson.

Hodges had joined the squadron at around the same time as

* Hamilton, *op cit.*

Hugh Verity, in November 1942, and they shared the same quarters a few miles from the station in a country mansion commandeered by the authorities for the duration.

At that time the squadron was getting over the early teething troubles although, according to Verity, there was 'an atmosphere of cinematic stunt-riding about the whole business of pick-up operations'.* So while Hodges developed and improved the less dramatic methods of dropping supplies and agents from the Halifaxes, Verity set out to standardise the highly individualistic techniques used for Lysander operations.

They had accomplished much together by the time Hodges was given overall command in the May of that beautiful summer. He was decorated with his second Distinguished Flying Cross and promoted to wing commander, while Verity picked up his first decoration, also a DFC.

They were the lucky ones. Flight Lieutenant Jack Bartrum, a pre-war, part-time flier who had known Verity since their days in the Oxford University Air Squadron, arrived at Tempsford on 6 May as a replacement for the Lysander flight.

Ten days later he was returning from a training flight when he stalled just before touchdown. Verity, who had just landed a Hudson, saw it smash down on the concrete runway and watched helplessly as his friend died in the blazing wreckage.

He had persuaded Bartrum to join the squadron, and as the Lysander burned he felt the chill which comes with the death of a man you have known and liked, and with whom you have shared the same hopes and fears. Verity, the son of a clergyman, was then twenty-five years old. Bartrum was about the same age.

'It was the ninth time I had seen a friend die in similar circumstances,' he told me many years later. 'By then there is no feeling of shock, just a numbness. It's not callous, it's self-preservation. There's a limit to how much grief you can take.

'I had reached the point of having a sort of casing around me. You just accept death as a fact and get on with the job as well as you can. But you never forget.'

Bartrum's death right on their doorstep was an ugly reminder to the aircrews that death was but a brief moment of carelessness away. And it was a reminder to Verity that his job was to ensure the Lysander Flight was run on what would be called today a 'cost-effective' basis: a maximum amount of work output with the

* Verity, *op cit.*

minimum of resources available, and carried out in the most economical way in terms of production and lives.

If Pickard was a swashbuckling buccaneer of the air who flew by the seat of his pants, Verity was a dedicated technician who took chances only when there was no other alternative. His manual on how pick-up operations should be carried out became the bible for both pilots and agents, and was itself to become a historical document when Professor Foot included it as an appendix to his official history of the SOE in France.

Verity's concluding summary is a masterpiece of British understatement:

> Finally, remember that Lysander and Hudson operations are perfectly normal forms of war transport and don't let anyone think that they are a sort of trick-cycling spectacle, for this conception has tended in the past to cut down the number of operations attempted.*

He also insisted on going by the book as far as landing procedures were concerned. Pilots were warned not to land if there was any irregularity in the flare path, or if an incorrect identification signal was flashed from the ground. Referring to Sticky Murphy's escapade† he wrote: 'In one case where this rule was disobeyed, the pilot came home with 30 bullet holes in his aircraft and one in his neck . . .'

Hodges, who had not made any pick-ups by the time he became squadron commander, was to rely very much on Verity's expertise as a veteran of eight successful Lysander operations. Two more months were to pass before he was to carry out his own first pick-up. The Hudson, especially, was not the sort of aircraft that took kindly to strange hands at the controls. Hodges knew all there was to know about a Halifax, but you could not simply slide into the cockpit of a Hudson and steer it through the night like a bus.

So the next Hudson pick-up after Pickard's departure was carried out by Mouse Fielden himself, accompanied by the station navigation officer, Squadron Leader James 'Waggy' Wagland, and Flying Officer Cocker, the wireless operator.

It was a very special mission for a Very Important Passenger, and the 39-year-old station commander did not intend to put the burden of responsibility for it onto younger shoulders. In any case, Verity was the only other available pilot with any experience of

* Foot, *op cit.*
† See pages 52-54.

flying Hudsons and he was otherwise engaged with the Lysanders down at Tangmere.

The group captain took off at 2250 hours on 15 May, knowing that no less a personage than the Prime Minister was taking a keen interest in the outcome. Consequently it was much to his chagrin that he was unable to locate the reception party lights in the Plaine de Chanet region because of fog. He returned to base to plan a second attempt.

Meanwhile, in France, the VIP went back into hiding. He was urgently wanted in England in the hope that he would be able to do something to relieve the strained relations between the British and de Gaulle. It was hoped, perhaps naively, that the Free French leader might feel indebted to General Joseph Georges, the man who had given him command of a division in 1940.

This was the VIP Fielden had been ordered to snatch out of France. As de Gaulle's military superior it was thought he would at least be able to influence the self-appointed saviour of France's honour and mellow his intransigent attitude towards the Allies.

It was a forlorn hope at best, but one which Winston Churchill thought worth trying.

General Georges, by then in his sixty-eighth year, was however a broken man. When the Germans broke through at Sedan he is reported to have collapsed in his headquarters and spent the rest of the campaign racked by sobs and indecision.

Hardly a man likely to have much influence on the actions of a high-principled soldier like de Gaulle.

None of this politicking in high places was of any concern to Mouse Fielden. Four days after the aborted Hudson mission he went out again and landed successfully this time with three outward-bound agents. After a delay of about ten minutes, General Georges turned up with five other passengers and all seemed set.

Then came the final blow to British hopes. Fielden decided he could not risk a direct trip home. The last part of the journey would have to be made in daylight, and in the comparatively slow Hudson he would have needed more luck than he felt fair to expect to avoid Luftwaffe fighters patrolling the Channel.

Instead, he headed south to land at the Maison Blanche airfield near Algiers. The idea was to return to England the following night, via Gibraltar. Which would have been an excellent plan if General Georges had not immediately removed himself from Maison Blanche to report to General Henri Giraud – a bitter and intense rival of de Gaulle!

The RAF's part in this reunion of the generals in North Africa only served to exacerbate de Gaulle's suspicions of Allied plots to wrest from him the leadership of the Free French.

On the same night as Fielden's unwitting gaffe, Verity also carried out *his* first Hudson pick-up as the squadron had by now acquired a second aircraft, P-for-Peter. He landed in a field near Lons-le-Saunier in the Saône valley, with Livry as his navigator and Eddie Shine, a flight sergeant from Yorkshire, doubling as wireless operator and turret gunner.

They left Tempsford ten minutes before Fielden and made their own rendezvous at about the same time, some hundred miles to the east of him. Verity, however, never thought of going anywhere else but straight home after landing his one passenger and picking up eight.

As Fielden was heading south with his precious general, Verity was risking the daylight Channel crossing. He arrived back at base at a quarter past six in the morning, forty minutes before O-for-Oboe touched down at Maison Blanche.

Nevertheless, the group captain had the last laugh. When he returned to Tempsford he set the pattern for future diversions to Algiers and Gibraltar by bringing back all the Mediterranean fruit he could carry, together with other luxuries unobtainable in wartime Britain.

The importance of the Hudson as an air-taxi could not have been more clearly demonstrated than by these two flights in the moon period of May. Four agents with specific missions had been put down in France, and fourteen passengers had been brought back.

One of Verity's passengers was Roger Lardy, who was bringing to London a report on the progress being made by his chief, Jean Moulin, one of the great and genuine heroes of the French Resistance. There is a monument to him at Chartres, the city whose Prefect he was when the Germans marched through the streets in 1940.

So proud was he that he cut his throat rather than submit to torture at the hands of the invaders he so despised, but luckily he was found in time and made a full recovery in hospital. The startled Germans admitted defeat and left him alone.

He slipped out of France in 1941 and reached London via Portugal to join de Gaulle. The two men struck an immediate rapport, and he went back to France by parachute early in 1942 as the general's representative on the Gaullist Committee of National Liberation.

According to Professor Foot,* Moulin was among the first to realise the need for air drops to be properly organised in order to realise the full benefit of the arms and supplies which the British could make available.

His aim was to set up a secret army, many thousands strong, which would be ready to rise as soon as the Allied invasion began. He returned to England with the secret army's military commander, General Charles Delestraint, in a triple Lysander operation masterminded by Verity on the same night in February that Pickard carried out the first Hudson pick-up.

After a short rest they were flown back the following month in a Lysander piloted by Flight Lieutenant John Bridger. Verity himself had almost killed them both attempting the flight a few days earlier.

He had failed to make the rendezvous at a field south of the Loire because of fog. He returned to find another thick blanket of fog covering Tangmere, but with fuel running low he had no option but to attempt a landing.

He came in soft and gentle, and just as he thought he was about to fly into the ground he jerked the controls sharply back to make what he later called† 'a three-point landing about thirty feet up.'

The runway was still out of sight under the fog as the Lysander pancaked through it, hitting the ground with a rending crash and snapping off a sturdy undercarriage hitherto considered unbreakable. The aircraft came to a halt standing on its nose.

The passenger – there was only one of them – scrambled out, courteously waving aside Verity's apologies and even thanking him for 'a very agreeable flight'. As his passenger loosened his coat collar, Verity could see a jagged scar across his throat, but it was not until many years later that he realised his companion on that so nearly disastrous flight had been Jean Moulin.

Verity's second Hudson operation was the only one by the squadron in June. One of his two outgoing passengers was Claude Bouchinet-Serreules, an aide-de-camp to de Gaulle, who was on his way to join Moulin. The BBC message used to alert the reception party near Mâcon was, 'Listen to my weeping heart'.

Quite an apt choice, thought Verity, as he looked down through the torrential rain obliterating all signs of the ground below. The squadron records show that he failed to get in on the first two attempts. On both occasions he had to use full throttle to climb out of danger and go round on another circuit, each time increasing the

* *Six Faces of Courage* by M.R.D. Foot (Eyre Methuen) 1978.
† Verity, *op cit.*

risk of discovery because of the noise of the engines.

He succeeded in putting the aircraft down on the third attempt, dropping his two passengers and picking up eight. Among them was Paul Rivière, who had distinguished himself by organising reception parties and was to become de Gaulle's chief of air operations covering a quarter of France during the rest of 1943.

Also among the passengers returning was Henri Frenay, leader of a large, anti-communist network who had been involved a few weeks earlier in an angry slanging match with Moulin. Each had accused the other of trying to build up a personal following for political motives instead of getting on with the job of working together for France.

Then there was yet another circuit leader, an admiral and an elderly French general, all of them going to pay homage to de Gaulle. When they were all safely on board, Verity decided to emulate Fielden's flight of the previous month by heading for Maison Blanche; a decision which caused some anxiety to navigator Livry, who had not considered it necessary to bring maps of the route they would have to take.

They reached the airfield safely, however, and forewarned by Fielden's mistake, Verity refused to allow one of his passengers – a distinguished-looking man with a military bearing – to wander off and report to the French authorities.

Meanwhile, Bouchinet-Serreules was on his way to Lyons to link up with Moulin and General Delestraint. But he was too late. Delestraint, a military man who had no flair for clandestine work, was picked up by the Gestapo in Paris, and Moulin was arrested a week later, together with a dozen or so leading Gaullists.

Delestraint died in Dachau. Moulin died two weeks after his capture, without betraying a name or revealing a secret in spite of fiendish tortures.

June, although successful for Verity personally, was a tragic month for the squadron. Two Halifaxes were lost together with their seven-man crews. One of the casualties was Hodges' successor in charge of the Halifax flight, a Squadron Leader Walker. To make up the depleted numbers, airmen who had completed their tours of duty were asked to volunteer to stay on station. Eight of them did.

'This was a good showing,' Hodges wrote in the squadron records.

Another Halifax with a new crew went missing in July as the tempo of operations was stepped up, and fresh crews had to be brought in to fill the gaps. A Hudson was also written off, but no one was in it at the time. Fielden had taken off for a field at Loyettes, not far from Lyons, but he was unable to make contact over the reception area so he diverted to Maison Blanche yet again.

The aircraft was parked securely in the airfield's dispersal area when a damaged Blenheim came in minus one propeller, and skidded smack into O-for-Oboe. Unable this time to take home a cargo of rationed goods, Fielden had to thumb a lift for his crew and two 'Joes' – RAF jargon for the secret agents – in a Lancaster.

The 'Joes' were Baron Emmanuel d'Astier de la Vigerie, who was one of de Gaulle's right-hand men, and Dr Jean-Pierre Levy, who became an important member of the *Conseil National de la Résistance* (CNR), which had been created by Moulin.

The two men were successfully landed in France a week later, on 25 July, in the Hudson P-for-Peter flown by Verity. It was another narrow escape for him. The weather was bad and the visibility poor, and to compound the difficulties a tree which had no business being there was off to one side of the runway. It was too close for comfort in a Hudson, but Verity made the landing safely.

By this time Rivière was back in France to organise pick-ups and he was at the field to greet the baron and the doctor before they were whisked away into the darkness.

Another eight passengers scrambled into the aircraft for the homeward flight. Ten minutes later Verity was airborne, heading once more for Algiers on the second leg of a round trip which was to last eighteen hours and ten minutes of flying time.

He was later congratulated for his skill in carrying out the mission so successfully, but the proximity of that tree prompted him to put in a report for the squadron records: 'The landing ground is not recommended for further landings.'

In case it should be thought that Verity was obsessed by trees, he was! Landing on strange fields at night was dangerous enough without added complications, and there are many recorded instances of pilots returning home with their aircraft bearing garlands of twigs, leaves and sections of hedgerows.

If it was a busy time at Tempsford, it was even busier elsewhere in the July of 1943. The Allies had landed in Sicily . . . Mussolini was about to be arrested and the Italian Fascist Party outlawed . . . 20,000 civilians were slaughtered in an RAF raid over Hamburg . . . the Japanese lost a vital air battle over the Solomons.

There were still five months to go before the end of the year, and already people all over the world were beginning to ask: Will it really all be over by *this* Christmas?

*

*2000 hours, 20 March 1945: The weather was foul, with the cloud
formation churned by thhe cold front moving eastwards in front of them, but
the navigator knew that somewhere down there lay Antwerp, with Brussels
over on the right.*

*He checked his figures against his charts and made a rapid calculation in
his head, as he did time and again on every flight. When his skipper's voice
came over the inter-com he was able to reply without hesitating that they
would be over Dresden shortly before midnight.*

*But it would be difficult finding the target on such a murky night. This
was as dodgy as any sortie the navigator had flown in bombers . . .*

. . . For Harry Johnson the mental agonies of bombing civilians
came to an end on 11 June 1943, when his Wellington turned away
from the glowing fires marking Dusseldorf and he set a course for
No 199 squadron's base. He had completed 28 bombing sorties,
and although he did not know it then he was to become 'tour
expired' and sent to No 24 Operational Training Unit – the same
one in which a pilot called John Affleck had once caused such a
furore by his criticisms.

His job there would be to learn the new techniques of navigating
while blind by a radar bombing aid called H2S by the boffins who
devised it, and 'Home Sweet Home' by the crews who used it to find
their way back.

As the Wellington V-for-Victor picked its way through the puffs of
black smoke dotting the sky he and the rest of the crew kept a sharp
look-out for the fighters which would be harrying them all the way
back to the coast, and he remembered again that sickening moment
last month.

They had been on their way back from Dortmund that time. Or
had it been Dusseldorf again?

They had just come through a flak barrage when an excited voice
had crackled through the headphones: 'Fire! There's a fire in the
bomb bay!'

They were approaching the coast at the time, but the sturdy
Wellington was still holding up, apparently unaffected, so the pilot
kept grimly on course, through the last curtain of flak, with its
jagged shards of metal picked out in flashes of orange and black.

Fear came at him then, a tangible thing, and with others of the
crew who could be spared from flying and observation duties he
tore at the floor of the fuselage to get at the glow twinkling inside the
bomb bay.

When they were safely back at base, Johnson wrote a letter to his sister Edith about the incident:

> I thought we were done for. But when we hacked our way through the floor we discovered that the 'fire' was an electric light which the bomb loaders had forgotten to switch off.

Amusing at the time, but fire was the element feared above all others by the men who fought the war in the air.

7

One of the three passengers squatting uncomfortably on the bare metal floor in the mid-section of the fuselage was already earmarked for death.

Wing Commander Bob Hodges was at the controls, and as the Hudson settled gently on a large meadow in a bend of River Loir north of Angers, he felt a surge of relief. He had made it. His first pick-up had gone without a hitch although he reported later that the weather was 'none too good' and that visibility was 'very poor'.

It was also the first Hudson operation to be organised by Henri Déricourt, who had only just returned to France himself after an inexplicable overnight stay in London the day before.

Why had he been recalled to London on 20 July for just that one night? The answer may never be known, but the possibility is that he went back for talks with British Intelligence regarding the approaches which had been made to him by SD officers in Paris.

Whatever the reason, he was considered trustworthy enough to be taken back to France by Verity's Lysander in time to organise Hodges' first Hudson pick-up the following night.

Both men had every reason to be pleased with the choice of rendezvous. Hodges was to describe it as most satisfactory, with excellent signalling and a well-lighted flare path which he had no hesitation in recommending for further use. And it *was* to be used extensively, both by the Hudson crews ferrying agents, and by the Nazi SD teams who watched the landings and followed the incoming agents to their next destinations.

As Hodges took off for home with only three anonymous Belgians on board, the obvious question arises: Why send a Hudson when a Lysander would have done the job just as well? The answer would appear to be that more passengers had been expected. All that is known for sure is that the Gestapo around Paris had become extremely active, and a number of arrests had been made.

The purpose of Hodges' flight was to transport two men who had been ordered by the SOE F Section chief, Maurice Buckmaster, to find out what was going on. The third passenger who stepped on to French soil that night must remain nameless. There is no record of him other than that he travelled on the same flight as Major Nick Bodington, of the SOE staff, and Jack Agazarian, a wireless operator who had already served one tour in the field with distinction.

As Hodges and his crew of Alan Broadley and 'Lofty' Reed were tucking into breakfast at Tangmere after an uneventful return trip with their three Belgians, Bodington and Agazarian were on their way to Paris. There, they found a shambles. The *Prosper* circuit, set up in the second half of 1942 to offset the betrayal of *Interallie* and the collapse of Pierre de Vomécourt's *Autogiro*, was itself disintegrating.

There had been a penetration which was to lead to literally hundreds of arrests – 400 has been recorded as a conservative estimate – and have repercussions in many of the neighbouring circuits. Bodington's job was to assess the extent of the damage and see what could be retrieved from the debris.

He was a typical SOE staff officer in that he was an Oxford man with a public school background; and untypical in that his chosen career was as a journalist in the Paris bureau of Reuter's news agency. He is said by Foot* to have been 'bold to the point of foolhardiness, brilliantly clever, a superb translator from and into French, yet lacking in authoritative weight'.

By the time he reached Paris, the lovely young Indian woman, Noor Inayat Khan, was operating one of the few F Section transmitters still undetected in that part of France.

Agazarian, a dashingly handsome young airman who had been a *Prosper* wireless operator before he was recalled the previous month, had accepted a 'request' that he should volunteer to go back with Bodington to provide another wireless link as it was not known exactly how many of the others had been compromised.

Even at that mid-way stage in the war, trained wireless operators were rare commodities. In any case, it was thought he would only have to spend a few weeks back in the field before he could be pulled out to be put in a safe job and pick up the threads of his life with his young wife, Francine. She had been brought out of the field with him at the end of his first mission in June. When the full moon rose in July he told her he would have to go back and so they kissed goodbye. It was for the last time.

Prosper's troubles may have stemmed from the fact that at one time it had been in contact with the *Carte* organisation, which was unwieldy, notoriously unreliable, and had anyway been penetrated several months earlier by the Abwehr.

*Op cit.

Then there was the shadowy figure of Déricourt. Oddly, he never came under suspicion at this stage, although he had used *Prosper's* radio links to keep in touch with London, and was a close acquaintance of the doomed head of the network, Francis Suttill.

More important, Agazarian had passed on to London the suspicions of Déricourt voiced by Henri Frager, the *Carte* second-in-command who had so nearly been caught accidentally in a schoolhouse by the education curriculum investigators of the Gestapo.

With hindsight, it would seem that the Baker Street headquarters staff of SOE were tardy in recognising the warning signs. But it must be remembered that the constant interchange and overlapping of circuits, of responsibilities, and even of the various enemy security organisations, all helped to create that 'fog of war' which had so confused the more conventional generals of the past.

Bodington, who was the F Section equivalent of a big industrial organisation's trouble-shooter, insisted on going into Paris to pierce that fog. Were the Paris SD men watching by that meadow near Angers when Hodges brought his Hudson down? No one will ever know now, although it is thought by most sources to have been unlikely.

It seems certain that neither of the two agents was followed after leaving the aircraft because they were able to wander unobstructed around Paris for a week. Both of them were experienced enough to know if they were being tailed. And Bodington was certainly too valuable a prize for the Germans to resist taking if they had known his whereabouts.

His problem was knowing where to start to pick up the surviving threads of *Prosper*. He had to presume that all the regular contacts had either been arrested or were under surveillance. Eventually he and Agazarian settled for an address which was passed on to them from London, who had obtained it from a radio which was still operating. This radio, however, had been turned and was now being worked by the SD, or played back as it was called, to the unsuspecting London end. Aware of this possibility, but having no alternative other than to try it, Bodington and Agazarian decided to toss a coin to see who should make the approach.

Agazarian lost. He stifled his doubts, called at the apartment, and was promptly arrested. In spite of the most hideous tortures the Gestapo could inflict, he refused to talk and was eventually executed by a firing squad at Flossenburg when the war had only six more weeks to run.

The methodical Germans went on to round up more *Prosper* contacts in a series of swoops which netted all the radio operators with the exception of Noor Inayat Khan. Time was running out for her. There was nothing Bodington could do to stop the rot so he made arrangements with Déricourt to return to London during the August moon period. He wanted Noor to go back with him as there was very little she could accomplish on her own.

Her reply was typical of this gentle woman who had seemed in training to be so unsuitable for clandestine operations. 'Not overburdened with brains,' was how one of her training officers unkindly endorsed her report. Be that as it may, she still managed to dodge the Germans for three months after *Prosper* began collapsing, and was caught only by chance when an informer discovered where she was living and tipped off the Gestapo.

For her courage she was posthumously awarded the highest possible civilian decoration for bravery, the George Cross. Part of the citation reads:

> She refused . . . to abandon what had become the principal and most dangerous post in France, although given the opportunity to return to England, because she did not wish to leave her French comrades without communications, and she hoped also to rebuild her group.

So Bodington left alone for London. It was his own escape from the *Prosper* debacle which convinced him that Déricourt was not the traitor, and that the growing suspicions of him in Baker Street were so much poppycock.

Yet there is some evidence that he and the hierarchy already knew at this stage that their landing ground organiser was leading a double life. SOE records show that he pencilled an office note shortly before he left to investigate the *Prosper* arrests.

It reads: 'We know he is in contact with the Germans, and also how & why.'

The problem so many years after the events is to know who was double-crossing whom.

Tempsford's pilots were blissfully unaware of the skulduggery behind the scenes, which was fortunate for their peace of mind. During that August, all previous operational records were broken without the loss of a single man or aircraft. Verity was awarded the DSO to mark his fourteen pick-ups and the others he had planned in the first seven months of the year.

The potential of the Hudson as an airbus had by now become

fully recognised. A training programme had been drawn up, but as yet there were not enough aircraft and not enough trained crews available.

Meanwhile arrangements were being made to replace the squadron's two Havocs and fit the Hudsons with the special wireless apparatus used to make direct voice contact with agents on the ground.

This conversion was intended to make the Hudsons cost-effective, a requirement which could not otherwise have been achieved as there was a limit to the number of pick-ups in which a light bomber would be needed instead of a Lysander.

Only two were laid on in August, and both of them were carried out by Hodges.

On the first he brought back ten passengers – many of them now legendary names – but the operation was so nearly a disaster. Hodges had few qualms about the operation as he knew he would be landing on the Déricourt meadow near Angers where he had made his first pick-up the month before.

He arrived to find the field covered in a fine mist, but he could see a signal lamp flashing through the gauzy curtain. He lost sight of the torch-lit flare-path on his first approach and had to go round again, knowing nothing of the consternation caused down below by the racket of his engines.

It was like a scene from a sort of Keystone Cops-cum-Western film. The meadow was full of people, charging around in all directions trying to round up a herd of bullocks and several horses maddened by the noise. As soon as there was some semblance of order, the aircraft approached and off the animals went again, thundering from one end of the landing strip to the other.

One of the 'cowboy' agents in the round-up was Major Robert Boiteux, a 35-year-old London-born Frenchman who had been variously a hairdresser in a fashionable Bond Street salon, a gold prospector, and a professional boxer. The church clock in the nearby village was striking ten when he arrived at the rendezvous to find his co-passengers milling around in confusion, with Déricourt nowhere in sight.

Eventually he arrived to split the group into three parties and lead them to the meadow where the Hudson was expected at around one in the morning. Boiteux was later to describe* the 'muffled howls of dismay' which greeted the sight of the local farmer's livestock running loose.

*Evelyn le Chêne. *op cit.*

He recalls how the agents 'desperately tried to clear the landing ground, shooing the animals to the edge of the field.' The horses shying a little, trotted over to the trees, but the cows moved only a few feet before returning full of curiosity.

Boiteux, who was *not* half-Jewish as the official SOE history and many other sources have indicated, makes the point that the round-up had to be carried out in complete silence to avoid attracting attention from the nearby village. But no sooner were all the animals cajoled to one side than the Hudson arrived. The herd bolted and they had to start all over again.

Hodges, of course, knew nothing of this because of the ground mist. However, he landed safely, avoiding the livestock, and his solitary passenger deplaned. He was Erwin Deman, a Viennese Jew who had fought with the French Army in 1940, then escaped from a prisoner-of-war camp to join SOE.

As he melted away into the night, the ten returning agents hurriedly clambered on board and slumped down, as Boiteux puts it, 'absolutely exhausted' by their efforts.

They had lived on their nerves for so long that the sudden lifting of tension acted as a gentle anaesthetic, he explains, and they fell asleep. Hodges could only have guessed at those tensions as he checked his instruments and prepared for take-off with Déricourt's hurried warning to watch out for the cattle.

Boiteux had with him his entire team from the 'blown' *Spruce* circuit, which had been operating around Lyons. They were: Marie-Thérèse le Chêne, Joseph Marchand, who was fifty years old and a manufacturer of perfumes, and one of his salesmen, Jean Regnier. The two men were later to organise *réseaux* of their own.

Boiteux had first been parachuted into the field from a Halifax flown by a Polish crew from Tempsford in May 1942. His companion, Robert Sheppard, landed on an outhouse roof next to a gendarmerie at Anse, near Lyons, and was promptly arrested.

Boiteux made himself scarce. His orders were to take command of *Spruce*, which at that time was being run by an erratic Frenchman called Georges Dubourdin. But the latter gloried in his role as a Resistance leader and had no intention of being supplanted by some Johnny-come-lately from London.

He made Boiteux's job impossible by refusing to give him details of where supplies were stored, or even when drops were to be made. This situation could not be allowed to continue. Eventually Boiteux managed to organise a supply drop of his own and received, among the grenades, explosives and sten guns – a consignment of itching powder.

Try as he might, he was unable to elicit from Dubourdin the details of a 10,000-strong secret army he was supposed to be controlling – for the very good reason that it did not exist.

Bodington was sent out from London to sort out difficulties, and his solution was to recall Dubourdin and leave Boiteux behind to rebuild the circuit from scratch.

This fall from grace was accepted with ill humour and the feud between the two men continued right up to the moment Peter Vaughan-Fowler put his aircraft down for one of the early Lysander pick-ups.

He became involved in an altercation with one of the men who materialised out of the darkness. He could have had no idea what all the fuss was about, but Boiteux remembers the scene vividly.* He arrived late at the field to find Dubourdin arguing excitably with the pilot. He was refusing to climb into the aircraft because he had not been given a parachute.

Boiteux, by now desperate to be given some clue about the activities of the circuit he was to command, demanded for the last time to be given details about the number of volunteers available and the whereabouts of equipment and explosives.

Foot's history records that Dubourdin said simply: 'Well, I'm leaving now; you are in command.'

Boiteux's biographer goes into more detail. Dubourdin is said to have given him a disdainful look before turning his back to resume his argument with the pilot. Boiteux's patience, never very reliable in such situations, finally snapped.

'Exasperated, I put my foot on his backside and pushed.'

And with the parting words, 'Get in, you stupid bastard,' he stamped angrily away from the field.

Curiously, another agent who left with Dubourdin that night in Vaughan-Fowler's Lysander, makes no mention of this incident in *his* memoirs.†

Ben Cowburn had been involved with Pierre de Vomécourt in the successful plot to outwit the Abwehr by tricking the traitress Mathilde Carré into going back to England. He was now returning to England himself at the end of his second mission, and in his graphic description of a Lysander pick-up, he mentions in passing that there *were* parachutes in the cockpit.

*Evelyn le Chêne. *op cit.*
†*No Cloak, No Dagger* by Benjamin Cowburn, (Jarrolds) 1960.

He describes how he and another man (now known to be Dubourdin) climbed into the aircraft and pulled a sliding hood forward over their heads.

> There were parachutes in the cockpit and we fumbled to adjust them. I found difficulty in getting my harness tight enough and hoped I would not have to use it. I . . . suddenly saw a small black shape which looked like a bird flying alongside us, opposite the wingtip.
>   This must be a fighter taking a look at us first. I carried the microphone to my face and was just trying to figure out which side was port or starboard when one was facing backwards when a white cloud threw the 'enemy' into relief, and I realised it was the streamlined insulator of the wireless aerial . . .

Cowburn, one of SOE's more effective saboteurs, worked before the war in the oil industry. He was a tough, no nonsense operator from Lancashire who appreciated in rather high-flown terms the value of the secret squadrons' air supply service:

> You beckoned and some of the glorious airmen of the legendary Royal Air Force mounted their great machine and came flying through the night, rushing the enemy defences with a 5,000 hp roar of defiance. They risked their lives, not to bomb some major target selected by a council of generals, but to find that little clearing chosen by humble country-folk.

Cowburn was another of the agents who once received a consignment of itching powder in a weapons drop. He felt insulted at first that Baker Street should apparently regard his *réseau* as no more than a gang of 'naughty schoolboys'. Then he recruited a woman working in a laundry which was under contract for washing the underwear of a German unit stationed nearby.

It is still believed in Troyes, where Cowburn's *Tinker* circuit operated, that at least one U-boat surrendered in mid-Atlantic so that the crew could be treated for what the captain believed to be a dangerous skin disease.

Such stories were a filip for the morale of civilian populations, but should be taken with a pinch, say, of powder!

However, to return to the main narrative, Boiteux and his *Spruce* team were soon made comfortable in Hodges' Hudson, where they fell asleep, lulled by the cognac-laced tea poured from Lofty Reed's thermos.

With them was another top agent who had just made a sensational escape from the Gestapo's clutches. By all the accepted standards, he should now have been dead or dying in the interrogation block at No 84 Avenue Foch, the notorious Paris headquarters.

Yet here he was, free, and on his way to where a knock on the door in the night did not bring the automatic reflex of fear.

Robert Benoist was a racing driver of independent means and owned a considerable amount of land south of the French capital. With the help of two other racing enthusiasts he had built a small but secure *réseau* called *Chestnut* to carry out sabotage operations.

But by July 1943 the Germans were moving in. The Abwehr's Peilfunkdienst (wireless direction-finding service) had improved their methods since the early hit-or-miss days and were gradually whittling down the possible locations for transmissions emanating from the Pontoise area.

Chestnut's operator was committing the suicidal error of sending messages too often from the same place, and when the Abwehr pounced on the last day of the month they caught him at his set. Within two days they had picked up Benoist's brother, Maurice, and his racing driver colleague, Charles Grover-Williams.

Benoist himself was arrested in a Parisian street three days later. It looked like the end. He was bundled into a car, but his cocksure guards were so busy congratulating each other that they forgot to handcuff him. As the driver accelerated away, with tyres screeching in the film gangster fashion which German security services so often imitated just for effect, Benoist threw himself against the man sitting next to him as they swung around a corner.

The door flew open and the two men rolled into the street. Cat-like, and with his life at stake, Benoist was the first to recover and before the car had time to stop he had disappeared down a back alley, heading for a friend's house and a change of clothing.

Grover-Williams was to die in Sachsenhausen, but he stayed silent to the end and *Chestnut* survived to do more useful work. Benoist, his cover blown, laid low at his secretary's flat to await the Hudson pick-up arranged for the August moon. For him, it was a hilarious anti-climax to find the pick-up field full of cattle.

Another agent on Hodges' homeward flight, Tony Brooks, had also narrowly escaped capture a few months earlier. In the midsummer of 1942, when he had just celebrated his twentieth birthday, he was parachuted into the field to become the youngest agent ever sent out by F Section. An Englishman with a Swiss education, he was living in France when war broke out and became involved with one of the embryo escape organisations on the Mediterranean coast.

He reached England in 1941 where he was snapped up by SOE and put through an intensive training course designed to give him some experience of working as a railwayman.

He had a bad start. His parachute was faulty and he landed in a tree, badly injuring a leg. However, that misfortune behind him, he was soon put in touch with a small but highly efficient group and together they formed a circuit known as *Pimento*.

His orders were to penetrate the railway system on the main lines north and west of Marseilles; a job he was to carry out with remarkable success. Early in 1943 his wireless operator was caught and Brooks himself looked likely to be arrested when he spotted Gestapo men, in their inevitable uniform trench coats and trilbies, waiting on a station platform as he was about to leave a train.

Luckily, a French policeman who was a member of the Resistance, realised the danger and moved forward to snap handcuffs over Brooks' wrists. The gendarme and his 'captive' then marched past the grinning Germans, out of the station, and into a police car. When they were out of sight the handcuffs were removed and Brooks was set free.

He continued operating until August, organising no less than thirty air drops. His receptions were always popular with the RAF crews because they were so efficiently organised.

He was pulled out of France on London's orders because he had earned a rest. That was how he came to join Boiteux, Benoist and the *Spruce* team in the cattle round-up as Hodges' Hudson was coming in to land.

In spite of their exhaustion, there was the holiday atmosphere of a charter flight on the way home. All of them had come close to death and had been living for months in the knowledge that every day could be their last of freedom. Now at last they could relax and let the RAF look after them.

Among the others on that flight was Octave Simon, a sculptor, who had been involved with the Resistance since 1940. He organised *Satirist* in the Sarthe region, and he alone managed to escape when it broke up in the wake of the *Prosper* arrests. He was to return to France in 1944, but walked straight into a trap and was executed at Gross Rosen concentration camp.

Yet another of the agents on the way to a huge breakfast at Tempsford was Victor Gerson, a Jewish textile manufacturer who was busily setting up the various *Vic* escape lines which were to bring so many shot down aircrew back home to safety.

For these 'Joes' all the tensions of living in the shadow of the

Gestapo were over, at least for the time being. Of the ten men who
returned to England with Bob Hodges, at least four went back to
France to fight again, and two of them never came back from the
camps.

The aircrews, under tensions of a sharper if less prolonged kind,
had no time to rest in those fleeting monthly phases of the moon.

Two days after Hodges' return on 20 August, Verity attempted
and failed to land a Hudson in one of Rivière's fields near Mâcon.
The operation, code-name *Trojan Horse*, was pulled off at the second
attempt the following night by Hodges. He took in an agent called
Louis Franzini, and brought back eight passengers, including a
flight sergeant called Patterson, one of the crew of a Tempsford
Halifax shot down the previous month.

An altogether more sinister gentleman was also brought back on
that flight: Armand Khodja, a deadly marksman who was to return
to France and assassinate at least eleven Gestapo and SD officers in
and around the Lyons area in February 1944.

This was the type of SOE murder and mayhem plot so detested
by the more traditional minds of the War Office, which preferred
making omelettes without breaking eggs.

Khodja was part of a small but highly effective RF Section *réseau*
code-named *Armada*, which was responsible for some of SOE's
most successful sabotage operations in the closing months of 1943.
Just before his pick-up, three members of his team had blown up a
canal lock system at Gigny. The damage took four months to repair.

This and other sabotage carried out by *Armada* teams – each one
never more than five strong – were to disrupt totally all water
transport through north-eastern France between the industrial
Ruhr and the Mediterranean. This was at a time when Germany
badly needed this vital access to the fighting in Italy.

The powerful torpedo-carrying E-boats and two-man submarines,
which could have carried out wholesale slaughter off the beach-
heads of Salerno and Anzio, remained bottled up in the North Sea
instead of where they were needed at Italian strike bases.

It was a classic example of how tactical action could have strategic
impact.

Two mainsprings of *Armada*, Jarrot and Basset, were picked up in
the next Hudson landing in September. It was Bob Hodges' third
successful pick-up and the thirteenth to be carried out by a Hudson.
Eight passengers were taken in, but in spite of risking a ten-minute
wait on the ground some fifteen miles from Lons-le-Saunier, only

the *Armada* duo and two other men turned up for the return journey.

Hodges recalls* that one man of the reception party made a last-minute decision to get on board with the others, but his return is not mentioned in squadron records.

Four of the men Hodges took to France on that night of 15 September were political appointees whose job it was to ensure that information from the various Resistance groups could be channelled direct to de Gaulle. The haughty Frenchman was still at that time embroiled in a bitter fight for the leadership with Giraud, a protege of the Americans.

The British, however, were backing de Gaulle. It was recognised that he had the support of most of the active resisters, with the exception of the communists. And even they were prepared to cooperate for as long as they received the weapons which only the British could supply.

But not all of his true followers really liked him as a man.

There was a time during those days in London when the Free French gathered in a popular little cafe run by a Frenchwoman in St James. This was, and still is the heartland of those exclusive clubs used by a certain type of Englishman.

The cafe, an island of Gallic nostalgia, was celebrating Bastille Day in the French manner, with liberty, equality and fraternity being toasted to the raucous accompaniment of patriotic songs and accordion music.

Then de Gaulle arrived.

The story is still told there of how the great man sat down to dinner, then immediately objected to sharing the dining room with junior officers. The enraged patroness stormed up to the table and drawing herself up to her full five feet two inches, ordered him off the premises.

In vain did his staff protest, pleading out of his earshot about the strains and stresses he was under while carrying out his duties for love of la belle France.

De Gaulle just sat there, unsmiling, his back ramrod straight.

'Out!' the woman insisted.

It was an order, not a request.

And like the good soldier he was, out the general went, retreating in good order by bowing stiffly as he left.

The nucleus of the men who would pave the way for de Gaulle's

*Verity. *op cit.*

return to France travelled on Hodges' September moon Hudson. One of them was Louis Mangin, who had just been appointed head of the zone covering the southern half of France. With him went Maurice Bourgès-Maunoury, Paul Leistenschneider, and H.H. Gaillard, regional military delegates, respectively, for Lyons, Montpellier-Toulouse, and Bordeaux.

If de Gaulle was at odds with the communists and others who did not share his political aspirations, he was also deeply suspicious of the loyalties of the most effective French intelligence network operating alongside, but apart from, SOE agents.

Known as *Alliance*, the organisation was held together by Marie-Madeleine Méric, now better known by the name of her second husband, Fourcade. The head of the network's military operations was Commandant Léon Faye, a French Air Force major.

Marie-Madeleine had agreed reluctantly to leave France after a spate of arrests in July 1943, and she was brought out by Vaughan-Fowler's Lysander on the 18th. She was joined in London the following month by Faye and a British-trained wireless operator they knew by the name of Frederick Rodney. He has also been identified elsewhere* as Frederick Rodriguez.

Their *Alliance*, which was known to the Germans as *Noah's ark* because its members took their code-names from animals and birds, was still functioning, and they began pulling strings to be sent back into the field to recruit and reorganise.

De Gaulle saw *Alliance* as a means by which his rival Giraud would have a personal intelligence-gathering agency. He never really believed that the network's one true allegiance was to France rather than to any one individual. He always suspected, perhaps with some justification, that the British only passed on to his HQ the *Alliance* information which they, the British, wanted him to know.

Marie-Madeleine and her comrades were bound by a close brotherhood of danger and death to the crews of No 161 Squadron. While many Frenchmen bemoaned the tardiness of the RAF in allocating sufficient aircraft to provide all the supplies they were demanding, she was grateful for anything and everything that was being done to help.

She alone of the French agents seemed to understand that you could not just wave a magic wand and expect to see the sky blossom with unfolding parachutes carrying men and materials. She once even made an excuse to herself to explain the non-arrival of pick-up

*Verity. *op cit.*

aircraft. When they failed to arrive for a full month she put their absence down to heavy casualties among the Lysander crews.

In fact, there were no less than nine Lysander and four Hudson pick-ups in that particular month, but all of them were for operations carrying higher priorities than those planned by *Alliance*.

As for casualties – there had been none!

At its peak, her network had a strength estimated at 3,000 resisters equipped with 30 radio transmitters. Like Topsy, it was like the vain frog which huffed and puffed and puffed and huffed – until it blew itself up.

Hundreds of resisters were arrested and shot before her policy of de-centralisation could stop the rot. No matter how often the Germans penetrated the organisation, she always managed to rally the survivors to rebuild and plague her tormentors.

Marie-Madeleine, or *Hedgehog* in *Noah's ark*, was as anxious to return to France herself as she was to stop Faye, the *Eagle*. She had a recurring nightmare that his next trip would be his last. Faye, exasperated by the bland excuses given by the British for not sending him, is reported* to have made a remark which illustrates a common denominator in men who are faced time and again with the possibility of death.

'I am dead,' he told her, meaning he had nothing more to fear.

The same point has been made many times to explain how bomber crews could go out night after night in spite of the appalling casualties over Germany.

This philosophy appears to be based on the premise that once a man has accepted his own death as if it had already happened, then he can function effectively because he has nothing more to lose.

Not explained is whether such a *machismo* theory could apply to Marie-Madeleine, or other women who faced unspeakable deaths like Violet Szabo and Noor Inayat Khan.

Theories on courage and its companion, fear, are academic. It will never be known if Commandant Faye really accepted the death that was to come to him in such a lingering, agonising way when he finally persuaded London to send him back.

'Damn their law of averages,' he told Marie-Madeleine. 'According to their calculations I should have been dead long ago. I am dead. This ghost's going.'

And he went on 15 September, the day Hodges returned from his third Hudson pick-up. Some unfair criticism was levelled at the RAF as a result of the operation. Faye and wireless operator Rodney

Noah's Ark by Marie-Madeleine Fourcade. (George Allen and Unwin) 1973.

were taken in a Lysander flown by Flight Lieutenant Robin Hooper, who was one day to be knighted and appointed British Ambassador to Greece.

The landing was made without mishap in the Compiègne locality. The two passengers deplaned and two of their comrades in *Alliance* climbed in for the return journey.

Two days later Marie-Madeleine received a message from her deputy, Paul Bernard, to say the commandant and Rodney had been arrested when their train pulled in to Paris. A few days later he sent another message angrily complaining that the two men had been captured because London had sent them with an inexperienced pilot whose stooging around the reception area had drawn attention to the operation.

Nothing could have been further from the truth. Hooper, who had been in the Diplomatic Service and had learned to fly before war broke out, had already completed one tour of clandestine operations with Halifaxes, and had completed three successful Lysander pick-ups.

Marie-Madeleine knew intuitively that the disaster had been caused instead by treason. She was right. A traitor who was later identified as Jean-Paul Lien – or 'Lanky', as he was known – had passed on to the Abwehr the time and place of Faye's arrival.

His arrest was the high point for the Germans in a remarkable month which saw no less than 150 *Alliance* agents put out of action. For Marie-Madeleine, then thirty-three years old, it was a time of heart-breaking anguish as one by one her wireless sets went silent. She was unable to sleep for a week and once, staring at her reflection in a mirror, she cried out aloud: 'I'm going mad. I have no right to go mad.'

The work of the Resistance was put back further in that black September by the bad weather conditions which made it impossible for No 161 Squadron to carry out operations. Yet the records state, rather contrarily, that a 'good performance' was put up for the period as a whole.

An attempt was made to reinforce the Halifaxes by using three Stirlings attached from No 214 Squadron, but out of six attempted sorties, only two were partly carried out and Hodges considered there had been insufficient time in which to assess their suitability or otherwise.

By now three Hudsons had been used on the station and their value had again been adequately demonstrated. Three new Hudson crews were brought in to begin training for the air-to-ground radio communication programme still being carried out by two Havocs.

This was at a time when Resistance groups all over Europe were clamouring to be given the tools promised by Churchill to finish the job. The two special Tempsford squadrons doing most of the work of pumping men and supplies through this aerial lifeline had no more than about thirty operational bombers and half a dozen Lysanders between them. But Bomber Command was at last coming round to the idea that a trained saboteur with local knowledge could in certain circumstances do more with well-placed explosives than a squadron of Lancasters. And at no risk to valuable aircrews and the friendly civilian populations around the target areas.

One of the most remarkable operations for this month was carried out in three Lysanders flown by Verity, McCairns and Vaughan-Fowler. They took eight people into France and brought eight back – and it took only nine minutes from the first touchdown to the last take-off.

It was the sort of job which by this stage in the squadron's activities would normally have been allocated to a Hudson, but reconnaissance indicated that the chosen field was much too small.

One of the pilots brought back Yves Rocard, a physicist formerly at the Sorbonne. He had sent SOE detailed sketches of German navigational stations used by the Luftwaffe to guide fighters to intercept bombers, and his technical expertise was of considerable help to the British scientists engaged in finding counter measures.

The last pick-up for September was carried out by Verity with his crew of Livry and Shine, the latter by then commissioned as a pilot-officer. Their rendezvous was a large field by the Saône about six miles from Tournus.

Verity found it difficult finding the reception area because of low-lying cloud formations which covered the usual landmarks, and it took him three attempts to line up the aircraft before he felt confident enough to bring it down for a landing.

Among the four agents he took in was Richard Heslop, who remembers the flight as 'a quiet, uneventful ride, the only hazards being the cold draughts which swept through the aircraft.'*

Verity had brought him back to England three months earlier after a year in the field. Now he was going back as part of a combined SOE operation to spend two weeks investigating the strength and durability of the Resistance around the Swiss frontier provinces of the Ain, Isère, Savoie, Haute-Savoie and the Jura.

* Heslop. *op cit.*

The French half of the mission was RF Section's Jean Rosenthal, a bespectacled Parisian who had been dealing in furs and precious stones when the Germans marched down the Champs Elysées. They made a formidable team.

Verity kept the Hudson's engines running as they made their brief farewells and jumped into a car parked in a nearby road. As the men of the reception party off-loaded 42 packages of supplies, eight London-bound passengers scrambled through the door and the aircraft took off. The change-over had taken just eight minutes.

. It could not have been quick enough for the redoutable Henri Guillermin. As sabotage leader of the Saône-et-Loire region, he had been busily engaged in wrecking a canal system with the *Armada* group and was now on the run with the Gestapo hot on his heels.

With the end of September came the accounting: the Hudsons O-for-Oboe and P-for-Peter had attempted seventeen pick-ups and completed fourteen of them in the nine months since Pickard had shown the way. Forty-three people had been taken to France and 95 brought out.

The cost: One empty Hudson damaged while parked off the runway at Maison Blanche.

During the same period the remarkable Lysanders – no more than six of them operational at any one time – had carried out 55 successful missions, putting 108 people into the field and bringing 174 back.

The cost: One Lysander crash-landed by Verity and badly-damaged; one pilot killed and his aircraft written off on a training flight.

In the previous year when Lysanders had been doing all the pick-ups, 21 successful operations had been carried out, taking 29 people into Europe and bringing 43 back for the loss of two aircraft.

The autumn leaves were beginning to fall from the trees around Tempsford . . . the Italians had just surrendered . . . the Russians had advanced back to Smolensk . . . the Germans were calculating the strategic effect of the damage done to the battleship *Tirpitz* by the Royal Navy's midget submarine frogmen.

John Affleck, now a pilot officer, added a DFC to his DFM for his work on dropping operations with the Halifaxes and was about to volunteer to join the élite involved in pick-ups.

On air bases elsewhere in England other men were applying for postings which would bring them to Tempsford as part of a new intake needed to cope with the extra demands to be made on No

161 Squadron as the countdown to the invasion of Europe began.

*

2100 hours, 20 March 1945: They were crossing into Germany now and England seemed a lifetime and another world away. It was the moment which bomber pilots regarded as a signpost and remembered for the heightened awareness of the senses. Down below lay Aachen and the Siegfried Line, with Montgomery's 21st Army Group deployed on the left and Bradley's 12th Army Group stretching away to the south on the right.

Buffeted by the turbulence, N-for-Nan droned on through thick cloud. Soon they would be crossing the Rhine where the Germans were waiting in their foxholes and emplacements and laagers for the final onslaught in the land battle. But for the crew there were more immediate problems in their private war.

Where were the nightfighters? Would the weather keep them grounded or were they already up and looking for them? The pilot checked his instruments for the umpteenth time. No problems there. Soon he would have to make a decision. Unless the weather improved there was no point in going on. But for the time being he had no option.

It was too soon to abort . . .

. . . Terence Helfer had made up his mind. He intended to stay in the RAF when the war was over. Flying was now in his blood in spite of all he had endured and the thought of going back to a City office and a career in accountancy had become even more abhorrent.

He could have been forgiven for trying to get back to Civvy Street as soon as was decently possible because his career on bombing operations had been extremely short-lived by the usual standards. He had done only ten operations – exactly one-third of a normal tour of duty – and in that short space of four months three of the aircraft he had flown had been destroyed.

There was his first operation which had ended three days late when he and his crew waded ashore at Margate. Then his third operation ended in near disaster when he landed safely only to have a Wellington land on top of his aircraft as he taxied along the runway.

There had been a punch-up in the mess afterwards when his crew angrily slugged it out with the men from the offending Wellington.

On his sixth operation he was returning from Emden when he ran out of fuel and was forced to make his second ditching, this time off the Norfolk coast a mile from Wells.

The last straw had been a 'milk run' to Brest when he came back with the starboard engine of his Wellington out of action and had to make an emergency landing at Middle Wallop with cars lined up to illuminate the runway with their headlights.

He and his unlucky crew – or lucky, as it turned out – went on only one more operation before their commanding officer decided they had done enough and arranged for them to be posted to other duties.

That had been in January 1942. They got out just in time. Bomber Command's casualties in the next few months were horrific, worse than anything experienced in the preceding two years of the war in the air.

Now, eighteen months later, he wanted to return to active duty. After hundreds of hours flying Lysanders with a gunnery target flight at Newmarket, he volunteered for another operational tour with a friend, Flying Officer W.M. 'Sugar' Hale. Four more months were to pass before their postings came through to join the special duties Lysanders at Tempsford.

And they never did get to fly them. Instead, they were selected for the newly-formed Hudson flight.

8

Pilot Officer Affleck felt a prickly ball of excitement churning his insides as Squadron Leader Verity opened the throttles to maximum boost and pulled the Hudson up in a long, shuddering climb, the propellers clawing the night air as he banked to go round again to make a second approach.

Below, Paul Rivière's reception party waited anxiously. This same operation had already been aborted once, the week before. The moon was on the wane so this time it had to be right or they would have to wait another month.

The aircraft had taken off from Tangmere early on the evening of 16 October 1943, and it was not yet midnight. Even though it was only the second time Affleck had experienced a pick-up attempt, he had been around long enough to know the dangers of spending too much time in the landing area. The town of Mâcon was only about six miles away to the south and if the Germans were sufficiently alert they could be at the scene in as many minutes.

Down they went again. Verity recalls* how he floated the aircraft over this meadow by the Saône before dropping down and pulling up sharply in unusually long grass. Affleck remembers† what was his first landing on French soil more dramatically. If memory serves him correctly they touched down with a jar which shook every bone in his body.

Philippe Livry, by now promoted a step to the rank of squadron leader, was sitting in his navigator's collapsible canvas seat with Affleck a little behind him. As the aircraft's wheels jarred down there was a loud crack as the impact snapped the seat supports. A full 15 stones of navigator catapulted backwards flattening young Affleck and pinning him to the cabin floor. Verity, too, remembers the scene, but was too busy bringing M-for-Mike down to a halt to do anything to help.

For what seemed like hours to Affleck he and Livry lay in a tangle of limbs and both had bruises to show for days after it. He was particularly chagrined because as a skilled pilot himself, albeit one without any experience of landing at night in an unknown field, he

* *Op cit.*
† Personal interview.

should have realised the six-ton Hudson would have to be brought down with an ungraceful bump to avoid eating up the limited runway.

For both Affleck and Flying Officer 'Brad' Bradbury squatting beside him, the successful if startling landing was a case of second time lucky. They had both been taken out by Wing Commander Hodges on a familiarisation flight to the same area a week earlier, but had been forced to turn back because visibility had not been good enough to make a safe approach.

Memories are fallible and it is perhaps for this reason that Livry himself makes no mention in *his* memoirs* of his heavy landing on top of the unfortunate co-pilot. His account of this very important operation differs in some details from the official records, and appears to be more of an amalgam of several Hudson pick-ups.

He describes his pilot accurately as Jamaican-born and about to start a career in the Diplomatic Service before war broke out. Verity's parents did in fact go out to Jamaica where he spent his early boyhood. The son of an English country parson, Verity also does not dispute the added description of himself as a man who likes to philosophise all day long . . . a man who says 'he doesn't understand war, and that the Germans are all men like other men, and that he doesn't like to kill them'.

But then Livry goes on to describe the gunner-wireless operator as a Yorkshireman whose ambition after the war was to run a pub – an ambition which Eddie Shine was to achieve.

Bradbury, however, and not Shine, was the gunner on this particular flight. Livry also recalls that four agents were being taken to France instead of the five reported in the squadron records, and he goes on to describe them:

The first was said to have helped us uncover the secrets of the V-1 rockets and was to be badly wounded on a later mission. This description could fit several of Marie-Madeleine Fourcade's *Alliance* agents.

A second passenger, more than sixty years old, was believed by Livry to have been the manager of a large London hotel. He should have known. He frequented enough of them.

Another was a well-known Parisian who had lost part of an arm after being blown up by a mine in 1940, and the fourth he described as 'a young girl, almost a child, smiling and charming' who was to be betrayed to the Germans on the eve of the Liberation.

His account does, however, give a graphic description of what it

* *Op cit.*

was like to face death night after night on those lonely flights in slow, almost defenceless aircraft.

> Suddenly, a few metres above us, a German plane crosses our path. We plunge into a cloud . . . just in time. The enemy turns to chase us . . .

They shook off the nightfighter and continued over the River Loire, following the silvery thread as it twisted and turned south, banking to port over a landmark to pick up the River Saône. It was dark and raining, not the sort of weather recommended for pick-ups. Then Livry spotted the landing lights in the distance – with a 'little, lonely signal' flashing the correct recognition letter.

> We go down to the landing lights . . . The pilot slows down the engine as much as he can, and the feeling of calm and nervous tension grips us. One last look at the instruments to check if the wheels and flaps are OK. The ground approaches quickly and we seem to be engulfed in the darkness.
>
> Suddenly there is that anxious throbbing of the engines, and we realise that we have gone too far. We can't land. There are a few seconds of uncertainty and the plane continues to drop lower. But we pick up speed again and it is OK.

That account ties in with Verity's decision to go round for a second attempt, but of course it could fit several other Hudson operations as it was so difficult to make a 'spot on' first-time approach.

The crew was not aware of it then, but it was particularly important that this second attempt should succeed. Not so much for the missions to be carried out by the five passengers they landed, but for the vital role in the war effort planned for one of the eight passengers waiting to be picked up for the return trip. It would have been difficult to believe it at the time.

He looked like a tramp. For such a distinguished personage he was an incongruous sight in that moonlit field, with his shabby clothes, his greasy cloth cap, and a huge, shaggy black beard. He shuffled diffidently into the aircraft with the rest, but in spite of the circumstances there was no mistaking his soldierly bearing.

After take-off, Verity handed the controls over to Affleck and went back into the rear compartment to meet his passengers. The 'tramp' rose slowly to his feet, bowed stiffly and held out his hand as one of the other passengers introduced him as Jean de Lattre de Tassigny, General of the French Army.

There was no way of knowing then that this man would one day

put his name to the German surrender document along with
Marshal Zhukov, Air Marshal Sir Arthur Tedder, and the American
Air Force General Carl 'Tooey' Spaatz.

This disreputable-looking fugitive who would be instrumental in
bringing a modern war to an end had started his military career as a
cavalry officer in what by comparison was an old-fashioned war –
blooding himself on horseback in a hand-to-hand duel with a
Prussian Uhlan in 1914. He carried the scar of this wound until his
death in 1952.

De Lattre was to describe his escape from France by Verity's
Hudson as 'a veritable miracle' – no pun intended – which
permitted him to play his part in the struggle for liberation.

He had remained at his post as Chief of Staff of the French Fifth
Army after the 1940 capitulation, but was very soon regarded as
suspect by the Vichy French authorities because of his often
declared sympathy for the Allied cause.

Eventually he was arrested and sentenced by a national tribunal
to ten years in jail. He served only ten months before escaping to go
into hiding with the Resistance. Six weeks later he was in Verity's
Hudson, drinking cognac from a tin cup handed to him by a
middle-aged Frenchman in RAF uniform who kept glancing at him
with puzzled curiosity.

Livry had been attending to his navigating duties when the
introductions had been made by Verity. So although the face
obscured by the bushy beard was familiar, he could not quite place
the name. Still searching his memory before take-off, he handed a
parcel to Rivière and asked for it to be delivered to his wife at
Audrieu with the brief message: 'Your husband is well.'

The parcel contained a pair of shoes and several bars of soap.
Soap, especially, had become a luxury in France. Then with a wave
he climbed back into the aircraft to plot the course for home.

Now, after sharing out the cognac which London-bound agents
traditionally presented to the pick-up crews, he stared at Blackbeard.
Only now, by the cabin lights, he could see the beard was actually
pepper-and-salt in colour. The eyes above the beard stared back,
but there was no recognition on either side.

Livry's attention was diverted to an emaciated figure of a man
who appeared to be at his last gasp. 'What happened – ' he asked.

'Gestapo.'

Nothing more had to be said. Livry discovered that this passenger
had just escaped from a prison with the aid of an elderly guard from
Alsace. The guard was also on that flight back to Tangmere,

according to his possibly not entirely correct account of it later.*

Meanwhile Livry, making his rounds of the cabin guests, discovered he was once more playing air chauffeur to Richard Heslop. It was for the third time in four months – and Heslop still had one more trip to make. He and Jean Rosenthal were returning to Baker Street to report on the outcome of their three-week investigation into the war readiness of Resistance groups in the Alpine regions along the Swiss frontier.

Everywhere they had been given the same message: 'Give us the guns and we'll do the job.' They were going back to London for just as long as it would take to pick up a wireless operator who would be needed to open that vital channel of communication so necessary for the delivery of supplies from the air.

The Hudson was coming in to land now and still Livry was puzzling over the identity of the man behind the bushy beard. It was not until they were all in the squadron's mess hall, hungrily attacking plates heaped with the inevitable but very welcome English breakfast of bacon and eggs that the general introduced himself and the mystery was solved.

Of course! Livry slapped his forehead. Their last meeting had been shortly before the German breakthrough when Livry was a staff liaison officer attached to de Lattre's headquarters.

The next Hudson pick-up came only two nights later when Heslop and Rosenthal were taken back to France in an incredible operation led by Bob Hodges. No less than eighteen people had been collected by Paul Rivière. All of them were waiting for transport to England and the only way they could be brought out in a single operation was by half a dozen Lysanders or two Hudsons.

The Lysanders were out of the question. A triple operation had once been carried out, but the Germans could hardly fail to notice if the so-called secret squadron began formation flying across the Channel with six aircraft at a time.

Hodges decided the time had come to put the Hudsons and the new crews to the supreme test by mounting a double operation. He flew the old, tried and trusted O-for-Oboe of the King's Flight, with the experienced Jimmy Wagland to show them the way. As the Chief Navigation Officer at Tempsford, Waggy always felt honour bound to put in some flying time in any operation considered a little dodgy. They took with them Lofty Reed and an Australian flying officer called McDonald who had just started training as a pick-up pilot.

* Livry-Level. *op cit.*

Affleck was in M-for-Mike with three flying-officers who were all
newcomers to pick-up operations: navigator Dickie Richards, his
close friend from their days on the disciplinary course at Brighton;
air gunner 'Goldie' Goldfinch; and Bradbury, the wireless operator
who had broken his duck on Verity's flight two nights earlier.

As a pilot officer, Affleck was out-ranked by every other man on
the operation, and he was very conscious of the fact that he still had
to put a Hudson down in France. Before, he had been no more than
a passenger sitting alongside Verity. Now the safety of everyone in
the aircraft would be his responsibility.

It was perhaps for this reason that Hodges was carrying the two
top agents, Heslop and Rosenthal, while Affleck was taking the
second string of Americans: Elizabeth Reynolds, the courier for
Heslop's embryo *Marksman* circuit, and Denis Johnson, their
wireless operator, who had been filched for the mission from SOE's
American counterpart, OSS.

The squadron records state simply that Hodges landed at 15
minutes past midnight, while Affleck put his Hudson down 15
minutes later after overshooting once. Not surprisingly, the eager
23-year-old did not want to make too much fuss about the fact that
on his way in for the second attempt he had inadvertently crunched
through the tops of trees bordering the field.

His young woman passenger felt considerably shaken by the near
miss. The crackling and grinding as the Hudson's underbelly struck
the treetops led her to believe a wing had struck the belfry of a
church she had spotted in the distance as they were banking for the
second approach. Affleck's pride would have been hurt if he had
known at the time about her relief at being alive.

He was himself relieved just to have pulled off what had been a
difficult landing under the hyper-critical eye of his squadron
commander, who was by now airborne again and watching the
proceedings below with satisfied approval. The new boy had made
it.

This success by Hodges and Affleck was to have a devastating
impact on the work of arming Resistance fighters in south-eastern
France. Heslop and his *Marksman* team were heading for that vast,
mountainous area which was to be of considerable strategic
importance when the Allied armies landed in the south the
following year.

Heslop's job was to organise the militant bands known as *Maquis*,
so-called for a word in the Corsican dialect, meaning 'scrubland'.
He had to arrange for the dropping and distribution of supplies,

and to keep a tight rein on the more aggressive leaders who could think no further than giving the *Boche* a bloody nose as soon as they had weapons in their hands.

As the two Hudsons headed for home a car set off from the landing ground and sped away into the night with dimmed lights. The reception party broke up, some of them no doubt speculating on the striking woman who had been the first to get into the car.

Elizabeth Reynolds, who was then twenty-seven, was accustomed to attracting the attention of men. Tall, with a long, aristocratic nose and gingery fair hair, she looked a typical product of the girls' public school she had attended in southern England. She was in fact American, but showed no trace of her background.

Heslop had been reluctant to take her because he felt even the most dim-witted policeman would be unable to mistake her for anything other than British.

But on the rigorous SOE training courses she had taken unarmed combat in her long, loping stride, and had proved as adept at handling explosives as she had once wielded a hockey stick. No matter what the situation, she always had a dignified bearing; a haughty arrogance which was once so much the hallmark of the English gentlewoman abroad.

As courier for *Marksman* she became a familiar sight in the Haute-Savoie and Jura, striding along the hilly roads between villages, her rucksack slung across her back, for all the world like an English eccentric on a walking holiday.

Her greatest attribute was a phenomenal memory. She rarely had to carry written messages. She would recite them carefully, memorise them, then repeat them verbatim when she arrived at her destination.

This knack could well have saved her life on many occasions. Other agents were caught at security checkpoints after being unable to explain away the possession of scraps of paper bearing cryptic messages. The 'Grey Mice', as the women's section of the German security forces were known, had no compunction about ordering Frenchwomen to strip to the skin for body searches whenever their suspicions were sufficiently aroused.

Heslop was to say later that she had done 'a fine job, for she had guts and imagination'.

It was to this courageous young woman that Affleck said a hurried farewell as he took off again for base, still carrying branches and leaves from the treetops in the Hudson's air intakes.

Hodges, flying the lead Hudson on the way back, had every

reason to feel jubilant. He and Affleck were bringing home a record number of passengers for a single operation. Unlike the bomber crews who could usually see the result of some of their work below, the clandestine nature of the special duties crews meant they could only guess at the extent of their contribution to the war effort.

Consequently on this flight, as on most others, they counted their success in bodies taken to and from England without knowing whether they really mattered in the long run.

In this case they did. One of the London-bound men was Vincent Auriol, who in 1948 became the President of France and awarded the Légion d'Honneur to Hodges and Wagland. The ceremony was carried out by the French Ambassador in England, René Massigli – who had himself been snatched out of France by Pickard.

The Lysanders and Hudsons of No 161 Squadron had made Occupied Europe part of a very small world.

Baron Emmanuel d'Astier de la Vigerie also had reason to be thankful for the first double Hudson operation. He had gone into the field eleven months earlier to take money and instructions from de Gaulle to assist Jean Moulin.

He was to be instrumental now in persuading Churchill that a greater effort would be needed to supply arms and ammunition to bring the *Maquis* of the mountains to full flower, before it wilted and had its potential wasted by neglect.

Heslop, whose *Marksman* team was settling down for the night in a safe house at a village by the River Ain, was to receive a large share of those supplies.

The last Hudson operation for October was again carried out by Affleck with his by now confident crew in what he reported to be a 'return journey made without incident'.

This time the destination was Déricourt's field near Angers, and three of his four passengers had important missions: Joseph Marchand was returning to organise *Newsagent*; Albert Browne-Bartoli was going in to set up *Ditcher* in Burgundy, a little to the north of him; Robert Benoist, also going back for a second mission, had orders to take charge of *Clergyman* around Nantes, and to blow up a power station which supplied much of Brittany.

Although for Affleck it was an operation 'without incident', he was too busy preparing for take-off to notice the atmosphere of tension among the four 'Joes' who were climbing into the aircraft for the return trip.

Three of them can be quickly dismissed: Francis Nearne, an

assistant to the head of *Stationer*, Maurice Southgate, and brother of two of SOE's women agents; Le Prince, who was working for General Giraud; and Alexandre Levy, a Jewish public service administrator in Paris who had decided to flee before the Germans rounded him up for dispatch to a concentration camp.

The fourth agent on his way home to London was Henri Frager. It is difficult now to follow the tortuous twists and turns in the tangled web of double dealing and double cross in which he was enmeshed.

For some considerable time Frager had been suspicious of Déricourt. He had arranged for warning messages to be sent back to headquarters by radio, but no action had been taken. Not content to leave it at that, he decided to go back in person and demand an investigation. But to get back, he had to ask Déricourt to make the transport arrangements for an aircraft pick-up. Imagine his dilemma.

As a precaution against betrayal he took along his trusted second-in-command, Roger Bardet.

'Watch Déricourt,' he confided. 'He could be working with the SD.'

But Bardet himself was a traitor. He had been recruited by Bleicher, the Abwehr's ubiquitous sergeant, who had already told him that Déricourt had an 'arrangement' with the rival SD.

Déricourt was furious when Frager turned up at Angers with Bardet. He rightly considered it to be a breach of security.

There was no place at a pick-up for non-essential spectators, he argued, knowing full well that Bardet was an Abwehr man, but unable to tell Frager this in case it should jeopardise his own status with the SD. A vociferous argument broke out before Affleck's Hudson landed, with Déricourt insisting that Bardet should go to London, and Frager contemptuously replying that he would do no such thing.

If Déricourt could have put Bardet on the Hudson, he undoubtedly would have tipped off London, thus clearing himself of the accusation which he knew Frager had been making about his own loyalties. Not surprisingly Bardet refused point-blank to get on the aircraft. It was not very difficult to guess what was on Déricourt's mind, and he had no intention of finishing up on the end of a rope in Wormwood Scrubs.

In this ugly scene with a cast of three there was one Frenchman working for the Germans, one working for the British, and one with a foot in both camps. The only truly honest patriot among them was the only one fated to die before the war ended.

Frager did not quite know what to make of Déricourt's insistence that Bardet should fly to England. But he was certainly not going to take orders from a man he believed to be an enemy, and he cautiously closed his hand over the butt of a revolver concealed in his coat pocket.

Déricourt, a man of considerable ability and charm, saw the move and changed his tactics. He agreed that Bardet should remain in France and talked persuasively for several minutes about the need to stay united for the sole aim of throwing the Germans out of the France they both loved.

'Why do you distrust me, Paul?' he asked, using Frager's field name.

The other man then apparently softened, and when the time came to climb on board the aircraft just brought down by Affleck, he turned to shake Déricourt's hand. His gesture was brusquely refused, and the Hudson took off with the crew knowing nothing of the drama which had just been enacted.

Evidence that Déricourt had not on that occasion informed his SD paymasters of the pick-up operation is indicated by the fact that none of the agents going into France was followed from the rendezvous. The next Hudson operation carried out in the following month was to be very different and would help to put £20,000 into Déricourt's bank account.

October generally had been a good month for No 161 Squadron although bad weather conditions had reduced the number of operations planned for the Lysanders and Halifaxes. And although the double Hudson operation had been an unqualified success, Bob Hodges decided not to recommend a repeat performance.

He logged a note in the squadron records to the effect that a double operation should never be laid on again 'except in an emergency, as it involves a great deal of stooging in the target area'.

It was in this month that a fourth Hudson arrived on station: N-for-Nan, the aircraft destined to become a tragic memorial on a hillside of the Ardennes.

It had been begged from the Air Ministry with the plea that more Hudsons were needed to relieve the extra workload planned for O-for-Oboe, M-for-Mike and P-for-Peter, which between them had carried out 18 successful sorties by the end of that month.

The Hudsons were now about to become the squadron work-horses, the only aircraft capable of both pick-up operations and of parachuting agents into the field. It was difficult to jump from a

Lysander because of its design, and the Havoc could not be flown slowly enough to make an exit from them either practical or safe. The four-engine Halifax was too big ever to be used for clandestine landings.

A third attribute of the Hudson was its adaptability. The Havocs had been carrying out what were known as *Ascension* operations which enabled direct radio contact to be made between an aircraft and an agent on the ground. Hodges planned to convert the Hudsons to carry this special type of radio equipment and to phase the Havocs out, to be used only as a reserve.

Regular *Ascension* sorties were made by Hudsons from the autumn of 1943 to make direct S-phone contact with agents, probably of the SIS, who were code-named *Bullet* and *Player*. There is no official record of SOE agents using the S-phone although the head of F Section, Maurice Buckmaster, records in his memoirs* an incident in which an officer went out from Baker Street to contact a man in the field.

The aircraft was circling the rendezvous, searching for the reception lights, when one of the crew spotted a dim glow from what were obviously small hand torches.

'Well! Look at those bloody awful lights,' exclaimed the exasperated RAF man.

His remark over the aircraft's intercom system was picked up by the S-phone and heard by those waiting below.

Back came the reply, in a broad Lancashire accent instantly recognisable as that of the agent they had come to contact: 'Aye, and yours would be bloody awful too, if you had the Gestapo as near you as we have.'

As October came to an end, Hodges reported that the first *Ascension* operation carried out by a Hudson had been an 'initial success' and training began in earnest to lay the groundwork for the invasion which everyone guessed was going to be launched in 1944.

The bad weather conditions continued in November, a month which was enlivened by a visit to Tempsford by the King and Queen. The squadron officers felt they had really arrived as an élite unit by this Royal recognition, but the Other Ranks who spent days polishing and painting in anticipation of the rumoured visit may well have had other views.

Six more Stirlings joined the squadron strength, but again Hodges had to report that results were 'not impressive'. The new

Specially Employed, by M.J. Buckmaster. (Batchworth Press) 1952.

Hudson N-for-Nan really got down to business, flying 14 *Ascension* sorties to make eleven contacts with *Bullet* and six with *Player*. Affleck carried out three of the sorties, and Hodges did one.

Flying Officer McDonald, who had flown with the squadron commander on the double Hudson pick-up the previous month, broke his solo duck by doing two of the *Ascension* sorties, while the remaining eight were carried out by the first non-commissioned Hudson pilot, a Flight Sergeant Smith.

The only Hudson pick-up during this month was carried out on the night of the 15th by Hodges, who took off a little after midnight for a flight lasting an hour and twenty minutes to Déricourt's favourite field near Angers. The reception was 'excellent' and the ground 'reasonably hard'. Afterwards the wing commander decided it had been 'a very straightforward operation'.

It was anything but. Unknown to Hodges, his crew, the five agents they landed, and the ten passengers who climbed on board for the return trip, the entire operation was watched from a safe distance by officers and men of the SD. They were led by Josef Kieffer, a former police inspector in Karlsruhe, a frontier town in the Rhine Valley.

A cruel, vicious, but extremely able man, he was too cunning to scoop everyone on the field into his net as he could have done so easily. Instead, he was prepared to forsake the pleasure of capturing the ten London-bound passengers for the greater achievement of following the five incoming agents to discover their contacts and, eventually, the missions they had been ordered to carry out by London.

Three of them were arrested that very night after travelling separately by train to Paris. One evaded capture for three days. The fifth would have been Kieffer's most important catch, but he was too wily an operator to be trapped by Kieffer's dull-witted scum recruited from the criminal underworld of Paris.

Vic Gerson was on his third mission in his second war and he had learned enough to know that the peacetime virtue of trust can be a vice in war. He was a survivor.

The nucleus of his escape line organisation was formed from the Jewish community around Lyons, and by the summer of 1942 it had links of safe hiding places in a chain stretching from Paris to the Spanish frontier.

His first exploit of significance was to organise an escape of several agents from the French concentration camp at Mauzac in the Dordogne. Among them were Georges Bégué, F Section's first radio man, and two of SOE's key operatives: Michael Trotobas and Philippe Liewer. Gerson returned to England to make a progress report, and was dropped back into the field from a No 161 Squadron Halifax to spend the first six months of 1943 setting up two more escape lines as insurance against German penetration.

He returned to London once more in the Hodges' Hudson which landed in a field of cattle; now he had been put down in the same field at Angers, unaware that Kieffer and his men of the Paris SD were on hand to admire the touchdown.

He and another agent, Edward Levene, somehow managed to give their shadows the slip. The latter was on his way to join Henri Frager's *Donkeyman* as a weapons instructor. But by this time the *réseau* had been penetrated by the betrayal of Frager's lieutenant, Roger Bardet.

This gives some credibility to the theories of the special duties pilots and others who believed after the war that Déricourt had been maligned. Could Kieffer not have been tipped off about the Hudson landing by Bardet? Possibly. Certainly there has been no evidence that Déricourt deliberately arranged for agents to be captured, and men who knew him well have always argued that whatever he did, he was acting under orders from British Intelligence.

At his trial after the war Déricourt admitted he had given the Germans the localities of eight landing grounds out of fourteen he could use for pick-ups or *parachutages*. But he insisted he never used the eight. The information he had given to Kieffer was only a bait to enable him to continue working unmolested for the British.

The fact remains, however, that four agents were captured on this November operation, and Déricourt was paid £20,000 at a time when the going rate for exposing British agents was £5,000 each.

Levene was caught at a blown safe house three days after his arrival. The other three were caught within 24 hours of leaving the Hudson. The most experienced of them was Jean Menesson, a lecturer from the Institut Français in London. He had first gone to France in 1942 to run an underground newspaper, and was on his way back for a second tour after a period of leave.

Paul Pardi was on his way to join the *Scientist* circuit as the liaison officer responsible for Lysander and Hudson pick-ups.

Kieffer's real coup of that night was the arrest of the third man, A.A. Maugenet. Both Menesson and Pardi remained silent during the initial interrogation under the imposing chandelier of the SD chief's lavender-carpeted office.

But the inquisitors at the Avenue Foch learned enough to discover that Maugenet had orders to link up with Diana Rowden, who had arrived three months earlier in a Lysander operation arranged by Déricourt. The head of her *réseau* was John Starr, who had been betrayed by a double agent the previous month and was still under interrogation at Avenue Foch when Maugenet was brought in.

Also at the notorious SD headquarters at this time was Commandant Faye, of *Alliance*. By tapping out Morse on the wall of his cell he had been able to contact yet another familiar squadron passenger, the gentle Indian princess, Noor Inayat Khan. She in turn was in touch with Starr, and Faye decided that all three should escape.

He told them it would be easy to loosen the bars set in crumbling mortar in the skylights of their cells, and when they were all ready they arranged to meet on the rooftop.

But they were in a trap. The street below was a cul-de-sac.

Noor, a young woman brought up in the caring ways of the Sufi sect, which her father introduced to Europe, spent much of her remaining life in chains. Kieffer was to say before he was hanged after the war that she had 'behaved most bravely' and that he had been unable to extract from her any new information about her activities.

She was thirty-one years old when she was murdered at Dachau, silent to the end.

Faye, whose spirit also remained unbroken in the six months he was incarcerated in the fortress of Bruchsal, was no more than a skeleton when he was taken out to face a firing squad in the grounds of Schwabisch-Hall prison. He was forty-five.

Starr, who gave his parole to the Nazis after the abortive escape attempt, managed to fade into the shadows of Mauthausen concentration camp and was one of the few F Section prisoners there to survive.

That was all in the future. While Faye was plotting the escape, and while the three agents from the November Hudson were setting off for Angers and the Paris train which was to carry them into a trap, Hodges was preparing for the return trip to base.

On board were five RAF bomber pilots who had been shot down and passed along an escape line into Déricourt's care, and five agents who had been ordered back to London.

One of them was Francis Cammaerts, a Cambridge hockey blue. He was looking forward to his first English breakfast in nine months when he turned to Déricourt for a farewell handshake. He never forgot the other man's reaction.

Déricourt looked him straight in the eye and said in a voice devoid of any emotion: 'I never want to see you again.'

Hurt, and not a little bewildered by this abrupt rejection, he climbed into the aircraft to think about it. Cammaerts, who had been brought up in England as the son of a Belgian poet, started the war as a conscientious objector and an avowed pacifist. He decided the war could get on very well without him and made his contribution by working on a farm.

The death of his brother in action with the RAF changed all that. From a man of peace he changed almost overnight into a dedicated anti-Nazi, and in 1942, at the age of twenty-six, he was recruited by SOE.

He was sent into the field in March 1943 in a Lysander piloted by Verity. On the landing ground he exchanged hurried greetings with Peter Churchill and Henri Frager. He then set off in the company of Georges Dubourdin, the former head of *Spruce* who had been so unceremoniously booted out of France five months earlier by Robert Boiteux.

His orders were to act as Frager's British liaison officer in *Donkeyman*, and to set up a new and separate organisation to be known as *Jockey*. Some innate sense of foreboding – a prerequisite for survival – warned him to tread warily. A cautious man himself, he found the cavalier attitude of his French contacts extremely unnerving and he suspected quite rightly that *Donkeyman* was insecure.

It was a powder keg and when it blew up Cammaerts was forced to wander around Paris, keeping what today would be called a low profile. Eventually he was able to contact Odette Sansom, who put him in touch with the man who had been running *Donkeyman* in Frager's absence.

It was Bardet. Again Cammaerts' intuition came to his aid. He distrusted the Frenchman on sight, and decided to have nothing more to do with the network. Instead, he set about his secondary job of organising *Jockey*, and in just a few months he had created several small, reliable units operating along the west bank of the Rhône from just south of Lyons to the coast.

His only major setback was the tragic loss of his courier, Cecily Lefort, who was arrested at a blown address which he had warned her against using.

By November he was running a tight operation and was ready to return to London to report. He was delighted to find Déricourt in charge of pick-up arrangements as they had met before on several occasions and he had come to enjoy the extrovert Frenchman's company.

As the Hudson took off he reflected on the untypically rude farewell and decided that Déricourt's apparent hostility was due to his strict sense of security. A stickler for security himself, he could appreciate the other man's attitude, so he settled down for home and breakfast, mollified by the belief that Déricourt was being no more than ultra-careful.

When the full extent of the Frenchman's duplicity became known, Cammaerts realised those parting words outside the Hudson had expressed the heartfelt wish of a man in anguish.

' . . . I never want to see you again.'

He had not been rejecting a friendship. He had been hoping simply that Cammaerts would never again be in a position where the Germans might capture him through information which he had passed as part of his double-dealing machinations in some overall intelligence plot.

A French-Canadian called Chartrand travelled back with Cammaerts just one jump ahead of the Gestapo. He was one of the few survivors among the leaders of *Butler*, a *réseau* which had carried out useful sabotage in the Sarthe region around Le Mans.

Three others returning on the November Hudson belonged to the disintegrating *Tinker réseau*, which had been disrupting rail transport in the important junction town of Troyes.

They were Pierre Mulsant, a timber merchant who was deputy chief of the circuit, his courier Yvonne Fontaine, and the wireless operator, John Barrett.

All three were to return to France the following year, but only the woman survived.

Although No 161 Squadron records show that ten people were brought back to England on the one and only Hudson flight in November – and five of them are now known to have been shot-down bomber pilots – there would appear to have been an eleventh passenger on this already overcrowded airbus: Charles Rechenmann, who was returning to England for more training in sabotage techniques.

He, too, was to die in a concentration camp after returning to his old haunts the following year to organise a team of saboteurs. But his death was not in vain. The men he trained were responsible for the destruction of vital factory equipment which the RAF had been unable to knock out in industrial Tarbes. Their activities were also a big enough nuisance for the Germans to divert combat units which otherwise would have been more effectively deployed along the Normandy front.

November was only a moderately successful month for No 161 Squadron because of the atrocious weather, and things were now beginning to go wrong. A Halifax had veered off the runway on take-off and smashed into a steamroller, injuring a gunner and wrecking the aircraft. It was a bad omen for the pilot, Flight Lieutenant Gray, and his crew.

Then there was the disappearance of Robin Hooper, missing somewhere in France. His Lysander had bogged down in a field at Châtellerault and he was now on the run – the first loss on a pick-up operation for fourteen months.

And there was worse to come.

*

2200 hours, 20 March 1945: The Rhine was behind them and somewhere down below lay the Westerwald, a beautiful hilly range of forest which before the war was thronged every summer weekend with hikers and campers and picnic parties, but which now concealed the battered remnants of Hitler's panzers.

If he thought about them at all, the gunner would undoubtedly have tried to shoot them out of their hiding places. He was like that. But he had never yet had a chance of using his beloved Brownings on clandestine operations . . .

. . . Tommy Thompson knew he wanted to be a flier as soon as he decided to go to war. He and Onslow had talked of nothing else in their room back home. Well, his brother had made it and now, in November 1943, he was somewhere else in England flying Mosquitoes.

Thompson himself had to be content as a back-seat driver in the rear turret of bombers. But for that crazy night in Canada at the flying school he, too, could have been a pilot.

After basic training he had been sent to Canada from New Zealand for flying lessons, but an excess of hospitality one night in the Mess had led to a hung-over error the following day and he had seriously 'bent' a trainer aircraft.

The RAF decided at the subsequent inquiry that his destructive urges could be better utilised so he was posted to an air gunnery course.

In those days the Air Ministry was concerned to note that an increasing number of young men from the former colonies were earning commissions, and generally lowering the tone of stations where they were based by indisciplined hell-raising. They even mixed socially with Other Ranks.

The Top Brass raised in the shires of England could not understand this new breed of officer.

Thompson did now know it, but in a memo sent to Bomber Command HQ a staff officer wrote in 1942: 'There are indications . . . that we are not getting a reasonable percentage of the young men of the middle and upper classes, who are the backbone of this country, when they leave the public schools.'

Hence a 'colonial' had to have an unblotted copybook if he wanted to survive training for jobs which by tradition went to the sons of the boys of the old brigade.

So Thompson was scrubbed out of flying school while his brother Onslow passed, albeit without a commission and officer status. Disappointed, but not disillusioned, Thompson stuck to his gunnery course. He earned the coveted 'AG' brevet with its single wing, won the DFM and completed 27 bombing operations by the end of April 1943.

Now, some six months later, he was waiting for a posting to a secret squadron where he had been told no obstacles would be put in the way of a 'colonial' who wanted to be an officer.

That would be something to write home about. He and Onslow had always shared everything, united as small boys in rebellion against their mother's almost Victorian upbringing which imposed on them a strict but very loving regime.

They had always been very much in awe of her, and even now Thompson dared not tell her that the woolly Fair Isle socks she persisted in knitting to keep his feet warm were now accumulating, unused, in a bedside drawer.

He knew what the other gunners would say if they caught him wearing fancy socks. A tough bunch, the gunners who had survived one tour . . . as tough and uncompromising as their unofficial motto: 'We Aim – Not to Please.'

PART THREE

. . . And the Waning

The breath of a night like death did flow
Beneath the sinking moon.
                    —SHELLEY.

9

Christmas was coming. The girls of the WAAF were planning a party and every coloured piece of paper and tinsel found on the station over the past few weeks had been carefully hoarded to make bunting. Was this going to be the last Christmas of the war, like the four others gone before?

The festive spirit, like victory, was in the air, but some familiar faces were missing and the frantic merrymaking in many cases was but a brittle veneer, ready to crack.

Jimmy Bathgate, a 25-year-old New Zealander, was shot down and killed in a Lysander over France on his ninth pick-up operation on 11 December. He had just been awarded the DFC.

Lofty Reed left for a special signals course at Pwllheli.

Philippe Livry, restless because he felt he was not getting enough action, pestered everyone he knew from wing commander upwards until he was posted to fly Mosquitoes with Charles Pickard's No 21 Squadron at Sculthorpe. Alan Broadley, with a new DSO, had already joined him.

Hugh Verity had gone and was now flying a desk in London with the Air Liaison (Operations) section at SOE headquarters. He had made 29 clandestine landings – three times more than the legendary Pickard – and made eight other attempts which failed because of bad weather or poor receptions.

He had taken 45 agents into the field – many of them vital to the work of the Resistance – and brought 94 passengers back. A further breakdown of his achievements show that he carried 54 passengers on his five Hudson pick-ups, and 85 on his 24 Lysander operations.

He had more than earned his desk. He was visiting Tangmere socially when Robin Hooper was brought back, rescued from France in an operation flown by Bob Hodges. But the jubilation at his safe return was tempered by the heavy casualties suffered by the squadron on that same Black Thursday of 16 December.

After 22 months with only a single fatality on operations, the squadron was unprepared for the tragedies on that night of disaster, when a total of five aircraft failed to return safely.

Flight Lieutenant Gray, who had survived the runway collision with a steam roller a few weeks earlier, crash-landed his replacement Halifax and was killed with two of his crew. The rest were badly injured, including wireless operator Eddie Shine, one of Verity's crew in the Hudsons. He was never to fly on operations again.

Flying Officer Harborrow was forced to ditch off the Suffolk coast and one of his crew, Flying Officer McMasters, drowned at his action station before he could be pulled to safety.

In the third Halifax out that night, Flight Sergeant Caldwell nursed his stricken aircraft all the way across the Channel before ordering his crew to bail out. Luckily they all made it without injury, except Flight Sergeant Morris, who hurt a foot.

Meanwhile, three Lysander pilots were on their way home from successful pick-ups: Hodges, who was bringing back Hooper and an agent called Jean Depractère; Flight Lieutenant Stephen Hankey, and Flying Officer J.M. McBride, with two agents each.

Hodges had taken Wagland along to do the navigating as he wanted to leave himself free to concentrate on flying on what the weather forecasters had warned would be a 'dirty' night.

They had tried the pick-up the night before on an operation code-named *Scenery*, but it had been abandoned because of bad weather. *Scenery II* has been successful and they were now on their way back, with the words of warning from Mouse Fielden still echoing in their minds: 'Be careful. We don't want to have to lay on *Scenery III*.'

The squadron commander had taken off before the other two Lysanders and on the return flight he found the weather was closing in fast. With the cloud base down to 300 feet he was just able to pick out the runway lights at Tangmere. As he put the aircraft down, visibility dropped down to zero.

The noise of the engine drowned the sigh of relief from Hooper in the rear compartment. With four on board he had been unable to see any of what had been going on outside the aircraft. He had spent the journey lying on the floor and his only worry was that Depractère would be airsick all over him.

Hankey and McBride were some two hours behind after a double operation to pick up their four agents. Hodges and Hooper broke off their reunion celebrations to make their way to the control tower when word came through that the two Lysanders were approaching the coast.

The fog was impenetrable. McBride was instructed to attempt his landing at Tangmere. There was nowhere else for him to go.

The men on the ground heard his aircraft coming in on the final approach, and through the gloom they saw it about to make what would have been a perfect touchdown when suddenly the radio crackled into life and McBride was heard to call out: 'You are flying me into the hangars.'

Tragically the young pilot had mistaken a red light on top of a control caravan for station obstruction lights, and he pulled back on his controls to make another attempt.

The distinctive buzz of his engine faded away into the distance and was never heard again.

Miraculously, the two agents he had been carrying were found staggering around a field a mile from the runway. The Lysander had gone in nose down and was still burning fiercely when Hodges and Hooper reached the scene.

It had been McBride's fourth operation and he had not been with the squadron long enough for anyone to remember his Christian name. He had been just 'MacB', to distinguish him from the other 'Macs'.

Stephen Hankey, meanwhile, had been diverted to the nearby naval base at Ford. He is believed to have gone out of control in the pea-souper and the wreckage of his Lysander was found on a hillside with the three bodies still inside.

Verity, who had taken time off from his duties at Baker Street to pay a social call on friends at his old squadron, slept soundly through it all and knew nothing about the deaths until he went in to breakfast that morning.

At this point in the squadron's operations it would be appropriate to question the justification for risking the lives of experienced aircrew and the loss of valuable aircraft by mounting pick-up operations to rescue shot-down pilots and other aircrew.

The answer can not be in doubt. If Hooper had been captured and his unit identified, the Gestapo would not have hesitated to ignore his prisoner-of-war status to squeeze from him all he knew about clandestine operations.

This alone was sufficient justification for his rescue, and the fact that it was effected in an operation to bring an agent out of France at the same time made it doubly so.

The same to a lesser degree applied to the five bomber pilots who were picked up by Hodges in November. The precedent had been set two years earlier when Sticky Murphy set out in a tired, old Anson to pick up John Nesbitt-Dufort in what was the forerunner of Hudson operations.*

The RAF could not just abandon such men on the run. For Nesbitt-Dufort and Hooper, capture would have been unpleasant

*See Chapter III

at most, but the odds were that they would suffer no more than the discomfort of a prison camp for the duration of the war.

For the families who gave them shelter, discovery would have meant deportation and death. Yet for all the risks there were always ordinary people prepared to make these sacrifices to rid themselves of the evil of the Nazi Occupation. The mass of them, as the American philospher Thoreau said in a different context a century earlier, were living 'lives of quiet desperation'.

For most of them there was no other way of fighting back; perhaps because they did not have the temperament for undercover work, or because they were too old to be of use in an active role, or because there was no active Resistance unit in their neighbourhood.

There were, of course, others who would have nothing whatever to do with shot-down airmen. It was asking a lot, after all, to put a man in a position where he and his family could be executed out of hand. There was always the possibility, too, that the bedraggled figure in RAF uniform asking for asylum in the middle of the night could be a 'plant' by the SD or Abwehr in an attempt to infiltrate an escape route.

Surprisingly, the decision to put War Office muscle behind these lifelines which had sprung up willy-nilly in haphazard fashion after 1940 met initially with considerable opposition in London. Escapers and evaders were considered small fry and not worth the effort of saving.

Like the Blimps of World War I who refused to sanction the issue of parachutes to aircrew in case they should use them when not really necessary, there were men of influence in Whitehall who believed that people had no business allowing themselves to be taken prisoner in the first place.

Fortunately that sort of Whitehall warrior was in the minority. But they *did* exist and their kind of mentality was to blight the early efforts being made by men of vision to bring some cohesion to the efforts of a small unit created in 1939.

It was given the departmental designation of MI9 and put under the command of a mere brigadier, Norman Crockatt. Like SOE, it was very much despised by the older agencies responsible for intelligence-gathering (MI6) and counter espionage (MI5).

Some intelligence chiefs were horrified at the thought of independent novices in the art of undercover work being allowed to roam loose across Europe, stirring up a hornets' nest of German activity which could be damaging to the professionals in the spying game.

Sir Claude Dansey, a grey figure behind MI6 and a man of Machiavellian intrigue, found a compromise much to his liking by offering Crockatt a deal by which British Intelligence contacts could be used to organise escape lines over the Pyrenees and by sea between Marseilles and Spain.

He wanted a foot in the door of Room 900 – as the MI9 headquarters were known – in order to give MI6 access to any intelligence coming out of Europe with escapers and evaders.

The result of the deal was that Crockatt had to sacrifice some of his organisation's independence, but as it was being run on a shoestring he needed all the help he could get. It came in the form of James Langley, a Coldstream Guards subaltern of outstanding courage who refused to allow the loss of an arm at Dunkirk prevent him from escaping from a camp.

One constant bone of contention was the use of No 161 Squadron for bring escapers and evaders back to England. Dansey, described by Langley* as looking very much like a 'benign uncle, with his white hair, blue eyes and general air of benevolence,' was dead set against the use of scarce aircraft which he believed could be put to better use by his own agents.

But so far as MI9 was concerned, escape by air was by far the speediest method, and by reducing the time a man was in hiding, the risks were reduced to the security of the escape lines.

A classic example is that of the squadron leader who got engaged at a dance at the Savoy on a Saturday, was shot down over France on the Monday, and was brought back in time for his engagement party the following Saturday.

Relations between MI9 and the pilots of No 161 were always of the best, although there were occasional hot-tempered rows arising out of a lack of understanding.

An agent might choose a landing ground which the RAF considered unsuitable, even dangerous; while a reception party could sometimes be left waiting vainly in a brightly moonlit field, not knowing the flight had been cancelled at the last minute because of bad weather over England.

Langley recalls summing up those misunderstandings in a poem he wrote in a Tempsford scrap book. He remembers, inaccurately, that it began:

The moon is blazing in the sky,
Will those buggers never fly?

Fight Another Day by J.M. Langley. (William Collins) 1974.

And ended:

> The moon is dying in the sky,
> And still those bastards will not fly.

Neither very poetic, nor very fair, as he himself, admits. Hugh Verity includes the correct version in *his* memoirs.* While not as strongly worded, it is nevertheless similarly uncomplimentary.

But as Langley points out: 'The fact that no offence was given or taken says much for the splendid spirit of co-operation that existed between the pilots and the chairborne officers in London.'

By the time of the Normandy landings MI9 had masterminded the return from Europe of more than 3,000 Allied airmen who otherwise would have been unable to take any further part in the war. It says much for those evaders that so many of them went back into action only to meet their deaths.

And a statistic often forgotten is that for every airman rescued, one civilian was executed in reprisals.

Francis Cammaerts, returning to France early in 1944 to organise his *Jockey* sabotage teams in preparation for D-Day, discovered for himself how the first heart-stopping contact with evasion lines could be made by aircrew on the run.

He told me how the Halifax taking him from Tempsford was hit by flak many miles from his rendezvous, and he heard the skipper calling on him to jump.

'It was an eerie, frightening experience. As I fell away from the plane I could see it was well on fire. The crew made sure I got out first, as it would not be very advisable for me, in civilian clothes, to get picked up with them when we landed.

'I seemed to fall through the clouds for ages. We were 10,000 feet up at the time, which was about 9,000 feet higher than the recommended altitude for the usual clandestine jump.

'I landed with a bump and made my way to a cottage where I knocked on the door and told the man who answered, "You must be a good Frenchman. I am a British agent." It was a risk I had to take.'

Cammaerts was alone and miles, as far as he was aware, from any Resistance group. He knew he was liable to be picked up at any moment by German units searching for the crew of the shot-down Halifax. He had no alternative but to use the only method of contact known to the ordinary airman.

*Verity, *op cit.*

The gamble paid off, as it so often did. 'The Frenchman was overjoyed to see me. He said he had always wanted to be with the Resistance, but he had no time as he had thirty acres of farmland to look after and a family to feed.

'He was able to put me in touch with local Resistance men – and by sheer chance it turned out they belonged to a group belonging to my circuit. I immediately arranged for them to search for the Halifax crew before the Germans found them. This they did, and they were very quickly put into a safe house.'

The usual drill at this point in evasion techniques was for RAF personnel to lie low until arrangements could be made to have them escorted down the line in the general direction of the Pyrenees. But Cammaerts has never forgotten the example set by the young rear-gunner of the Halifax, a nineteen-year-old called Len Gormall.

'It was all very much a big adventure for him to be in France, surrounded by Germans,' he recalls. 'The local resisters were about to go on an operation to rescue some men who had been arrested.

'He insisted on going along. He argued that his knowledge of guns would be useful. It was not very good security because he could only speak a smattering of schoolboy French and it would have been all up with him if he had been questioned.

'However, the local men dressed him up in a gendarme's uniform and took him along for a rescue operation which was a complete success. From that point on he was regarded as something of a lucky mascot.

'The locals could not do enough for him and his name is still remembered in that locality. His skipper was not at all keen on his taking part in Resistance activities, and at one stage ordered him not to.

'I made it quite clear to this squadron leader that the boy should be left alone, and that if he didn't recommend him for a gong when they got back home, I would see to it that unless he gave this guarantee, he personally might have to stay in France longer than he anticipated.'

Such a story should have a happy ending. The crew eventually got back to England safely and Gormall, who was anxious to get on with the war achieved his ambition of becoming a fighter pilot.

He was shot down and killed over Holland shortly before the war ended.

Another story of an evader which has never before been told involves yet another Halifax rear gunner: Flight Sergeant John

Frederick Quirk Brough, or 'JFQ' as he was sometimes called.*

He was just twenty-one years old and awaiting promotion to flight lieutenant when his aircraft took off from Tempsford on the night of 3 November 1943. The pilot, Flight Sergeant Hodges – no relation to No 161 Squadron's CO – took the usual route, crossing the French coast at Cabourg, then dropping to a few thousand feet to make a low-level run for the supply dropping zone in south-eastern France.

They reached the rendezvous on time but there was no sign of the recognition lights. They circled the area for perhaps thirty minutes, the crew alternately searching the ground for pinpoints of light, and the skies around them for the tell-tale exhaust or silhouette of an enemy night fighter.

The pilot decided to make one more sweep before aborting the mission and returning home. Brough remembers the events which followed only hazily.

'We had just commenced our last run when the aircraft gave a violent shudder, stalled and crashed into the ground. At this stage I must have blacked out, because when I came to I was lying on the side of a mountain. By a miracle I was unhurt.

'I scrambled down to the wreckage of the aircraft a little below me, but I was unable to get anywhere near because of the flames. There was nothing I could do. I must have blacked out again, and this time when I recovered I was lying by a stream.

'I had no idea of the time by then because my watch had stopped at twelve minutes past midnight. I staggered down the mountainside until I spotted a French farmer. He took me to his cottage. There was a woman inside nursing a small child. I could only speak the little French I had learned at school, and they had no English, but we managed to communicate by sign language.

'He gave me breakfast of bread and roasted chestnuts, then he took me to a wood where he made me understand I would have to remain in hiding until nightfall. He came back for me later and introduced me to a French woman who took me to her house at a nearby village called Marcols-les-Eaux and provided me with hot food, a hot bath, and a bed.'

It was there, two nights after his crash, that he was interrogated by some very tough-looking and suspicious Resistance men. They said the Germans were not searching for him because they had found seven bodies in the Halifax – the normal crew complement for the bomber.

* Personal interview.

Who, they wanted to know, was he? Brough explained that the aircraft had been carrying a passenger, a United States Air Force captain who was learning the techniques of night navigation and supply dropping.

The Resistance men were still dubious, but if Brough were a German agent surely the Germans would have made a show of searching for a missing crewman? However, they could not afford to take chances. They took him to the town of Valence where he met a Scotswoman who had married a Frenchman before the war and had managed to keep her nationality and loyalties concealed from the authorities.

She asked him various questions about life in England, while arrangements were being made to contact London by radio to check his credentials. When the word came through that he was a genuine evader he was fitted out with a blue sports jacket, grey flannel trousers, and given a beret as a concession to the Anglo-Saxon belief that all Frenchmen wore them.

Then, complete with a set of brand-new but deliberately soiled identify papers, he was walked around Valence, in and out of wine bars and cafes, to get him acclimatised to a world where field-grey uniforms and jackboots were commonplace and everywhere.

The next stage was a train journey to Lyons. It was uneventful and without checks until he and his escort reached the main line station where his identity cards were scrutinised briefly by gendarmes at the control point. There were no questions.

The end of the line for the time being came at a château on the outskirts of Lyons where he met two important figures of the Resistance: Raymond and Lucille Aubrac, in hiding with their three-year-old son Jean-Pierre, known to them all as 'Boo-boo'.

While the WAAF contingent at Tempsford were throwing their Christmas party, Brough was celebrating with the Aubracs and waiting for news of a Hudson pick-up which had been laid on to get them all out of France. The weather was atrocious, and when a pick-up was eventually laid on, all their hopes were dashed by a last-minute cancellation.

The young air gunner went off to hide in the hills with a band of *maquisards,* and often found himself on reception parties for supply drops carried out by aircraft from his own squadron.

'It was a strange feeling to be standing in a field, looking up and waiting for the sound of the engines, then seeing the aircraft and knowing that with any luck I would soon be back up there with them again.'

In February, nearly three months after his crash he was on his way home in a Hudson flown by John Affleck.

It was not until after the end of the war that Brough was able to piece together what had happened on the flight which was so nearly his last. His Halifax had clipped a large rock perched on top of a mountain in the Haute Loire. The tail section where he had been lying huddled over his guns snapped on impact and he was hurled clear of the blazing wreck as it tore its way down the reverse slope.

A memorial stone marks the spot today.

Brough was twice lucky; lucky to survive the crash and lucky in that the Resistance group which found him was already organising a pick-up for the Aubracs, who were then on the Gestapo's 'Most Wanted' list. Otherwise, as a not particularly essential air gunner, he would have been put on the long and arduous route to safety travelled by so many other aircrew over the Pyrenees.

The London end of these escape routes was handled by MI9 staff officers like Jimmy Langley and Airey Neave, the Colditz home runner, with Donald Darling in Lisbon and Gibraltar smoothing out the kinks in the lifeline running through Franco's neutral but hostile Spain.

But the real work at the sharp end was done by the organisers whose lives were constantly and literally 'put on the line'.

Several of them found the Hudsons to be a handy method of transportation. Victor Gerson, whose *Vic* line operated between Lyons and Perpignan, has been dealt with in the last chapter.

Erwin Deman, a Viennese Jew who fought in the French Army, escaped from a POW camp in 1940 and made his way to England. His fluency in French and German made him a natural for SOE and by August 1943 he was on his way back to France, a solitary passenger in the Hudson which Hodges brought down in a field of cattle.

Within eight weeks he had set up an escape line called *Var*, running through Brittany with a headquarters at Rennes. It was one of the few successful routes by sea, using as a jumping off point a small beach near Dinard below a villa owned by Cecily Lefort, the international yachtswoman who was a courier to Cammaerts' *Jockey réseau* before her capture and eventual death in Ravensbrück.

Women played a vital role in the escape lines. It was a field of the Resistance where their natural attributes could be employed to the best advantage. As an escort to a party of airmen, perhaps in the guise of a nurse, a woman was less likely to excite suspicion; she could carry bulky equipment in hand and shopping bags without being questioned; she could often charm her way out of tricky situations as men the world over are susceptible to flattery.

Mary Lindell was one such woman. She went back to France by Lysander on 27 October 1942, at the age of forty-seven. A nurse in World War I, she had become the Comtesse de Milleville by the outbreak of hostilities in 1939.

She planned the escape of several British officers after Dunkirk, but the Gestapo caught up with her and put her, so they believed, out of harm's way. She escaped to London in July 1942, and was very soon making a nuisance of herself, pulling strings in high places, in her determination to get back into action.

Sir Claude Dansey was morbidly suspicious of anyone who had been a guest of the Gestapo and he was dead set against her being allowed to return. But as a woman brought up in the tradition of Nurse Edith Cavell, that tragic escape line organiser of the other war, she would brook no arguments in her insistence on going back to set up the *Marie-Claire* line.

A woman of direct, often irascible temperament, she was the type of English eccentric who strode into rooms and barked instructions rather than show weakness by making requests.

Airey Neave recalls* how a Lysander pilot (it was Pilot Officer John Bridger) was introduced to her before take-off from Tangmere on a night in October 1942. He took both of her hands in his and said: 'I just wanted to say thank you for going over there. I can't tell you what we feel about it, but all the boys have tremendous admiration for what you are doing.'

After a series of adventures, which included organising the escape of two of the 'Cockleshell Heroes' who made the memorable raid on Bordeaux harbour, she was arrested in November 1943 and was sent to Ravensbrück.

But the plucky *comtesse* survived all the horrors there and returned to Paris where she is still living, well into her eighties.

Another woman who made a significant contribution to the escape lines is Andrée de Jongh, known as Dédée. She and her father, a Belgian schoolteacher, set up one of the most effective routes.

Called *Comet*, it stretched down from Brussels, through Paris, to link up with *Marie-Claire* at Ruffec, continuing down to the Gascony coastal resorts of Biarritz and Bayonne, from where it was but a short step across the mountains to San Sebastian in Spain.

In 1942, at the age of twenty-five, she made contact with Michael Creswell, the MI9 man code-named *Monday*, after conducting a

*Saturday at MI9, by Airey Neave. (Hodder and Stoughton) 1969.

party of evaders over the frontier. Such was her dynamic personality she was able to convince him that she was capable of organising an escape route if she had official recognition and support from London.

Again, after initial opposition from Dansey who suspected she was a Gestapo 'plant', she was accepted and later given unqualified assistance by the other two of the MI9 triumvirate: Neave, as *Saturday*, and Donald Darling, as *Sunday*.*

Dédée and her sister Suzanne had been brought up by their father on tales on Nurse Cavell's resistance and execution, but the new generation of resisters faced problems which could well have daunted even that brave spirit.

Edith Cavell's escape routes had to stretch no further than the Dutch border, a mere fifty miles at most. *Comet's* organisers had to blaze an unmarked trail south, down the entire length of France. Yet within a few weeks of starting operations they had reconnoitred a possible route, almost all of it by rail.

In spite of some early arrests of members of her group, including her sister, Dédée managed to survive until the beginning of 1943. She had been running the gauntlet too long. She was captured after a tip-off by an informer as she and a small party of RAF evaders were resting at a farmhouse in the coastal foothills of the French Pyrenees.

Her father, Frédéric de Jongh, was arrested five months later and executed by a firing squad. Suzanne died shortly after the war ended as a result of the scars left by her treatment in German captivity.

Incredibly, Dédée, a slim and shapely blonde with eyes of blue that really did sparkle, came back from the nightmare of Ravensbrück to build a new life, still serving mankind, as a nurse in an African leper colony.

Comet itself survived the family's arrests and was never extinguished. The last evader crossed the Pyrenees on 4 June 1944 – two days before the Allies landed in Normandy.

The *Pat* line, sometimes known as the *Pao* line after the pseudonymic initials of its driving spirit, Patrick Albert O'Leary, was bigger in scope but in action for a shorter period. Neave estimates that *Comet* brought about 1,000 men back safely, while *Pat* passed 600 through central and eastern France before the Germans could smash it.

Déricourt used a *Pat* route when he left France in 1942 to join

Secret Sunday, by Donald Darling (William Kimber) 1975.

SOE. One of the original workers in it was Andrée Borrel, who later became courier to Francis Suttill in *Prosper*. There is nothing sinister in this connection. The collapse of *Prosper* and the destruction of the *Pat* line were just coincidences in the small world of the Resistance.

The man known as O'Leary became involved in clandestine activities by accident. The outbreak of war found him serving as a medical officer in a Belgian cavalry unit. His name: Dr Albert Guérisse.

He escaped to England and became second-in-command of a 'Q' ship operating off the French Riviera.

One night, after he was inadvertently left behind on a night landing operation, his 'Q' ship was torpedoed and sunk, leaving him stranded in France.

After various adventures he linked up with an embryo escape line early in 1941, and eventually became the chief organiser. He was captured in the spring of 1943, but endured the deprivations of several concentrations camps until he was able to return, unbroken, to his home in Belgium.

He never forgot his old comrades and the RAF crews who made so many sacrifices to drop men and materials to his organisation. No finer tribute could have been paid to the tragic crew of No 161 Squadron's N-for-Nan than that he should have read their memorial address by their isolated graves in the Ardennes 25 years after the war ended.

The squadron's Hudsons and Lysanders brought back no more than about fifty escapers and evaders because, after all, that was not their *raison d'être*.

But the knowledge in RAF mess halls that there was an organisation in existence to bring shot-down crews back to safety gave an enormous fillip to morale. The escape lines were able to return to duty about 3,000 valuable aircrew from Western Europe – it cost around £10,000 to train a bomber pilot – all of them men who would otherwise have been lost to Bomber Command at a time when heavy causalties were beginning to break the back of the air offensive.

Robin Hooper was one of the lucky few who were brought back on the 'express' route by air, just in time in his case for the festive season which was to be the prelude to the beginning of the end for Germany.

Christmas came and Tempsford had its party, and Hodges logged the records with the uncharacteristically emotive note that the squadron had been 'most unfortunate' in a December which had 'resulted in one of the most tragic pages in the unit's history'.

Then came the new year of 1944, a year and yet a lifetime since Charles Pickard had broken his wrist falling from a beam during a wild celebration in the Mess. This time the New Year's Eve merry-making was more restrained.

The old crowd had gone and the new men had not yet settled in, and several of them were still getting accustomed to the novelty of wearing officer's uniforms.

The run of tragedy continued in January. A Flying Officer Smith and Flight Sergeant Robertson were killed with their crews when two Halifaxes detailed for air-sea rescue work collided in mid-air.

By now it was known in high places that the invasion of Fortress Europe was to take place in the summer and the squadron's work of supplying the Resistance with the means to fight was given priority.

Four more Halifaxes were sent to Tempsford, with two more Hudsons. Gone were the days when No 161 would have to make do and mend with insufficient men and machines.

The new crews were being pushed hard through a programme of pick-up landing techniques. The Hudsons lost their independent 'utility' status to become an official unit as 'C' Flight, commanded initially by Squadron Leader Len Ratcliff, who was to become the last man to command the squadron.

Ratcliff, a short, sturdy young man of twenty-five, had already completed one tour of operations with a bomber squadron, and had carried on to distinguish himself as commander of No 161's 'B' Flight of Halifaxes.

Like many others who joined the RAF at the outbreak of war, he had seen the writing on the wall after Munich. He decided that as he did not want to drown, the Navy was out. And with his generation's fears of what war in the trenches could be like – as told to them in gory detail by their elders – there was no attraction in joining the army.

He knew where the real war would be fought and so he learned to fly with the Volunteer Air Reserve, winning his wings in time to be among the first to join the RAF when war was belatedly declared. Three weeks later he got married.

This was the man who was to weld the Hudson flight into a cohesive force, completing the job started by Pickard, developed by Verity and refined by Hodges . . . a man so small that three-inch wooden blocks had to be fitted to the foot controls of Stirlings before he could fly them.

Len Ratcliff DSO, DFC, and bar, AFC, Croix de Guerre, No 161 Squadron's last active service commanding officer.

'Take-off', the oil painting by Dame Laura Knight for which Flying Officer Ray Escreet was a model. He is the airman on the left foreground holding a pen. The aircraft is not a Hudson: Escreet modelled for it before joining No 161 Squadron.

Yet for all his diligence and personal courage, there was nothing he could do to save the Hudsons and their crews from the disasters which were ahead.

He was to see his command virtually destroyed because of the nature of the closing stages of the war.

It had to be fought over Germany where the defences were better than over France; longer distances were involved, thus increasing the dangers; new crews did not have the same time as their predecessors to become experienced in clandestine work.

But the German operations were still in the future when Ratcliff was given the job of welding the new flight into a team. He met two of his first recruits on 21 January. An Oxford trainer landed at Tempsford after a 20-minute flight from Mildenhall. Two newly-commissioned young pilot officers stepped out onto the runway.

They had been together since the previous March, flying patched-up Stirlings back to their home bases after overhauls and repairs at the maintenance depot.

Both knew the golden rule: 'Never Volunteer.' Both had broken it to become aircrew. Now they were to break it again by applying to join a special duties squadron.

One of the men was Ray Escreet. He had broken the rule on another occasion to earn himself a unique if anonymous place in the RAF's Hall of Fame. He could still remember that day at Mildenhall when his flight commander had called for volunteers who could appreciate art. No one had stepped forward because they all knew the one about the pianist who volunteered for an unspecified job with a piano, only to find himself humping it up a flight of stairs to the officers' mess.

Anyone who volunteered for an 'artistic' job would surely be handed a pot of paint and ordered to brighten up a barracks block. But he put his name down after all, and that was how he came to meet the gentle old lady who had been commissioned by the Air Ministry to paint a bomber crew at their Action Stations.

She was a Dame of the British Empire, and a confidante in their prime of such diverse characters as Augustus John, George Bernard Shaw and that other, pseudonymic Shaw known to the world as Lawrence of Arabia. She was also a painter of international repute in her own right.

From an hotel at Malvern in Worcestershire she had just written to tell him she had now finished the painting for which he had been one of her models.

It was dated 12 December 1943.

Dear Mr Escreet,

    I am writing a belated letter to thank from the bottom of my heart for your help and kindness to me when I was painting the picture. Now, when twilight approaches, I think of those many evenings when I dragged you away from a nice cup of tea, and asked you to sit in discomfort while I scratched with a pencil.

    Please forgive me for not writing before to tell you how very much I appreciate your generosity in giving up your time. Ever since I came back, every day seems to have been filled with one thing and another. Also I was rather tired, and at night, for weeks, in dreams, went over the complications I had memorised, inventing others which never existed.

    Now, thank goodness, that obsession has gone, but memory of my splendid friends remains as strong as ever. My only distress is that I have not yet been able to do the drawings of yourselves, which I promised to do. All being well I shall come over to the station early in the New Year, when I trust it will be possible to do these.

    I loved being with you all and being in touch with the magnificent work you are all doing. Ordinary life in contrast seems very ordinary, and strangely enclosed, although there is lots of space around us here – I suppose it is that one's imagination follows one's friends into the skies.

    Although I have never been in the air, now I have the sense of something missing, and of being tied down. I do hope I am not boring you in telling you this, but I want you to know how much I appreciate the privilege you gave me to see into your lives which is (sic) so different, and, shall I say it? – above the rest of us ordinary people.

    Good luck to you all, and the best of wishes.

Yours most gratefully,
Laura Knight.

Her painting, called 'Take Off', now hangs in the Imperial War Museum. But Dame Laura never did get down to the station at Mildenhall. Or if she did, it was too late. Her letter reached Escreet just as he was about to be posted to Tempsford, as a pilot officer.

When he first arrived there in an Oxford trainer, with another officer whom I do not intend to identify, they parked the small aircraft off the main runway and took in their surroundings.

So this was where the secret squadrons went about their mysterious business. At a glance they could take in the two big hangars and several barracks blocks painted in drab olive green and brown camouflage. Over in the distance, about 500 yards away, they could see an odd, barn-like structure, looking just a little incongruous out on its own, with what appeared to be a pigeon loft next to it.

They were to discover later that the 'barn' was where the secret agents were fitted into their flying gear and given a last-minute once-over by an escorting officer to make sure they were not carrying anything incriminating which could blow their cover stories.

As Escreet and his companion looked around, a khaki-coloured car approached and they straightened their caps and ties self-consciously. It was as if they were going to be interviewed for a job. Which, in a way, they were.

They were both bored with the routine, day-to-day grind of the maintenance base. Their only excitement in the past nine months had been an overshoot on the runway when they were making a delivery to Llandow in Glamorgan. The brakes had failed and their Stirling rolled to a halt in the back garden of a house bordering the airfield.

An elderly woman had promptly appeared in the doorway clutching a teapot.

'I don't mind you dropping in for tea,' she said, 'but I do wish you'd given me some warning.'

That was two months ago. Now they were hoping to get back into the real war. The car they had seen approaching now stopped and the WAAF driver offered them a lift to the squadron office.

They climbed inside, marvelling at the luxury of having a pretty chauffeuse, and were driven down a road running alongside one of two runways which crossed diagonally.

The girl pulled up outside a drab building and the two young officers went inside to meet Hodges and Ratcliff and to explain why they wanted to join the squadron.

No, they said, they had never flown Hudsons, but yes, they would like to give it a try.

They were then dismissed and four days later their postings were put up on the notice board at Mildenhall.

For Ray Escreet it was the beginning of a second tour of operations.

*

2300 hours, March 20, 1945: They were approaching Erfurt now, some 200 miles deep inside Germany, and with the memorable exception of a bombing raid on Berlin back in 1943 it was the longest sortie the wireless operator had ever flown. Outside the night was black, relieved occasionally by patches of moonlight shafting through the clouds, and he knew that if they were to complete the operation the weather would have to improve in the next hour, otherwise they would never find their rendezvous near Dresden . . .

. . . She peered through the curtains in the bedroom for the umpteenth time that day, as she did every day she knew Ray would be coming home. She was always there, too, when he left. Frank was always chiding her about it. She could not explain the happiness that filled her just to see her son striding down the avenue and turning into the gate; a happiness followed by a fear as each day flew by to the moment of yet another farewell.

When she saw him she always hurried downstairs to put on the tea, and as he came through the door he would sweep her up in a big hug and she would notice a little ruefully just how well he looked even without home cooking.

There was a time when she had thought, selfishly, at least he is safe now. No more operations, no more little red flags to be stuck into the wall map.

Escreet, meanwhile, had been wondering how he should break the news about his new posting. He and his skipper at the base maintenance unit had volunteered to join a unit known only by rumour. A secret squadron. All he knew about it was that there was plenty of excitement and bags of leave. Anything was better than the boredom of stooging around Mildenhall and crashing aircraft into old ladies' back gardens.

Soon he would be commissioned and starting a brand new life as an officer. What would Ruth make of that? Ruth Taylor was a plotter at an RAF early warning station on the Humber. He had been at the Pavilion dance hall in Withernsea when he caught sight of this beautiful girl with fair hair coiffed in the WAAF style. They met and danced and she said she came from Sark, and he had not been too sure exactly where Sark was, but he said nothing.

He had been in civvies and she had been frankly dubious, thinking he was shooting a line, when he told her he was aircrew. Before their first real date he had spent half an hour preparing his uniform, pressing knife-edge creases in his trousers and carefully ironing the chevrons flat against the sleeves of his tunic. His mother had stared in amazement. He had never ironed so much as a hankie before.

His father just smiled. He knew. He had also worn a uniform once.

Frank Escreet was secretly delighted to see Ray getting out of the habit of wearing civilian clothes on leave. There had been that time the year before when a soldier was overheard in a pub calling his son 'a bloody conchie'.

Ray's uncle had walked over to say, ever so quietly, that while the soldier had been asleep in his bed at Catterick Camp a few nights earlier, Ray had been over Germany in a Stirling bomber. The soldier left the pub in a hurry, too embarrassed even to apologise. They had allowed Ray to remain blissfully unaware of the incident.

Now, as he watched his son preparing to go out with a young WAAF he felt full of pride that he should have such a boy. And when that leave ended and the time came for Ray to go, he understood the reasons when he told them he would be reporting to a new unit at a place called Tempsford where he would be taking part in more active duties.

'But not bombing,' he assured them. He said nothing about any possible danger. Just that he would be made an officer and would be getting, as someone had once told him, 'bags of leave'.

10

The words seemed to hang in the air, suspended by disbelief.

'Quiet, please. We've just been told Pick is dead.'

The banter fell away then stopped altogether, and the silence in the Mess was like an electric charge, invisible yet still tangible with a menace felt by them all.

Even those new crews who had never known him had come to believe the legend which put him among the Immortals.

After leaving Tempsford the previous May, 1943, Charles Pickard had spent a restless two months agitating for a transfer. By then a group captain, he felt his abilities could be better utilised on more active service. He had no patience for the role of playing mother hen to the crews of clapped-out Ventura bombers.

His perseverance paid off and he was posted to command a Mosquito squadron at Sculthorpe where he very soon became an exponent of the low-level, precision attacks which had become the trademark of those fast and manoeuvreable aircraft made of wood.

He made but one concession to the possibility of death by writing a letter to a friend, Lord Londonderry, who had been an Air Secretary in the 'thirties. He was not unaware of the good fortune which had blessed his career while eluding many of his contemporaries, and the letter was his tribute to those men who were equally competent, but who did their job in the shadow of his limelight.

> Finally (he wrote) I cannot speak too highly of Bomber Command, particularly the men who are least mentioned; the wireless operators and the gunners; their risks are greater than anyone's, yet they are the least rewarded.

The letter was kept in a drawer of his desk, to be posted only in the event of a certain eventuality.

As 1943 was coming to a close, Pickard was joined by two old friends, posted to Sculthorpe at his and their own requests: His navigator from the early days, Alan Broadley, and that older navigator who knew France like the wrinkles on his face, Philippe Livry, who had asked for a transfer because he preferred hunting

Germans to the clandestine sorties where he had to go out of his way to avoid them.

Together all three went out on a raid which destroyed the V-1 rocket sites at Peenemünde in an operation which was reckoned at the time to have put back Hitler's revenge raids on London by at least six months.

Soon it was February, a month of signposts in Pickard's war service: in February 1941 he was filming the part of the hero-pilot of F-for-Freddie in the propaganda film; in 1942 he led a squadron of Whitleys on the Bruneval raid; in 1943 he landed the first Hudson in a pick-up operation which again had no precedent in RAF manuals.

Intelligence reports from France indicated that the Germans intended to execute many of the 700 or so Resistance fighters held in the civil prison at Amiens. Hundreds of them were earmarked for death in front of firing squads; many of them belonged to Marie-Madeleine Fourcade's *Alliance* organisation. Pickard had taken several of them into the field himself.

Livry recalls* how Pickard approached him one morning and said: 'Philippe, we have friends in prison in Amiens who can escape if we help them.'

The plan was to make a pinpoint attack to breach the walls of the prison. It was a plan born of desperation because the risks were appalling; not only to the aircrews, but to the prisoners and the civilian population living in houses around the jail.

But if the walls could be brought down, there was a chance that some prisoners could escape in the confusion.

Air Vice Marshal Sir Basil Embry, commanding No 2 Bomber Group, had pulled the strings which jerked Pickard out of his non-operational role with the 'Flying Pigs' squadron. He knew there was only one man qualified by temperament and training for such a daring operation.

Pickard jumped at the chance. The deadline for the raid was 19 February, the date set for the executions. With only eleven days to go the plans were finalised and the crews briefed down to the last detail. But as so often happened, the weather intervened and the days ticked by, draining the morale and adrenalin of the keyed-up Mosquito squadron.

Then 18 February dawned bright and clear and the order was given to go. Pickard, with Broadley at his elbow, took off at the head of eighteen aircraft, and led them unerringly to the target.

*Livry-Level. *op cit.*

There was a confusion of noise, of exploding bombs and bursting shells, and the screaming of engines, and then the silence on the way home. Livry remembers hearing the leader of the third flight calling over his radio: 'The oranges are ripe.' It was a signal that the raid had been a success.

Later it was learned that the walls had indeed been breached, but at a terrible cost. Eighty-seven prisoners had been killed. Of those involved in the mass escape, 182 were immediately recaptured, but 255 managed to disappear into the maze of side streets around the prison and remained free in spite of rigorous house-to-house searches.

Pickard was never to know the extent of his success. He made his own run over the target, and as he was turning for home he saw a Mosquito going down out of control. He followed him down to provide cover, and as he dived a prowling German fighter fastened on to his tail.

It was all over in seconds. Raked by a burst of fire, his tail section was shattered and his Mosquito turned on its back, crashing into a wood and bursting into flames. The pilot of the other Mosquito survived a crash-landing and spent the rest of the war in a prison camp.

Pickard and Broadley were found dead in what remained of the aircraft. By a tragic coincidence, it was also code-named F-for-Freddie . . .

Back in England a letter was delivered to Lord Londonderry . . .

Dorothy Pickard smothered her own grief to nurse the sheepdog, Ming, which had become desperately ill on the night her master failed to return . . .

At Tempsford there was many a drink taken that night in memory of the irrepressible Pick who would never again be around to entertain with his boisterous brand of high spirits.

The citation to one of his three DSOs surely sums up this man who so typified the spirit of the age: 'By his courage, self-sacrifice and devotion to duty, this officer has set an example which although attained by few, is admired by all.'

The war went on.

In France, the onset of better flying weather led to renewed efforts to arm the Resistance, and Francis Cammaerts jumped out of a crippled Halifax to begin an adventure in which the young rear-gunner Len Gormall became a Resistance hero.

At Tempsford, it was a month of 'firsts'. Ray Escreet had his first operational flight in a Hudson on an *Ascension* operation to contact an agent code-named *Bullet* by radio-telephone. His pilot was newly-commissioned Pilot Officer Johnnie Scragg, with the ribbon of a brand-new DFC already on his tunic.

It was Scragg's first Hudson sortie after only a few weeks with the squadron, and a few days later he became the first to use the technique of parachuting agents from a slide fitted to the rear of the aircraft. He dropped two of them over a rendezvous near a distinctive bend of the River Loire.

The Hudsons were now the most versatile aircraft of World War II, the diversity of their operational roles to be equalled only by that great but later workhorse, the ubiquitous Dakota used by the Americans.

Len Ratcliff, as commander of the new Hudson flight, did not waste any time before chalking up *his* first pick-up, and it was in an operation loaded with drama.

Henri Déricourt had by now come under the deepest suspicion. Too much had been going wrong, and too many agents were voicing their distrust of his loyalties.

London decided the time had come to bring him out of France for interrogation before any of the more excitable Resistance men took matters into their own hands. An operation was laid on to bring him out – ominously code-named *Knacker*. To allay any forebodings Déricourt may have had it was decided that the operation should be delayed until he had a group of agents gathered for a routine pick-up. He would then be brought back on the same flight, without any warning.

Whispers of what SOE was planning filtered along the RAF grapevine and reached some of the Tempsford pilots. Robin Hooper, who had been posted to SOE headquarters as an air liaison officer after his adventures in France, felt shocked and incredulous when the F Section chief Maurice Buckmaster told him Déricourt had been accused by a French *réseau* of passing information to the Germans.

This wave of shock went right through the men in the know. Déricourt was trusted implicitly by all the pilots. They knew him by name, unlike most of the other agents they had carried. They had drunk with him in the Mess and in London pubs; some had entertained him as their guest at their homes, and all shared with him that camaraderie of the air enjoyed by all men who have ever known the thrill and danger of flying.

With the exception of Paul Rivière, there was no other landing

ground organiser to match his efficiency and knowledge of what
was needed for pick-up operations and supply drops. If Déricourt
was a traitor, was it possible to trust anyone?

At Baker Street, Buckmaster vigorously defended his man, but
agreed reluctantly that the allegations were too serious to be
ignored. The operations officer, Major Gerry Morel – himself one
of Déricourt's staunchest defenders – was delegated the task of
bringing him back. At gunpoint if necessary.

Ratcliff was briefed to fly Operation *Knacker*, and although he
realised SOE was considering a kidnapping, he personally never
believed it would come to that. He thought there would be no
problem in simply persuading Déricourt to return to clear his
name.

Meanwhile, in Paris, the object of all this scheming remained
oblivious to the danger and busied himself making arrangements
for the operation's reception party.

He was told to expect ten incoming agents, and he had nine
passengers waiting to leave. Some of them had been hanging about
for several weeks because the bad weather had resulted in so many
cancelled operations during the previous two months.

Among them was Robert Benoist, who had given up his attempts
to set up *Clergyman* around the Nantes area.

This, his second mission, had been dogged by ill-luck, culminat-
ing in the capture of his wireless operator, the brave but reckless
Dubois. He is believed to have been tracked down by a direction-
finding team put on his trail as a result of a courier boasting at a
football match that he was carrying a wireless transmitter on the
pannier of his bicycle.

When the Germans caught him at his set he managed to kill one
and wound another, but he was pumped full of bullets – no less
than nine were removed in hospital by astonished doctors – and he
made a miraculous recovery only to die much later in a concentration
camp.

The loss of Dubois and the means to communicate with London
to lay on supply drops made it impossible for Benoist to carry out
any of his sabotage plans, so he asked Déricourt to arrange his
passage back to Tempsford.

He was to return to France a few weeks later in March, taking with
him Denise Bloch, another wireless operator, who made the trip by
Lysander as she had not yet been given any parachute training.

Benoist eventually disappeared in the *Nacht und Nebel* of Buchenwald. Denise was executed at Ravensbrück.

Another agent bound for the February Hudson which took Benoist to Tempsford was Philippe Liewer, the organiser of *Salesman*. He and his assistant, Robert Maloubier, had been operating cheekily under the Germans' noses along the Seine from Rouen to the closely-guarded coastal defences around Le Havre.

They had built up a resilient organisation and, with security as one of their priorities, they had avoided the disasters which overtook neighbouring *Prosper* and *Alliance*.

Maloubier was one of SOE's most effective saboteurs because the teams he trained not only put an electricity sub-station out of action for six months, but they also destroyed a small German gunboat. This would usually have led to savage reprisals and the execution of many innocent hostages but for the fact the Germans believed the raid must have been carried out by British commandos.

Which was unfortunate for the sentry on guard that night. He was shot for neglecting his duties.

As for the ship's crew, they were so delighted at not having to go back to the perils of the sea that they celebrated long and loud and were still hung over when they learned they were to be transferred to the army and sent to the Russian front.

Another awaiting Ratcliff's Hudson was Henri Borosh, a wireless operator for the *Vic* escape line, and three women. One of them was the wife of Felix Gouin, a politician who was to become a post-war prime minister of France.

The second was Madeleine Lavigne, an agent with only a year to live. She was parachuted back into France in time to be in Paris for the liberation, where she died of natural causes.

The third was the woman who ran a restaurant used by Déricourt to assemble his parties before taking them to the landing ground. The rendezvous for the February pick-up had been used several times in recent months. Déricourt may have felt perhaps the vessel was being taken to the well too often, so he was ordering her to London and safety before anything broke.

Two other agents who were due to catch the same flight were arrested as they were leaving Paris to link up with others at the restaurant. Their non-arrival would have convinced Déricourt that the time had come to get the restaurant manageress out of the country in case the Germans had decided to shut down his operations.

The time came for Déricourt's party to leave for the landing ground. Ratcliff was on his way in P-for-Peter, with Flying Officer Dickie Wooldridge as his navigator. The pre-arranged personal message broadcast by the BBC signalled all was well, and they touched down shortly after midnight after an uneventful flight.

Ratcliff was not quite sure what to expect. He had been given no specific orders except to stand by and await developments. He knew he would have to be ready for any eventuality. Morel, his solitary passenger, was wearing an RAF uniform as a precaution against being captured. His cover story was that he was one of the crew of a shot-down bomber.

As the Hudson trundled to a halt he got out and Ratcliff could see him remonstrating with Déricourt after the preliminary greeting. The effect was spoiled somewhat when Morel's spanking new officer's cap was blown from his head in the backwash from the propellers, and he had to scramble muddily in an undignified manner to retrieve it.

Déricourt was suspicious as soon as he realised there were no other incoming passengers when he had been warned to expect ten.

'What do you expect me to do with all these bicycles?' he complained.

There were eleven of them, hidden some distance away from the landing ground, and he pointed out to Morel the obvious truth that the field would be well and truly 'blown' if they were just left lying around for the Germans to find.

The SOE major pondered the point while Déricourt climbed into the Hudson to have a word with the pilot. At this stage it would have been simple indeed for Morel to have covered Déricourt with his revolver and ordered Ratcliff to take off. He wrote in his report later: ' . . . had I wished to retain him there by force, there would have been no difficulty in doing so.'

But he missed his opportunity. Instead, Déricourt was able to persuade him that he would have to get rid of the bicycles and put his affairs in order before leaving for London, and he promised to return on the next Lysander pick-up.

Ratcliff recalls* that Déricourt was quickly aware of what Morel was up to, but he insisted that it was impossible for him to return without clearing up 'certain obligations'. He did not say what they were.

'I had never gone along with the idea of a kidnap in the first place. I didn't think it was in keeping with the spirit of our work to drag the chap away by force. If we were prepared to use his landing fields – and I used them on several occasions – I felt we should not doubt his word.

*Personal interview.

'Trust was the basis of our dealings with him. As I was sitting there at the controls, talking to him while waiting for something to happen, I just could not believe he was a traitor.

'I think Morel was a bit disappointed that I didn't tap him on the head and take off while he was still in the cockpit. But we had no plan to take him by force. There was no possibility that I would be able to restrain him and fly the aircraft at the same time.

'Although I knew he was under suspicion when I went to collect him, I never anticipated anything other than a friendly reception. The thought that he was working with the Gestapo never seriously crossed my mind.'

Foot suggests* that Morel could have solved the dilemma of the bicycles by loading them into the Hudson, but this would have meant keeping the aircraft on the ground while they were collected, and the pick-up drill was quite emphatic about the need to spend as little time on the ground as possible.

Consequently Déricourt was allowed to leave on the understanding that he would be picked up the following week. He kept his word. In what was his last clandestine operation he laid on a reception for a Lysander flown by Flight Lieutenant Leslie Whittaker at a field east of Tours. With him he brought his 'certain obligation'. It was blonde and pretty and married to him.

It should have been obvious to SOE that he would never have abandoned her to the mercies of the SD. If he had been in league with the Germans they would not have taken kindly to his desertion and his wife most certainly would have been packed off to a concentration camp at the very least.

So Déricourt returned to England voluntarily, suspecting he might have to fight for his life or freedom. This was hardly the action of a guilty man. After persuading Morel to go back in the Hudson alone, he could easily have defected to the SD and put himself under Kieffer's protection.

He had been playing a dangerous game, but he had powerful friends in British Intelligence and so he took the gamble of returning. His interrogation revealed that he was, in fact, in touch with the SD, and had supplied them with documents and reports made out by agents in the field.

He had been giving the Germans access to selected items in the air mail carried by the pick-up pilots to and from London in exchange for a guarantee that they would not interfere with his operations.

*SOE in France. op cit.

Kieffer had been only too delighted to make the promise. On the excellent principle of the intelligence services that it is often better to keep an eye on an enemy agent to learn from what he does than to pick him up and perhaps learn nothing, the SD chief had allowed him to work unhindered.

SOE officers have always maintained they knew nothing of this convenient arrangement, and indeed it had a subtlety which was alien to the minds working in Baker Street. It bore the hallmark of the altogether more devious MI6. There was a furious outcry from F Section when it was decided 'higher up' that Déricourt's usefulness in the field was finished.

Morel said he was 'absolutely revolted' by the ruling, and Buckmaster wrote a testimonial insisting that 'his efficiency in Hudson and Lysander work was staggering and it was his very success that raised the ugly idea that he was controlled . . . he never once let any of our boys down and . . . he has by far the finest record of operations completed of any member of SOE.'

Déricourt was in a dilemma. He had obviously been working with the Germans – but only on orders from the spymasters in London. However, it would have been indelicate for this to have been admitted at a time when French men and women were being executed in their hundreds, some of them possibly as a direct or indirect result of Déricourt's double dealings.

After his interrogation he was allowed to go to ground somewhere in England, and he did not surface again until after the D-Day landings. This lends some substance to a theory* that he was involved in the complex deception plan designed to convince the Germans that the inevitable invasion would be in the Pas de Calais area, or anywhere other than Normandy.

When Déricourt next appeared publicly it was as a Spitfire pilot, and he spent the last eight months of the war in hospital, recovering from burns after being shot down.

After the war the bogey of betrayal materialised again and he was brought to trial in France accused of treason and facing death by execution.

One after the other, powerful voices were raised in his defence. The British sent Bodington and he affirmed he would have no hesitation in employing Déricourt again should the need ever arise in similar circumstances.

The court heard from others, like the highly-respected General Henri Zeller, a leading member of the Resistance who had been

*Bodyguard of Lies by Anthony Cave Brown. (W.H. Allen) 1976.

snatched from a tricky situation by a Déricourt pick-up; and Philippe Livry-Level, the Hudson navigator who was by then a Deputy for Normandy and using for all time both his cover and real names in hyphenated form.

Déricourt was acquitted on all charges and was last heard of officially in 1962 when he was reported to have been killed in Laos in an air crash.

But I have been told by a source I can not disclose that somewhere in Spain there is an elderly gentleman with a fund of wartime stories enjoying his retirement with his wife, her greying hair still showing touches of blonde . . .

On the night Déricourt was refusing to return in Ratcliff's Hudson, John Affleck was out in a second aircraft, circling a field some 250 miles to the east, searching for reception lights near Châlon-sur-Saône. Four nights later he made a second attempt to find the elusive lights and came up against the same sticky problem which had so nearly beaten Pickard a year earlier, on the third Hudson pick-up.

This was the 21st, but it was so nearly the first disaster. As Affleck was taking off from Tempsford, Flight Sergeant John 'JFQ' Brough was hoping this time he was going to be lucky. He had been in hiding since his Halifax had crashed three months earlier, and was on his way to the reception area now with resisters and villagers from nearby Villevieux.

When the aircraft was due they all stood in a long line holding torches, and when the engines were heard the organiser flashed a signal. The recognition signal came back without delay and they switched on their torches to guide the pilot down to what appeared to be firm grass.

Brough remembers* how Affleck first made one circuit, then came back to switch on a bright landing light before landing safely.

He watched as the Hudson P-for-Peter taxi-ed to the end of the field, turned and headed back to the starting point.

It was then that the port wheel sank deep in glutinous mud.

Rivière was the landing ground organiser and it is possible that the considerable number of successes he had achieved had made him careless, because it was very much out of character for him to signal a Hudson to land with the field in such a waterlogged condition.

Affleck, however, did not waste time in recriminations. The reception party alone was not large enough to manhandle the

*Personal interview.

aircraft to drier ground so help was called for at the village. Soon about two hundred men and women were assembled and to fervent cries of 'Allez-oop' – being the sum total of the crew's mastery of the French language – the Hudson was manoeuvred into place.

But every time the main wheels were dragged clear of the mud, the tail wheel became embedded, and vice versa. In spite of the bitter cold and driving flurries of snow, Affleck was glad he was wearing plimsolls. His feet may have been wet, but he fully expected he would have to make a run for it.

Flying boots, apart from being an encumbrance to a man on the run, would not have been a very suitable choice of footwear for an RAF officer trying to pass himself off as a French peasant.

The first attempt at a take-off was a failure. The aircraft was unable to build up enough speed. A team of six horses and twelve oxen was brought to the field and hitched to the Hudson. Everyone heaved and strained and cursed and shouted words of encouragement, but the Hudson remained firmly embedded.

Affleck glanced at his watch and decided to dig deep channels in front of the wheels, meanwhile making a mental note that if he was still on the ground at three o'clock that morning he would destroy the plane and go into hiding with the Résistance.

As an off-stage accompaniment to the hubbub of voices, lowing of cattle and the periodic racket from the engines, he could hear the occasional wailing of a small child, and what sounded like a man nagging at his wife about the delay. They were his priority passengers and Affleck could not help wondering how anyone could have a domestic row in such a situation.

He would have wondered even more if he had known how much the man owed his wife, who was heavily pregnant and was still having to cope with a small boy at her side.

Raymond Aubrac had good reason, however, to be so nervous and irritable. He was a surviving member of the *Conseil National de la Résistance* (CNR), the Gaullist organisation created by Jean Moulin. When Moulin, General Delestraint and several other leaders were arrested by the Gestapo the previous June, Aubrac was isolated in Lyons and very soon came under suspcion.

The Gestapo pulled him in for questioning and to all intents and purposes he was a dead man. His wife summoned help from a local *maquis*. By then it was November and she was six months pregnant, and it was as much for her unborn child as for her husband that she led the band into action.

The series of snapshots here broke all the rules of good security. One of the crew of this Hudson got to work with a box camera to capture these remarkable pictures of Resistance fighters unloading the aircraft on a field at Pau, near the Franco-Spanish frontier.

It had been a double operation, but only Flight Lieutenant Terence Helfer managed to reach the rendezvous. Wing Commander 'Mouse' Fielden, flying the other Hudson, turned left too soon over the Bay of Biscay and was forced to turn back to Tempsford after being fired on by flak batteries guarding Bordeaux.

Helfer pressed on and was able to land several agents at Pau. Their job would have been to organise Maquis bands to harry the rear of German Army units then heading north towards the Normandy beachhead.

The return flight was a calculated gamble. Taking off at dawn, shortly after these pictures were taken, he had insufficient fuel to fly the long way around over the sea and instead went overland at a height of 500 feet to reach home safely.

(*Left*) Flight Lieutenant John Affleck, DSO, DFC, AFM, Croix de Guerre and Dutch Flying Cross.

(*Below*) Taking photographs of Hudsons was not encouraged at Tempsford for security reasons, but here, standing in the shadow of one, are (*left to right*) Wing Commander Lewis Macdonald 'Bob' Hodges, DSO and bar, DFC and bar, who was to become an Air Chief Marshal and Deputy Commander of Allied Forces in Central Europe in 1973; Squadron Leader James Wagland, Station Navigation Officer at Tempsford; Flight Lieutenant 'Lofty' Reed, a wireless operator who became a pilot and reached the rank of wing commander in the post-war RAF; Flight Lieutenant Joe Corner, an air gunnery officer.

Wielding a sten gun, she rescued him from under the noses of his escort as he was being driven through Lyons. A brave and dedicated woman, Lucille Aubrac then made plans to have her family whisked to safety, and it was while in hiding at Villevieux that she met young John Brough and arranged for him to share the comfort of a Hudson flight back to England.

Now, with only an hour to go before Affleck's deadline for take-off, she was beginning to feel labour pains while at the same time coping with her tired and tearful three-year-old 'Boo-boo' and a querulous husband.

Affleck takes up the story*: 'I tried to ignore the nagging voices and decided to make one more attempt after the channels had been dug in front of the wheels.

'By then it was snowing hard, and the aircraft felt heavy and sluggish. At full throttle we were picking up speed too slowly and as we approached the end of the field we were doing no more than about fifty knots. We were never going to get into the air.

'Then we hit a slight bump. It was just enough to push us upwards and we cleared a boundary fence with what must have been only a few inches to spare.'

Brough, the survivor of one air crash, had every reason to regard Affleck's take-off as 'a marvellous piece of flying'.

The journey back was without incident, except for the increasing discomfort felt by Madame Aubrac, and as soon as it was safe to do so Affleck radioed ahead for a medical officer to be on hand at Tempsford.

Two nights later, on 11 February, she gave birth to a daughter at Queen Charlotte's Hospital in London, and kept a promise she had made to her comrades of the Resistance.

Before leaving she had told them if the baby were a boy he would have the word *Maquis* as one of his names. If it were a girl, she would think of something else, similarly appropriate.

The baby was christened Catherine Mitraillette – or Little Machine-gun . . .

The first Hudson casualties occurred in the following month of March and involved one of the eight new crews brought in from Coastal Command to learn the techniques of clandestine operations.

Flying Officer Baughan lost control and crashed at a point four miles from the village of Henlow shortly after taking off on a training flight. The aircraft was completely burned out. Baughan

*Personal interview.

and all his crew, Flying Officer Brocklehurst, Flight Lieutenant Gillander and Flight Sergeant Brewer, were killed.

The squadron also got a new commanding officer, the fourth since its inception. Bob Hodges was posted to the RAF Staff College and his place was taken by Wing Commander Alan Boxer, a New Zealander who was later to be knighted and become Secretary of Defence Services as an air vice-marshal twenty-one years later.

Hodges had carried out eight successful pick-ups, six of them in Hudsons, taking 23 agents into France and bringing 50 passengers back.

No pick-ups were attempted during the month Boxer took over command of the squadron, but a total of seven agents were dropped into France by parachute in sorties flown by Affleck, Ratcliff and Scragg.

Ratcliff's two agents were probably Pierre Mulsant and John Barrett, who are known to have parachuted back into France on the night of 3 March to set up *Minister* for operations around the Marne, east of Paris.

They were joined a few days later by their courier, Yvonne Fontaine, who had been flown out of France with them the previous November in the Hudson flown by Hodges. Together they organised five drops of supplies in the following two months – a total of sixty containers packed with sten guns, rifles, grenades and explosives.

Their activities behind the lines came to an end soon after D-Day when they were captured going to the assistance of a uniformed party of Special Air Service (SAS) troops trapped in the forest of Fontainebleau.

Yvonne escaped, but the two men were hustled away to die later in Buchenwald.

Pilot Officer Johnnie Scragg went out on the same night as Ratcliff with an old acquaintance of the squadron: Robert Boiteux, the *Spruce* organiser who had escaped from France the previous August on the memorable occasion Hodges put a Hudson down in a field of cattle.

Boiteux was going back this time to organise the *Gardener* network around Marseilles. With him went a wireless operator, Gaston Cohen, and his assistant, Roger Aptaker, a tall, handsome 21-year-old.

His biographer* gives a vivid account of the perils which faced the aircrews and agents on those missions across the Channel.

*Evelyn le Chêne. *op cit.*

Boiteux recalls the trip down the Atlantic coast of France as being uneventful until they reached Bordeaux. Then all hell broke loose.

They hit a concentration of flak and the aircraft lurched from side to side as Scragg – although he is not named – took evasive action.

> He dived, he climbed, he banked, he did the lot . . . Once when he banked, the angle was so acute that Cohen hit his head against a girder of the casing. He groaned, and a thin streak of blood appeared on his forehead.
>
> The cut was not a serious one; what was serious was the fact that he was obviously concussed and could not, therefore, drop with us. By the skill of our pilot we eventually emerged from the flak and were able to resume our course for the rendezvous.

Boiteux intended to leave Cohen in the aircraft, but the delay caused them to be late and they could not see any signal lights over the target area.

He weighed up the pros and cons of dropping blind, but like the excellent operator he was, he decided the risks involved were far greater than the possible gains. They returned to Tempsford and went back the following night in an American Dakota.

Scragg's account of the sortie was a brief note in the squadron records to the effect he was unable to find any reception after making two runs over the rendezvous.

Boiteux was one of those Frenchmen who never forgot where Britain had stood in those dark days of the war. When it was all over he said of the days following the liberation: 'What rankled with me was that in all the newspapers of that period of heady freedom, in all the speeches reported, in all the stories about the Resistance, from its first days to its last, there was no mention that a few Englishmen had stood at the sides of the resistants, nor of where those vital arms and other supplies had come from, nor how they had reached France and found their way into the hands of Frenchmen.

'In the whole of France during the entire war, the English agents sent out by SOE never reached a number which could have turned the tide alone, but they came when both England and France had their backs to the wall and when all seemed lost for both countries, and they came at a time when it was almost a suicide mission to do so.

'They brought arms, instructions and a sense of purpose to hundreds of French patriots; and together they planned, trained and lived for the day which was now being so wildly celebrated. I thought of my fellow English officers who would never return to England . . . I thought of the pilots who on every flight risked their lives in the slow, low-flying aircraft to bring in the arms.'

Scragg's next mission, two days later, was his last. He dropped two agents safely and completed a tour of 30 operations. He was due for a well-earned rest on less hazardous duties.

Ray Escreet could also have left the squadron had he not chosen to volunteer for more than the usual tour. When he had arrived at Tempsford the month before he already had 28 operational sorties in Stirlings to his credit.

His 29th was on 2 March, his first Hudson mission over France in P-for-Peter, flown by the pilot who had been posted to the squadron with him from the Stirling base maintenance unit at Mildenhall.

Their first outing was a failure. The target area was covered by eight-tenths cloud and they were unable to pick out any ground detail. In a second attempt four days later they were again unsuccessful and the pilot was one of the two posted back to their former units that month because they were considered unsuitable for clandestine operations.

To be RTU'd – or Returned to Unit – was always embarrassing for the individuals concerned, and consequently I do not intend to name them. But there was no disgrace involved, and to be so categorised could not in any way be considered a reflection on a man's courage. After all, they were volunteers in the first place.

Affleck recalls that one of the two who did not make the grade with No 161 Squadron went on to become a very much decorated officer with a bomber squadron.

Ratcliff, as the Hudson flight commander, had the unenviable task of telling the two officers that they were being posted out. He always insisted that pick-up pilots must be a breed apart from other fliers: his requirements were that they should be highly individual-istic, superb pilots, yet capable of working as part of a team.

If they did not measure up to his extremely high standards they were RTU'd before they killed themselves, their crews and the valuable agents they would be carrying.

It should be noted here that RTU did not bear the same stigma as the initials LMF – Lacking Moral Fibre. A man who was posted out of a secret squadron would probably find himself back in a Main Force squadron flying operations over Germany.

But a man said to be lacking in moral fibre was considered by deskbound bigots to be a coward. Such cases were often punished by courts-martial and a prison sentence, and it has been calculated that about one man in seven would fail to complete an operational tour of duty for this reason.

Such savagery on the part of the authorities who kept well out of the firing line is inconceivable today when it is recognised that courage is a quality that can be sapped by constant exposure to danger. A few LMF cases were lucky enough to have their symptoms sympathetically and intelligently diagnosed, and they were sent away to convalesce. These were often men disgusted with themselves, who wanted nothing more but to overcome their fear and return to their units.

None of the Hudson crews, according to the records, were ever found to be lacking in moral fibre; they were just politely told to leave because they were not temperamentally suited for clandestine operations.

Escreet therefore found himself consoling his friend, the pilot with whom he had flown for eleven months, and wishing him better luck at his new posting.

He was now without a regular skipper. He went up on one flight with Baughan, just eighteen days before his death in the training flight disaster over Henlow, and flew a second with John Affleck. But Affleck already had a regular crew. They had done four pick-ups together and were a tightly-knit team.

In the exclusive fraternities of wartime aircrews Escreet was now an outsider and might have remained a utility wireless operator had not fate taken a hand with the posting into the squadron of Flying Officer Terence Helfer, accompanied by Pilot Officer Forrest 'Tommy' Thompson.

Lines of chance which had their origins in Yorkshire, London and Waipiro Bay, finally converged at Tempsford. Another line, leading back to the Lockheed aircraft factory at Burbank, California, brought them all together on 26 March 1944, when they flew operationally for the first time as a crew on an *Ascension* in the doomed Hudson N-for-Nan.

On that same day Harry Johnson, the navigator from County Durham who was to become the fourth member of the crew, was on a routine cross-country flight in a Wellington of No 26 Operational Training Unit. His line of fate would not converge with theirs until the summer of that year.

The squadron records for March 1944 are optimistic about the future in spite of the deaths of Baughan and his crew:

> Taking everything into account the result for this month's efforts makes very good reading, and the squadron is now in a strong position to keep up with future demands.

The establishment has been finally settled and the strength has been made up accordingly. The bodies being received for both 'A' (Lysander) and 'C' (Hudson) Flights are entirely new to this type of work and thus the training commitment is pretty heavy. Unfortunately, owing to the lack of sufficient training aircraft, the process is somewhat hindered.

In fact, the squadron had four Hudsons available at any time, with one in reserve. April was a quiet month for them, with Affleck busily engaged in training the new crews up to the required standard.

Ratcliff moved over to take command of the Lysanders, which carried out twelve pick-ups, and Squadron Leader Reg Wilkinson became the Hudson Flight commander.

The squadron records refer this month to 'an unfortunate incident . . . for which there is no satisfactory explanation'.

The Hudson M-for-Mike had gone missing on a cross-country training flight from Tempsford to Wales and back via Cornwall.

Boxer recorded in the log that it turned up 'to everyone's amazement' after a forced landing – at the Gothenburg military airfield at Stockholm. All four of the crew were later reported to be interned.

Ratcliff discovered what had happened. The pilot, a non-commissioned officer, had wandered off on a north-easterly course, instead of heading north-westerly, and he mistook the water he was soon flying over for the Irish Sea. It was actually the Baltic.

With that basic error undetected, he became hopelessly lost. The navigator, who was an officer and technically in command on this training flight, had apparently set the compass incorrectly, or had failed to check the pilot's setting.

They wandered around in circles, searching for an identifiable pinpoint like the Isle of Man, until they ran so short of fuel that they had to make a landing at an airfield which appeared magically in view where no airfield should ever have been.

The navigator survived the war to take his pilot's licence and fly passenger airliners for BOAC.

On 8 May Eisenhower named the date for the invasion, and although word was not allowed to filter down to men in the front line, No 161 Squadron knew something was going on.

With less than four weeks to go, southern England resembled a gigantic ant-heap. Convoys were crawling along country lanes packed with men and materials; tanks were laagered in woodland clearings; guns of all calibres were bristling among the hedgerows.

In moonlit fields all over southern and western France men craned their necks and listened intently for the tell-tale drone of solitary aircraft bringing them yet more of the tools Churchill had promised to help them do the job.

The Hudsons carried out 12 successful parachute sorties, 19 *Ascension* flights, and one pick-up. It was carried out in N-for-Nan by Affleck, who took with him one of the new pilots, Flying Officer Harold Ibbott, in an operation to carry eight passengers in each direction.

· One of the 'Joes' he took in was Marcelle Somers, the mother of a Gaullist section wireless operator called Josiane, the youngest SOE agent ever put into the field. She was just nineteen. Marcelle was to arrange her daughter's reception when she was parachuted into the field two months later. Both survived the war.

On that same night of Ibbott's clandestine baptism the Lysander Flight had its fourth fatality in five months. Les Whittaker, the pilot who brought Déricourt and his wife back to England in February, was shot down and killed after flying too low by mistake over a Luftwaffe base near Chartres.

Also on that night of 3 May, Flight Lieutenant 'Sugar' Hale carried out his second Hudson mission in M-for-Mike, dropping three agents and four containers to a *réseau* of saboteurs who would be responsible for delaying the arrival of German troops at the Normandy beachhead.

Hale, who had joined the squadron with Helfer from the Lysander flying school, would come back from only one more mission.

The most notable passengers ferried into Tempsford during the pre-invasion month were an old friend of the squadron, Philippe Liewer, and his courier, Violette Szabo. They were picked up together in the Châteauroux locality in a double Lysander operation flown by Flight Lieutenant Bob Large and Flying Officer J.P. Alcock.

Liewer was an SOE jack-in-the-box so far as the squadron was concerned. He had been in and out of France on a regular basis since 1941. Two months after returning to England by Ratcliff's February Hudson, he went back again with Violette for a three-week reconnaissance of the Rouen area in an attempt to find out why so many arrests had been made in circuits adjoining his highly-effective *Salesman*.

When Large and Alcock picked them up they were returning to make their report. Violette was lucky to get back at all as a tyre of

Large's Lysander had been ripped by flak and on landing the aircraft did what the pilot later described as a 'ground loop'.

Both emerged unscathed, but Large later reported that his lady passenger attacked him with an umbrella. Their inter-com link had been switched off during the flight and after the crash she apparently thought the 'Lizzie' had crashed back in France and that the pilot was a potential enemy.

Violette was the widow of a French army officer who had been killed fighting at El Alamein after their only child was born. She was to parachute back into France with Liewer soon after D-Day, but she was captured three days later after a gun battle. Eventually she was executed at Ravensbrück and, like Noor Inayat Khan, she was posthumously awarded the George Cross.

While the Lysanders bore the brunt of pick-up operations in May, the Hudsons were by no means idle. Helfer, Escreet and Thompson were now flying regularly as a crew, with Flying Officer Harold 'Crafty' Binns as their navigator. His somewhat unsavoury nickname was a tribute to his ability to get by with the minimum of effort. Middle-aged when war broke out, Binns was a typical product of the peacetime air force. He knew every dodge in the book, and used his lifetime of experience and know-how to climb up through the ranks.

He was a fixer; a man who could wangle a mug of tea out of the cookhouse when the Naafi canteen was shut or 'organise' a 48-hour weekend pass at short notice. In the army he would have been an 'old sweat' and in the navy, an 'old salt'. He was also a very brave man.

Helfer also went out occasionally with other crews to build up more flying experience, and on 21 May two of his crew were Flying Officers Gall and a Canadian called Penhale.

Ten days later Gall was 'missing, believed killed'. He was in a Hudson shot down over Tilburg in Holland. Flying Officer Johnny Maskell was also posted 'missing', and both were later confirmed KIA – killed in action. The pilot, 'Sugar' Hale, and Flying Officer Mike Hughes, were found dead in the wreckage. They were the first Hudson casualties on operations.

Another Hudson pilot, Flying Officer J.W. McDonald, had been killed the previous February only days before the Hudsons were formed up into a separate Flight of No 161 Squadron. He was actually killed in a Lysander when he landed too fast and crashed on what would have been his third pick-up.

In the four months of 'C' Flight's existence, three of the nine new pilots had been killed – two of them with their crews – and another pilot and crew were in a Swedish internment camp. As two pilots had been returned to their former units, only Helfer, Ibbott and Flight Lieutenant John Menzies remained of the new boys.

They were suddenly veterans, the sole survivors of the February intake of Hudson pilots.

Neither the new squadron commander, Alan Boxer, nor the recently-appointed 'C' Flight commander, Reg Wilkinson, had any experience of pick-up operations in Hudsons. Ratcliff had completed one, and had two other pick-ups to his credit as the officer in command of the Lysanders.

Only the blunt, no-nonsense Scot, John Affleck, had any real experience of putting a large aircraft down in a small field at night in hostile territory. While still in the comparatively lowly com-missioned rank of flying officer, he had already added both the DSO and DFC to the AFM he had been awarded as a sergeant pilot. And he was just twenty-four years old.

Small wonder then that before leaving the squadron, Bob Hodges had felt compelled to write in recommending him for the DSO: 'As a captain of aircraft he is outstanding, and has at all times shown the greatest enthusiasm for operational flying.'

His expertise after five pick-ups was to be needed by 'C' Flight in the weeks to come, when he was given the job of training yet more 'green' crews coming in as replacements.

*

2330 hours, March 20, 1945: It was all over. The skipper had made the inevitable decision to abort and as they turned for home the navigator knew it was now up to him to get them back safely through the aerial minefields of flak which always awaited the unwary.

They would go back the way they came, crossing the Rhine between Koblenz and Cologne. He plotted the route to allow for westerly headwinds gusting up to Force Six – around 40 knots. The morning weather report indicated they would be heading back into the turbulence of a second cold front which he calculated would now be moving across the English Channel.

He snapped off the blue lamp above his navigator's table and sat back. It would be around four the morning before they got home . . .

. . . He was bored stiff. There were times when he convinced himself that running old Mr Woods' pharmacy in Sunderland had given him more excitement doling out aspirin.

Not that Harry Johnson particularly craved excitement. After 28 bombing sorties and a total of 148 night flying hours in ops, there had been no complaints from him the previous July when he was posted out of the front line and into the haven of No 26 Operational Training Unit.

Now it was nearly Christmas. For the last four months of 1943 he had been doing nothing but learn the drill for navigating blind on instruments in the latest Mark X Wellingtons. It was a cushy number; he could do it, so to speak, with his eyes shut.

The war was going on elsewhere, but he felt out of it and the days of just waiting around until the next training flight seemed interminable. He had put in for a posting to a special duties squadron, and he knew if he was lucky it would lead to a temporary commission. But time kept dragging and still there was no word from the squadron office.

His off duty hours were spent polishing up his conjuring tricks and entertaining his crew-mates; or carving the balsa wood model aeroplanes suspended from the ceiling above his bed.

Then there was reading. He devoured any and every book left lying around. His schoolteacher sister Edith always said he could not possibly take in a book because he turned the pages so quickly.

But he had always been a fast reader and he never failed to feel a sense of disappointment when he came to the end of a book because the time had gone so quickly. Books were at a premium in the sergeants' mess. He could never get enough of them to keep himself occupied. Perhaps his brothers, Stan and Jim, would send him some for Christmas.

He took little part in the social life of the station. Older in appearance and more serious-minded than his contemporaries, both in the RAF and at school, he enjoyed camping and cycling and rambling in mixed parties, but he was too shy to ask girls to go out with him on dates.

Now he was thirty years of age, his hairline was receding prematurely and the others in his crew – all young men full of boisterous high spirits – looked on him almost as part of another generation. Edith was right. She had often told him he was too quiet and reserved. What was it she had said? Something of a dreamer?

Well, one day he would show her what dreams were made of by landing in a field in France and bringing her back a present of a bottle of real French perfume.

Edith Johnson still has that bottle of Schiaparelli. It is called 'Shocking'.

11

Flying bombs were falling on London while across the Channel the Allied armies were rolling inexorably across the Normandy country-side. Caen had fallen to the British and Canadians, the Americans had marched into St Lô, and Hitler had survived the assassination attempt by the July bomb plot conspirators.

At Tempsford there had been a pause to draw breath when the invasion began. For a time the work of the special duties squadrons was done. The agents were in position, the Resistance fighters were well-supplied and armed, and the day for which they had been waiting all those years had now dawned.

Some of the 10,000 tons of weapons, ammunition and equipment delivered to France from the concealed air base at Tempsford were at last being put to the use which Churchill had envisaged back in 1940 when he issued the clarion cry to 'set Europe ablaze'.

Everywhere in France pin-pricks of irritation were frustrating German counter-thrusts aimed at the expanding beachhead. Small bands of *maquisards* were setting up ambushes at crossroads, cutting telephone lines, blowing up bridges and railways.

Some 150 underground radios were transmitting intelligence on German troop movements, and teams of SOE saboteurs had successfully carried out all but 100 of the 1,050 planned disruptions of rail traffic.

The *Pimento* circuit, led by the young Tony Brooks, stopped all rail movement between Toulouse and Montauban so that only one north-bound train got through after D-Day until the liberation three months later. Brooks, who had been a passenger in Hodges' Hudson the previous August, also ensured that every train leaving Marseilles for Lyons was derailed at least once along the route.

Jockey, organised by Francis Cammaerts, had similar successes east of the Rhône valley, and he had just been appointed head of all Allied Resistance operations in south-east France. Cammaerts' men also fought to hold open the only good road north from Cannes so that in August the invasion forces landing on the Riviera coast were able to push forward at an unexpected speed to Grenoble, thus outflanking the German defences in the lower Rhône.

Cammaerts himself was captured by what he told me was a

ridiculous fluke. He and two comrades were stopped at a road block, which did not worry them unduly.

German troops were usually baffled by French identity cards, and as long as they bore impressive and official-looking stamps, they rarely failed to pass the sort of cursory inspections given at random road checks.

But on this occasion a Belgian working for the Gestapo was inspecting the papers and he insisted that they turn out their pockets. Cammaerts realised with a feeling of angry shock that he was carrying his share of a consignment of money parachuted to them from England.

Baker Street had been careless. The notes were still brand new, with consecutive serial numbers. His two companions were also carrying their allocation. This one mistake alone was enough to condemn them. With the Third Reich disintegrating the Gestapo agents were in no mood for wasting time in interrogating their prisoners for information which anyway would be out of date, such was the speed of the Allied advance.

They locked them up in a nearby police station and, unknown to Cammaerts, made arrangements to have them shot out of hand the following morning.

Cammaerts owes his life to his 29-year-old courier, Christine Granville. She was informed of their arrest and immediately began negotiations for their release. Her boldness was to earn her the George Medal.

She called at the police station with a bribe of two million francs, or about £10,000, and gave the Germans a choice. Either they took the money and allowed Cammaerts and his men to go free, or she would see to it personally that everyone responsible for their deaths would be executed in turn when the area was liberated.

With an Allied army on the doorstep the Germans took the hint – and the money.

Christine, the half-Jewish daughter of a Polish count, lived to see the end of the war only to be murdered in a London hotel by a frustrated, would-be lover in 1952.

A tomboyish girl who had been in trouble at her convent school for shocking the nuns by climbing trees without knickers, her exploits began after the fall of Poland when she helped to set up escape routes from a base in Budapest.

She joined Cammaerts a month after D-Day when she parachuted into the Vercors area just in time for an abortive uprising by a band of *maquisards*. The Vercors was a rocky plateau, rising jaggedly from the farmland south-west of Grenoble and measuring about 30 by 12 miles. It was a natural base for guerillas and concealed one of the largest *maquis* of around 3,000 men.

Mao Tse-Tung, in his fight against the Japanese, had already laid down the rules for guerilla warfare. Guerillas, he wrote, should always have the ability to run away from a passive position.

The French command in London ignored this maxim, obsessed as they were by the ideal of France being liberated by Frenchmen. So the ill-equipped *maquisards* of the Vercors fought to extinction against the two regular divisions the Germans threw against them.

Cammaerts and Christine Granville were among the few who got away while the Germans were busily carrying out vicious reprisals of massacre and rape.

No 161 Squadron played little part in the invasion itself, but the Hudsons – by now there were five on operations with one in reserve – flew a total of 22 sorties to make radio contact with Resistance groups behind the lines.

N-for-Nan was the workhouse, flying ten of these *Ascension* operations. Terence Helfer, with Ray Escreet and Tommy Thompson, flew a successful mission called *Student Braid* to drop a specialist team of saboteurs. Their navigator, 'Crafty' Binns, was posted that month to No 138 Squadron and his place was taken by Pilot Officer John Weddell.

He was not to remain part of the crew for long. In July Harry Johnson, now with the rank of pilot officer, was posted in to the squadron and began his Hudson training prior to joining Helfer's team. Helfer himself must have felt he had a charmed life. Only he and Ibbott were left of the eight pilots who had joined the squadron the previous February.

The last of them, Flight Lieutenant Menzies, failed to return on 5 July from a sortie over Holland and was posted 'Missing, believed killed' with his crew of Flying Officer Bunney, Flight Sergeant Withers, and Flight Sergeant Eliot. The four agents on board also died.

Helfer knew he was being groomed for more dangerous work when he went on what was both his and the new commanding officer's first pick-up operation. Wing Commander Boxer had chosen to break his duck the most difficult way possible by attempting a night landing for the first time without the benefit of moonlight.

Helfer went along to learn as a back-up pilot in this, the first and last pick-up during what was called the 'Black' period. Unfortunately, details of this Operation *Tenerife* may remain forever unknown. There is no file on it in SOE archives and the full SIS records have not yet been made available to the general public if, indeed, they ever will be.

However, it is known that Hudson P-for-Peter was landed on a grassy strip of a disused airfield at Le Blanc, midway between Poitiers and Châteauroux, on the night of 27 July, in spite of the fact that the Germans had criss-crossed it with a plough just two days earlier.

The reception party carried out makeshift repairs in record time – as the aircraft was on the way, in fact – but it was nevertheless a bumpy landing with an even more hazardous take-off. Two agents and a consignment of urgently-needed medical supplies were taken in, and four evading aircrew were brought back.

Several weeks later, after the area had been liberated, Boxer and Helfer, together with their crew of Flight Lieutenants MacMillan, Johns and Lofty Reed, accepted an invitation to return to the area for an uproarious luncheon party thrown by the local mayor.

It was on this trip that they met an indefatigable heroine of the escape lines: Françoise Dissart, a white-haired woman in her sixties who was one of the few survivors of the *Pat* line still active on the day of liberation.

She lived in a flat near her dress shop not far from Gestapo HQ in Toulouse. With her cat, Mifouf, as her constant companion, her all-black clothing, her chain-smoking set off by a black cigarette holder forever clamped between her teeth, she was something of a witch-like figure to the young evaders entrusted to her care.

She never let them down. As the Germans were methodically smashing the network so painstakingly set up by Albert Guérisse, she continued to avoid arrest, secure in her pose as a crotchety old woman who wanted no part of the war.

She was among the guests of honour introduced to the RAF officers at the mayor's party. In fact, she told them proudly, she would be returning to Tempsford with them on instructions from MI9 – to collect a decoration from the king at Buckingham Palace.

The only other Hudson pick-up carried out in July 1944 was completed by John Affleck after one unsuccessful attempt when he identified the correct field, but was unable to see the reception party lights.

He went in again the following night, on 5 July, with Squadron Leader Reg Wilkinson, the new flight commander who was still learning the ropes, and a crew of Flight Lieutenant R.W. MacMillan, Flight Lieutenant Joe Corner, and Flying Officer Saunders.

One of their passengers was one of the great heroines of the Resistance, Marie-Madeleine Fourcade. She had finally browbeaten intelligence chiefs in London into accepting that her place was back in France with her comrades of the *Alliance* network.

The fact that the operation laid on to take her back was code-named *Baggage* may reflect the wry humour of some staff officer who had been on the receiving end of this energetic Frenchwoman's sometimes acerbic tongue.

She arrived at Tempsford to find aircraft lined up wing-tip to wing-tip 'as far as the eye could see.'* She was told they were part of a formation about to depart on a bombing raid. Affleck had been briefed to fly with them part of the way, in order to avoid drawing attention to himself on enemy radar.

She remembers how

we were driven to the tarmac, where I could see the burly outline of a Hudson, its paintwork chipped by machine-gun fire. I fell for it at once. I had the honour of being the first up the ladder into the fuselage, where I bumped into all kinds of containers piled up by the entrance, and went sprawling.

Also on the flight were seven agents, including Pierre Giraud and Raymond Pezet, the latter travelling as Marie-Madeleine's husband as part of their cover story.

'The runway began to speed past under our wheels,' she wrote. 'Then the big machine heaved itself off the ground ponderously, while around us the bombers rose with similar effort.'

One of the crew drew curtains across the windows as they approached the French coast, but not before the agents had time to be impressed then startled by a firework display of flak and tracer rising to meet them and the bomber stream ahead.

Marie-Madeleine learned later that this first attempt at Operation *Baggage* had to be aborted because the reception committee had heard about the raid and thought it wiser to lie low rather than draw attention to themselves by being out and about at a time when all law-abiding citizens should have been taking shelter.

The second attempt was successful, and with a quick farewell to Affleck and his crew, she set off with Pezet on foot, both of them carrying heavy hand luggage, to hitch a lift to the south of France.

Before the month was out she had been captured, but in one

*Fourcade. *op cit.*

of the most dramatic prison breaks of the war, she escaped from an army barracks guardroom by stripping naked and squeezing through the window bars, her slender body lubricated by the sweat of fear.

She remembered to take her cotton dress with her, otherwise she would have created something of a sensation during her subsequent flight through the streets.

A few days later the French and American forces landed on the Riviera and she linked up with them to join the headlong advance northwards.

She spent Christmas in Paris with her children – a boy of thirteen and a girl of eleven – for the first time since 1940.

While Marie-Madeleine was engaged on her hectic last mission, the Hudson crews were carrying out a record number of nine pick-ups recorded for August. It was as if No 161 Squadron were running holiday charter flights – and still the work carried out fell below expectations.

The fact that so many operations had to be 'scrubbed' is attributed by the squadron records to the rapid advance of the Allied armies. No sooner was an operation planned than it was made redundant by rapidly changing events.

In a somewhat fractured English, Wing Commander Boxer recorded in the monthly log:

> The fruits of the past year's efforts have materialised to a highly successful degree, shown by the excellent work carried out by the *maquis*, and other collaboration in the defeat of the enemy, which could only be brought about by through (sic) the medium of the organisation with which this and other squadrons have been working with.

Boxer himself flew three of the operations, the first of them a 'double' with Harold Ibbott, who was making his first solo pick-up with a 'new boy' crew of pilot-officers in M-for-Mike: A.R. Barr, W.B. Kaus and R.H.D. Wiltshire. Boxer, in P-for-Peter, took along the crew he had on the 'Black' period pick-up with the exception of Helfer who, as a pilot, was now too valuable to be risked flying as a mere passenger.

The two aircraft were put down on a field near Poitiers, just behind the shrinking German lines, with a cargo of rifles, sten guns and ammunition for the eager *maquis*, and picked up twenty passengers for the return flight, some of them carrying vital information about German troop movements and morale, both of the French and of the enemy.

More importantly, they took in a party of eleven highly-trained Special Air Service (SAS) troops to provide a hard core for the loosely-organised Resistance units which came under the umbrella of the French Forces of the Interior (FFI). This small unit was to have joined an advance party of the SAS which had been dropped into the field on D-Day and had been harrying German communications on road and rail routes between Poitiers and Tours.

By the beginning of July they were about fifty strong when they clashed with a battalion of an SS Division. A third of them were captured and executed on the spot. Boxer's party, code-named *Bulbasket*, were much-needed reinforcements. The entire group was eventually rescued in September by an SOE operation in which two Dakotas were used.

On 7 August, the day after Boxer and Ibbott's 'double', Reg Wilkinson pulled off his first Hudson pick-up with a crew of Dickie Wooldridge, now a flight lieutenant, and two replacement flying officers, Marneweck and F.J. Harry Champion. They put four agents into France and brought thirteen people out, in what was the second pick-up carried out in N-for-Nan.

Three nights later two Hudsons took thirteen agents (or possibly SAS troops) to France, but were able to bring back only four passengers. Boxer flew his tried and trusted P-for-Peter, with MacMillan, Champion and another newcomer, Flying Officer G.H. Ash. The second operation was carried out by Affleck in M-for-Mike.. He was without a gunner at the time so he borrowed 'Tommy' Thompson from Helfer to make up a crew with Wooldridge and a new pilot officer called Hall.

It was Affleck's last operation with the squadron before being posted to the Bomber Development Unit. He had carried out 23 bombing sorties with No 77 (Scottish) Squadron, 32 supply drops with No 161 Squadron's Halifaxes, and six successful Hudson pick-ups. He had landed 29 agents safely and brought 33 passengers back.

One he could never forget, not without some revulsion tainting his admiration. This particular agent was known as 'The Postman' because of his regular forays to and from France. Called 'Frenchie' to his face, he never spoke a word, not so much as a *'Bonsoir'* or *'Au revoir.'* But there was little doubt at Tempsford about his line of work. A huge man, he looked every bit the assassin he was. Any French official who appeared to be co-operating too eagerly with the Germans would receive a visit late at night. A few weeks later the word would go round the Tempsford mess that a certain *maire* in the vicinity of a recent dropping zone had been mysteriously done to death.

Apart from a nine-month break with a training unit and a short spell on a disciplinary course, John Affleck had been in the thick of action since the August of 1941. Most of his contemporaries were dead. Eventually he became a civil aviation pilot with BOAC, but before the war ended he had one more Hudson flight to make.

It was in January 1945 he was ordered to fly to one of the old secret landing grounds where a propaganda film unit was due to meet him to reconstruct for posterity the incident in which a village had turned out to dig his bogged-down Hudson from the mud.

But the foul weather which was bedevilling so many real-life operations at that time intervened to leave him grounded at Dijon and the film unit stranded at Tempsford. So the action had to be shot in a field in Bedfordshire with Terence Helfer making his film debut at the controls.

The film *Now it can be told* stars Jacqueline Nearne. She was a genuine SOE heroine, parachuting into France from a Halifax in 1943 and returning by Lysander fifteen months later. But she looks distinctly uncomfortable trying to act a role she had carried out so confidently when it was the real thing!

In view of what was to happen to the Hudson flight in the closing months of the war, it is likely that Affleck's posting came through in time to save his life. Oddly, in spite of his decorations and distinguished service – with a French Croix de Guerre and a Dutch Flying Cross still to come – he finished the war still as a flight lieutenant; a comment, perhaps, on the long memory of RAF disciplinary records which never allow past misdemeanors to be forgotten.

While August saw the end of Affleck's link with the squadron, it was also an important month for Helfer in that it marked the beginning of a partnership which was to end tragically on a Luxembourg hillside seven months later. It was on 4 August that Pilot Officer Harry Johnson became the third and last navigator of his crew, joining Escreet and Thompson who had been with him since March.

By then Johnson had flown only one operation with the squadron, and that was as a passenger in a Halifax. He had also flown three times with Helfer on training flights before he was considered to be up to the standard required of clandestine duty navigators on whose skill and judgement the success of operations so often depended.

Their first flight together as a crew on operations was in Hudson J-for-Jig. First they had a 30-minute trial run by daylight to test the aircraft for defects, and to give Johnson the feel of the plane. Everything went smoothly and Operation *Columbine* was *on*.

They left Tempsford at 2210 hours and were over the target on time, in the smaller hours of the morning. Twice they saw lights flashing the correct identification signal, but although they circled the area for several minutes – each one of them seeming to last an hour – they could see no sign of reception lights to guide them down to the makeshift runway.

Helfer knew his orders, the strict orders laid down so many months éarlier. So they turned back and made for home rather than risk the necks of the tensed agents sitting glumly in the passenger compartment. Their first operation had been a failure, but through no fault of their own. They never discovered what had gone wrong, but the likely explanation is that the reception party, as so often happened, were using bicycle lamps or pocket torches which were not bright enough to pierce the ground haze.

They had to wait another five days for their first success. Flying N-for-Nan in weather described as 'none too good' they dropped two agents and a weapon container into Holland just a month ahead of the massed Anglo-American airborne assault which ended in failure at Arnhem. They heard later that this operation, code-name *Rowing*, was only a partial success. One of the agents, a woman, broke her leg on landing and was unable to complete her mission.

Later that month Escreet went on leave where he learned to his amused surprise that his mother had broken her vow to give up smoking because of all the excitement of the Normandy landings. The rest of the crew went out on a successful *Ascension* with Flying Officers Smith and Dick Jarman. These operations lasted two hours and were flown at 25,000 feet on a track over the Channel parallel to a line joining North Foreland, Dungeness, Beachy Head and Selsey Bill.

Smith recalls that one contact was broken off abruptly in mid-sentence and the sound of small arms fire could be heard in the radio headphones. He never found out what had happened to the agent.

Escreet was not out of the crew for long. Helfer had no intention of losing this enthusiastic young Yorkshireman who recorded his personal war against Nazism with map pins. He was back with the crew for a dropping operation on the 28th, but again they had to abort after pin-pointing the field in Belgium only to be frustrated once more, this time by the absence of any lights whatever, either identification or reception.

That eventful, epoch-making summer was coming to an end, and it was on a balmy afternoon on the last day of August when Helfer and his team clumped into the briefing room in their flying gear to be told they would be going out on their first pick-up that night.

Thompson, who had been on Affleck's last operation, knew what it would be like. Helfer had also been in France, but only as a spare pilot where all he had to do was sit next to Boxer and watch how it was done. This time he would be in charge and any mistakes he made would be his alone, and other men would be depending on him.

It was to be a hectic night for the Hudson crews. Two operations were laid on, both of them requiring two aircraft to take in a total of nineteen passengers to two different localities in France. Boxer told the assembled men that he would fly M-for-Mike as the lead plane in Operation *Xylophone*, with a crew of MacMillan, Hall and Johns. Helfer would follow in K-for-King.

The flight commander, Reg Wilkinson, would take the lead for the second operation, *Dauntsey*, with Weddell, Champion and Pilot Officer Ronnie Morris, who had been a sergeant and one of the men who survived that disastrous night the previous December when three Halifaxes were destroyed. The second aircraft in *Dauntsey* was to be skippered by Ibbott, who would now be taking part in his second pick-up, with his crew of Barr, Kaus, and Wiltshire. Yet another newcomer, a Canadian pilot by the name of Chris Ragan, was briefed to go with Ibbott to learn the ropes.

Later that evening, when the warmth of day was cooling in a stiff breeze blowing across the Bedfordshire farmland, eight agents clambered into Boxer's aircraft and six went into Helfer's. Ibbott, in J-for-Jig, took three, and Wilkinson carried two in what was N-for-Nan's third pick-up operation.

Only one of the four Hudsons out that night brought passengers back to England. Boxer and Helfer landed some time after midnight, and were very soon back home to a dawn breakfast and mugs of tea laced with rum after discovering they had no return passengers. Ibbott came back with four, and all Wilkinson had to carry was one Top Secret letter.

Unfortunately, there is no trace of any files on either *Xylophone* or *Dauntsey* in SOE archives. These were either operations carried out for other intelligence agencies or belonged to a category of SOE files which went mysteriously missing or were accidentally destroyed by an office fire after the war.

Whatever the fate and intentions of the ingoing agents, the fact that there were only four who wanted to go to England can be attributed to the changing nature of the war.

De Gaulle was back in Paris and the Germans were pulling back to the frontiers of the Fatherland just as quickly as they had boiled over it four years earlier. There were very few agents who actually wanted to leave France when the nation was in the ecstatic turmoil of *La Libération*.

This account of Tempsford in that summer of 1944 would be incomplete without mention of Per Hysing-Dahl, a lieutenant in the Royal Norwegian Air Force who by then had completed a full tour of thirty operations with the Halifaxes. He immediately volunteered to join the Lysander 'A' Flight and completed seven successful pick-ups as well as carrying out several parachute dropping operations and *Ascension* sorties with 'C' Flight's Hudsons.

On one homeward flight he was shot down over the Normandy beachhead and his account of the incident in the squadron records is a masterpiece of brevity:

> Flak came up and aircraft and engine hit in several places, and also received hit in hand by shrapnel. Engines cut 20 miles out to sea and glided in at about 70 mph. Found myself sitting in cockpit with water all around. Undid harness and rose to surface.
>
> Saw three passengers swimming around. My own Mae West wouldn't inflate and I proceeded to inflate dinghy. Finally got three passengers on it. Four hours on water before pick-up. One passenger did not survive the ordeal.

That was Hysing-Dahl's last special operation with the squadron. He was posted out of Tempsford in August and survived the war to become a distinguished member of the Norwegian Government and Chief of the Parliamentary Defence Committee.

By the time the September moon rose bright and clear, the last sniper had been cleared out of Paris, the American First Army was about to crunch over the first few yards of German soil at a bridgehead over the frontier by the ancient town of Aachen, and the British Second Army had swept into Brussels.

An era was coming to an end, but there were still two more pick-up operations to be carried out on the night of 5 September. They were both 'doubles'. One of them was led by Boxer and the other by Group Captain 'Mouse' Fielden, whose last pick-up had been made fourteen months earlier.

Boxer's operation ended in tragedy. It was laid on to supply the 1,200-strong Armagnac battalion of the *maquis*, which was running short of arms and ammunition after scores of running battles.

Led by Commandant Parisot, a major in the French Army at the outbreak of war, they had just marched triumphantly through the liberated streets of Toulouse and were thirsting for battle. They had been recruited, supplied and fortified by SOE's *Wheelwright* network organised by George Starr.

Starr's courier, Anne-Marie Walters, has described* Parisot as a man of sparkling personality and constant good humour; a man whose obvious ability as a leader made him the most popular character in the *maquis*. Now, with the Germans on the run, new recruits flocked to join his men of the Armagnac and he made plans to further harry the Germans by striking at their rear.

But he needed more weapons to equip them, so Starr contacted London and the double operation *Dullingham* was laid on.

Boxer took off at 2045 hours and found the field in the Dordogne area easily enough. The landing strip was clearly marked in accordance with the usual drill, and the correct identification signal was flashed as he made his approach. At the last minute Boxer switched on a landing light fixed to the nose of N-for-Nan to make sure there were no unexpected obstacles.

He could not believe his eyes. There, directly in front of him and frozen for a split second in the harsh glare, was a group of about twenty people, beginning to scatter at the point where he intended to touch down.

His reflexes took over and he banged the throttle open to give the engines maximum boost. For a few more seconds the aircraft continued sinking and there was a bump as it hit the ground before the straining engines pulled it back into the sky for him to make another circuit.

His second attempt was successful and his three passengers deplaned. There was only one for the return journey. Behind Boxer came a Canadian pilot, Flying Officer Bob Ferris, carrying the load of stores so urgently needed by the Armagnac battalion. He took off again a few minutes later with four passengers.

The operation had been a success – but behind them they left two dead men in the moonlit field. One of them was Commandant Parisot.

The *maquisards* had lost their beloved leader with victory in sight. A bitter irony, indeed. Boxer returned safely to report:

On attempted first landing, owing to incorrect lay-out and number of

* *Moondrop to Gascony*, by Anne-Marie Walters (Pan) 1951.

people in the way, bumped over them and two killed. Second landing OK.

It was an accident caused by the carelessness of the reception party; an accident unforeseen, and in the past prevented, by the 'Pick-up Bible' in which Hugh Verity had laid down the drill for operations.

His instructions are published in full in Foot's history of SOE in France and it is sufficient here to refer only to a relevant part of it:

> Your approach should be fairly steep to avoid any trees or other obstacles and you should not touch down before light A or after a point 50 yards from it . . . Landing a Hudson, even on a good night, is difficult on an operational flare path and pilots should not be ashamed of themselves if they muff the approach the first time and have to go round again.

When Boxer made his approach a group of people had been standing on the right of light A and the only explanation is that they were inexperienced *maquisards* who had turned up at the field for the excitement of watching a night landing rather than men trained in clandestine landing techniques. Parisot himself, as leader of the unit, should never have been within a mile of the landing ground.

While Boxer and Ferris ere heading towards home and approaching the French coast, Fielden and Helfer were preparing to nature. They were to fly right across France towards a landing ground surrounded by mountains and forest.

Fielden, in M-for-Mike, took off at 0310 hours on 6 September, followed by Helfer five minutes later in L-for-Love. Escreet, who had by then done a total of 38 operational sorties – ten of them with No 161 Squadron – had been left behind and his place was taken on the radio by Flying Officer Dick Jarman.

Their destination was Gex, a small town on the Swiss frontier, eight miles from the lakeside at Geneva. Bad weather put Fielden badly off course and he aborted, making a U-turn to fly back to land at Brussels. He was unable to break radio silence because of the proximity of Luftwaffe nightfighter bases so he had no way of knowing that Helfer was pressing on steadily towards the rendezvous.

This operation, with the forbidding code-name of *Failsworthy*, was the last pick-up ever carried out by the squadron and until now the details have never before been made public by the Defence Ministry.

The squadron log records that Helfer took out nine passengers.

Foot's history of SOE puts the number at eight. The secret archives bring the numbers carried further down, to six – but add that a jeep was also part of the cargo!

If correct, the jeep must have been in a do-it-yourself kit form, ready to be assembled after landing, because it would not have been possible for it to be loaded into the aircraft all ready to go.

The Hudson may well have been a versatile aircraft, but it was not quite up to the requirements of a 'roll-on, roll-off' car ferry service. It is more likely that the jeep – or vital spare parts of one, such as tyres, wheels and engine components – were being carried in Fielden's M-for-Mike. He is known to have been carrying nothing but stores, while Helfer in L-for-Love was transporting the personnel.

Alternatively, as wartime records are not renowned for their accuracy, it is possible that the jeep was already waiting at the secret landing ground. It could have been 'liberated' or borrowed by the *maquis* from advance units of the American Seventh Army which had landed in the south and was by then rolling up the Germans northwards through Lyons.

On the day Helfer landed at Gex and picked up seven passengers for the return flight, the Americans were battle-locked in a fierce counter-attack by the XI Panzer Division at Bourg-en-Bresse, just thirty miles to the west. The heavily-armed combat team flown to this battle zone in L-for-Love had orders to create havoc in the enemy rear and so assist the Americans and the French army corps fighting on their left under the command of another one-time Hudson customer, General de Lattre de Tassigny.

This combat team was an inter-allied SOE mission code-named *Etoile* (*Failsworthy* was the code-name given to the air operation), and was commanded by Richard Broad, who had started the war as a lieutenant in a Scottish regiment. He had avoided having his career come to an untimely end by becoming an evader on an early escape line when the 51st Highland Division was trapped at St Valéry in 1940.

His second-in-command was Gerry Morel, the SOE operations officer who had tried to snatch Déricourt out of France and who was still courageously fighting ill-health on a diet of biscuits and milk.

Helfer put them down without problems to a reception party headed by Richard Heslop, the head of *Marksman*, who was later to run what became known as 'Xavier's Air Express Service' into a former Luftwaffe airfield at nearby Ambérieu.

Elizabeth Reynolds, his American courier who looked so English that Heslop always had fears for her safety, had been ordered home by him shortly after D-Day – knapsack, tweed suit and all. He had decided to send her back partly for her own sake, and partly to relieve the anxiety of those who knew and admired her. She pleaded to be allowed to stay to finish the job she had started eleven months earlier, but Heslop was adamant.

She had been in France since that night in October 1943 when she was brought in by John Affleck's first Hudson operation, via the tree tops around the field at Lons-le-Saunier. But she had no intention of leaving when the liberation she had fought for was so close at hand. She disobeyed his orders and went to visit her invalid mother in Paris – and she was arrested by the Gestapo. She was lucky. She was set free by the prison authorities at Fresnes when the Germans pulled out of Paris.

Heslop was still wondering about her fate when the *Etoile* mission stepped out of L-for-Love after a farewell handshake with Helfer and his crew. Broad explained that his orders were to co-ordinate the activities of local French resisters with those of the 2nd SAS batallion in the Vosges region, north of Belfort.

Broad, Morel and their four (or six? or seven?) companions piled into the jeep and a prison van which Heslop's men had commandeered, and set off north along what is now called Route Nationale 5, passing through scattered elements of German units until they linked up with the HQ of the American VI Corps at Lons-le-Saunier a day later. The following day they headed towards Baume-les-Dames, bumping into some regular French troops who told them that the locality had just been re-occupied by units of the retreating XI Panzers.

They were advised to take a side road leading to Lomont, but they had travelled no more than a few miles when the jeep and van came under heavy machine-gun fire. Four of the mission officers were wounded. But a troop of American armoured cars arrived in the nick of time like the 7th Cavalry and put the solitary machine gun and crew out of action.

The wounded men were driven back over side roads and put in the care of an American medical unit. Broad and Morel were then forced to rest for a few days while awaiting a supply drop of arms and ammunition for distribution among the men of the FFI.

The drop was made on 9 September, and for the next few weeks, what was left of the *Etoile* mission toured the area in an attempt to unite rival Resistance bands and bring some cohesion to their efforts.

They returned to England on 20 October, their mission fulfilled in that the area had been liberated and the FFI disbanded as an independent force and incorporated into the regular French Army.

By then, Ray Escreet was back in Helfer's crew and wondering what to do next. There was speculation at Tempsford about the squadron's future. All active service operations were now limited to Norway and Denmark, and the days on the station were long and uneventful.

They could not know that momentous decisions were being made in London – decisions which would cost the lives of many aircrew and agents.

They would soon learn of these decisions, but for the time being the squadron was given a rest during a period of reorganisation. The flight of Halifaxes was transferred back to the Main Force of Bomber Command for the intensified nightly onslaught against German cities. Their place at Tempsford was taken by the obsolete Stirlings, which were by now fit only for sorties over lightly defended areas like northern France.

There *was* a pointer to what was in store for the squadron, but few people realised it at the time. On 8 September an attempt was made to infiltrate two agents into Germany for the first time by air. Bob Ferris, in M-for-Mike with an all-Canadian team of Flying Officer A.F. Penhale, Pilot Officer J.E. Traill, and Warrant Officer R.G. Hutton, located their target a few miles east of the Rhine and gave the two agents the green light to jump.

One of them refused at the last minute. Although the other was willing to go, Ferris decided to bring them both home. This abortive attempt is important only in that it gave an indication of what the intelligence planners in London had in mind.

The squadron commander, Alan Boxer, must have had an inkling but he did not commit it to paper. Instead, his report for September in the squadron records reads in part:

> With the almost complete clearance of France of Axis troops, and the entry into Belgium and Holland by Allied forces, the majority of the special work required of the squadron has now come to a successful conclusion, and only commitments in Denmark and Norway now remain to work on.

The wing commander was more concerned about what he described as the 'very high reputation' of his squadron's training scheme. This reputation 'fell to pieces', he wrote, because of three accidents of a serious nature caused by carelessness shown by three pilots:

> This relapse was very largely due to the departure of all the old crews before the date originally planned, resulting in the scheme of conversion being thrown completely away.

It needs to be stated here that the Hudsons and their crews were not involved in this criticism. Apart from flying what was to be the last Hudson pick-up of the war, Helfer and his crew – with Escreet back once more in place of Jarman – spent the best part of September and October on mundane transport duties, flying military personnel and equipment to and from Belgium in L-for-Love.

About the only excitement for the Hudsons in October was when Flight Lieutenant 'Buster' Webb had what was described as a 'slight mishap' on a transport flight to Brussels due to an open door on P-for-Peter. Helfer had to fly across to bring him back with his crew while the aircraft was being repaired.

It was routine chores of this nature that prompted Escreet to discuss with Thompson the possibility of transferring from the Hudsons to join one of the élite Pathfinder squadrons which were then leading the vast bomber armadas on the pulverisation raids deep in the heart of Germany.

They were two of a kind, Ray and 'Tommy'. Both needed the excitement which came with action: Escreet because it seemed he had known no other way of life since leaving school; Thompson because he was homesick and longing to see and smell again the green hills around his family's farm above Waipiro Bay.

There was another reason for Thompson's hurry to get the war over and done with. When he returned to the farm he would be leaving his brother Onslow behind in an English grave. But he would be taking back with him the tall and beautiful Bedford girl who had just become his bride.

For the crew in general and himself in particular, the Hudson L-for-Love had become, unofficially, Lucky-in-Love. It had brought them home safely from the squadron's last pick-up at Gex – a round trip of nine hours as they played a deadly game of hide-and-seek with the Luftwaffe around the Alpine peaks of the Jura.

When they landed back at Tempsford after that hazardous flight across the breadth of France it was to learn that Britain's wartime blackout restrictions had just been lifted, and the lights put out in 1939 began to come on again.

For Tommy Thompson life held every promise in that autumn of 1944.

*0030 hours, March 21, 1945: The first day of spring was officially just
thirty minutes old as the gunner eased his aching shoulders and back. His
eyes were tired. For nearly six hours now he had been squinting through the
perspex panels of the dorsal turret, ceaselessly quartering every section of the
sky within the limits imposed on his vision by the Hudson's structure.*

*Air gunners had always had the rough end of this war, spending their
flying time wedged in tiny compartments surrounded by miles of lines
carrying fuel and hydraulic fluid and electrical currents, with belts of
ammunition making a lethal cocktail which could blow them to eternity in a
split second.*

*Fire was always the dominant fear in an air gunner's mind, especially in
twin-engine bombers with their cramped fuselages which made the wearing
of parachutes impracticable. His was even now stowed a few feet away. It
was impossible for him to wear it and operate the gun turret at the same
time . . .*

. . . The band was playing a quickstep and he could see her standing
at the far end of the dance floor; slim and blonde and wearing a
black, knee-length dress of taffeta with a silver-leaf motif. Their eyes
met and he smiled, and she felt ridiculous standing there, a full
head taller than most of the other young women around her.

But she could not help smiling back, and she watched a little
nervously as he started across the floor towards her, more than six
feet tall and handsomely dark-looking with the sort of tan that
comes from years of exposure to weather other than the typical
British summer.

As he came closer she noticed first the 'New Zealand' shoulder
flash, then the ribbon of the DFM above the left breast pocket of his
tunic.

There had been plenty of Canadians around Bedford, and an
ever-increasing swarm of Americans with their gifts of candy, gum
and nylons. But New Zealanders, even at this late stage of the war,
were something of a novelty.

He shouldered his way through the crush of dancers and as he
stopped he said something, and she replied, and weeks later neither
could remember what the other had said, but it did not matter
much because by then they felt they had known each other for
years.

The Last Waltz had come too soon, but when they parted they
arranged to meet again, and she went back to her parents' home in

Britannia Road wondering if they ever would. He had tilted his cap at a jaunty angle and set off for his quarters at Tempsford, determined to see more of this striking girl so unlike the others he had met in England.

That had been in the early summer of 1944, not long after he had joined the secret squadron. Now they were married. It had been a simple register office wedding. No fuss, no trimmings. Just a wartime ceremony with her parents as the only witnesses.

He told her to call him Tommy. Everyone else did. Only his mother called him by his real name – Forrest.

It was a name he had never liked. When they made plans for the wedding he said he would not be inviting the men in his crew. He wanted to keep the war in a separate compartment of his life. She did not question it. She was in love.

It had been a quiet war for Olive Mathers, in spite of living in a county town like Bedford, surrounded as it was by air bases and packed at weekends with young men making the most of 48-hour passes.

The terrifying majesty of war passed overhead night and day, and while part of it she always felt apart from it. A secretary by day, she was spurred on to do her bit by posters urging civilians to 'Lend A Hand On The Land', and so she spent many of the summer evenings in the fields, helping farmers to get their crops in.

She wanted a child. Tommy had his doubts. He had seen how the young wife of a friend had gone to pieces after his death in action, and how she had become of no use to herself or her baby.

Their life together was happy, and she had eased him through the bad patch when he learned of the death of his brother. No one really knew what had gone wrong. When his Mosquito had inexplicably crashed on take-off, Tommy had not known how to break the news to their mother. But someone had to.

Their only tiff had been a silly thing. He had acquired a Ford Seven, a battered old banger similar to one run by the crew's navigator, Harry Johnson. It had belonged to an officer called 'Scotty' who had been killed on a Halifax sortie.

Olive pleaded with him not to have it. She felt it would bring bad luck, driving a dead man's car. In any case, it refused to start on cold mornings and regularly had to be towed into a coughing, spluttering life by the neighbourhood milk van. But Tommy turned her protests down with his infectious smile and had told her not to worry.

And like thousands of other young wartime brides she had put her fears in a tightly-locked corner of her mind, and went ahead with her plans for making woolly clothes for the child she wanted by this man she would love long after the war had ended.

12

Luck finally ran out for a crew of L-for-Love on 26 November. Reg Wilkinson had already made the first successful penetration of Germany in a Hudson when he and his crew – with the addition of Flying Officer R.M. Ritchie – dropped two agents on target on 3 October.

With that experience behind him he elected to make the next trip in the aircraft which Terence Helfer had been flying on transport duties. He reached the target on time and the solitary agent on board slid out safely through the hatch.

But L-for-Love never reached home. It was shot down over Belgium and Wilkinson died in the crash three miles from Houffalize with Champion, Ash and Weddell. Ritchie, who had been on the previous trip for experience only, heard the news in the mess.

Helfer, by now promoted to flight lieutenant, became the new commander of the Hudsons, which had just been re-designated 'A' Flight after the withdrawal from service of the redundant Lysanders.

Wilkinson and his men were the squadron's first victims of a new Allied policy which had its origins two years earlier in President Roosevelt's ill-considered demand for the Unconditional Surrender of the Axis, made after the Casablanca Conference.

In Britain the words Unconditional Surrender had become a catch phrase applied to all activities in life from the performance of a football team to the response of a WAAF to an airman's amorous advances.

More seriously, it meant that Jerry had not only to be knocked for six, but he had to be knocked out of the game altogether and for all time. And that meant the invasion of Germany with all the bloody casualties it would entail.

The battle through France had not been easy, in spite of an active Resistance movement and a friendly population in the enemy rear. The campaign up the spine of Italy had been long and vicious, although the Allies had been able to count on the support of partisans harrying German communications and troop movements.

How then could the frontal assault on Germany be contemplated with so little support and intelligence available? The lessons of France and Italy were clear: the intelligence agencies would have to insert agents into the enemy heartland.

The Americans went about the job with an enthusiasm typical of their 'Can Do' attitudes. The war-weary British appeared to be more reluctant. Their war had been going on too long. While their intelligence apparatus in Germany was adequate for gleaning *some* information, it was admitted in high places that there would be problems once the armies crossed the Rhine.

For much of the war the British had been able to read the mind of the enemy through routine radio signals transmitted by the Germans through what they believed to be their foolproof Enigma coding machines. It is now known that a British team based at Bletchley had the capability of deciphering these signals sometimes within hours of their being sent out.

However, the further the Germans were pushed back towards their homeland, the more reliance they placed on ordinary telephone lines and less on radio communications. The up-to-date information which field commanders often had at their fingertips regarding German intentions was drying up with every advance they made.

So it was that in the autumn of 1944 the Allied High Command dithered over intelligence policy. The Americans said Go. The British, jealous of the senior position they had always had in European operations, said No.

But the Americans, comparatively new to the game of espionage, and full of dash, went ahead independently. On 2 September a German socialist called Jupp Kappius, wanted by the Gestapo since fleeing from Germany in 1937, returned by parachute to become the first American-trained agent to be dropped in Germany.

He was recruited by OSS, offspring of the British SOE and a forerunner of the CIA. His job was to create an underground organisation to carry out acts of sabotage, to encourage Left-wing elements to rise against the regime, and to foment rebellion among the conscripted foreign labour force which kept the wheels of German industry turning.

Unlike the agents who had been operating in the Occupied countries, Kappius was alone, ringed by enemies in the most brutal and effective police state the modern world had known. From this small beginning, the Americans were able to infiltrate a total of some two hundred agents into Germany to build a loose organisation where none had existed before.

Quite an achievement for a nation which was a newcomer to espionage and various other forms of underground skullduggery.

The British were reluctant to follow, but they had no option. The very real doubts about the wisdom of parachuting agents into a vacuum were set aside, and agents who had been standing in the wings were made ready to be dropped into Germany.

Some time late in the summer of 1944 Wing Commander Boxer was alerted to prepare his crews for sorties into Germany. Exploratory missions were flown and by November, with one successful operation marked down to Reg Wilkinson, four Hudsons were ready to make the run into Germany on the 26th.

Bob Ferris and his Canadians dropped one agent from N-for-Nan; 'Buster' Webb went out in H-for-How with a new crew of Flying Officer Watson-Smyth, Flying Officer Smith and Warrant Officer Gough, to drop two agents; Harold Ibbott dropped another two from P-for-Peter.

When Wilkinson took off on that bitterly cold evening, his target for the night was Arnstadt, a small town in the foothills of the Thuringian woods just south of Erfurt. The rendezvous was reached and correctly identified and his passenger – an agent of Polish-German extraction – parachuted out safely.

L-for-Love turned for home after covering 200 miles in what was then the deepest penetration ever made by No 161 Squadron's Hudsons into Germany. Wilkinson and his crew must have felt the worst was over when they flew across the Belgian frontier just north of Luxembourg. They had about two hours flying time left when a nightfighter found them.

They were buried in the cemetery at Evere, an airfield near Brussels. There would have been some sort of sense to it if it could be said they had not died in vain. Unhappily, their lives were wasted. Their passenger achieved nothing of any importance.

I have been able to discover that his orders were to head *east*wards from Arnstadt, cross the Polish frontier, and organise sabotage operations around Breslau, presumably to assist the advancing Russians.

All that is known of him is that he turned up in Hanover, more than 300 miles *west* of his scheduled theatre of operations, a year after the war ended. He reported for duty only to put in a claim for his back pay. Then he disappeared and never returned to collect it.

As 1944 drew to a close the squadron lost its last surviving link with the old days when Mouse Fielden was hospitalised by an accident and was later posted to another RAF station at Woodhall Spa. Before leaving he gave Helfer an expensively-bound World Atlas as a farewell present. His replacement as the station commander was

Group Captain E.J. Palmer, an Australian who had been working in the Air Ministry.

Helfer and Ibbott, both of them with pick-up experience, were now the only pilot survivors of the original Hudson flight formed with such enthusiasm at the beginning of the year. Ronnie Morris had joined them during the summer, with Ferris, Ragan and D.T. 'Olly' Oliver coming in as autumn replacements.

Three of them would be dead by the spring as a result of the decision to put agents into Germany.

By December all of them had experience of dropping agents by parachute into the less-heavily defended targets in Holland and Belgium. But Germany, as the Americans were saying, was a different ball game. The nightfighter squadrons of Messerschmitt 110s and Junkers 88s, equipped with their own airborne radar, were operating over their own territory. They could be scrambled and in position for an aerial ambush only minutes after tell-tale blips appeared on ground radar screens.

For most of the war the Germans had been forced to defend themselves from aerial attack, no matter how successful their ground and naval forces were at the time, and as a result they had been able to refine and develop their methods to a degree which the Air Staff could never have foreseen.

After years of survival and attrition their defences were as formidable as any which could be devised within the limitations of their available resources.

British strategic policy for war in the air had always been based on the premise of Lord Trenchard, the founding father of the RAF, that the bombers would always get through. So they would, if sent in sufficient numbers. But the appalling casualties suffered by Bomber Command showed that many would not get through, and those that did often dropped their loads wide of the target.

The special duties squadrons had different problems. Solitary aircraft flying low to dodge the radar screens might have a better chance of reaching their target intact, but once detected their light armament would give them little chance against cannon-firing fighters capable of speeds around 100 mph faster.

The length of the gauntlet which No 161 Squadron had been running in and out of France would be doubled to penetrate Germany, and with the added hazards of more effective radar and a more determined enemy defending their homeland.

When OSS decided the time had come to put agents into Germany there was immediate and unexpected opposition from the US Army Air Force, whose special duties crews had received their final training at Tempsford.

Like the British, American Intelligence had two squadrons of bombers available for clandestine operations. They belonged to the 492nd Bombardment Group and by the end of 1944 were operating out of Harrington, an Eighth Air Force base outside London. Their aircraft were the sturdy, B-24 Liberators, which were both faster and more heavily-armed than Hudsons, Halifaxes and Stirlings.

They were too big, however, for pick-ups and before the Liberation of France all OSS agents had to jump into the field unless a lift could be cadged in a Hudson or Lysander of No 161 Squadron. After D-Day, a flight of American Dakotas was available briefly, and made 20 landings in France to take 62 agents in and bring 108 passengers back.

The Americans' secret sorties were known as *Carpetbagger* flights after the unscrupulous Yankee adventurers who moved into the southern states of the defeated confederacy, seeking their fortunes and political power when the Civil War ended. The problems for the Americans came after the liberation of France. The *Carpetbagger* squadrons were posted back to the main bomber force and the crews experienced in night flying were gradually replaced by newcomers from the States. Only a few aircraft were left to carry out the occasional OSS operation.

But when it became apparent that the war would go on for at least another year the *Carpetbagger* squadrons were reformed from bomber crews which were trained only in the techniques of American daylight flying in rigid formations. They knew little about night navigation in lonely forays through hostile skies.

Moreover, the 492nd Bombardment Group had a new commander: Colonel Hudson H. Upham, who was reported with diplomatic delicacy by an OSS organiser to be 'a very fine officer, recently arrived from the United States with no experience of our type of activity, and unwilling to make definite decisions.'*

In short, Colonel Upham was refusing to allow his untrained men to fly into Germany because of the high risks involved. He did, however, make one concession. He would permit operations in the lightly-defended south-west corner of Germany, and for a time OSS had to be content with that restriction.

The British had no such difficulties. It would have been better for the agents and air crews if they had. But once the decision had been

* *Piercing the Reich* by Joseph Persico. (Michael Joseph), 1979.

made to infiltrate Germany, the RAF gave its usual full co-operation at squadron level to SOE and SIS. While the Air Ministry always had the final say on whether a mission should be carried out or not, the decision was based on weather conditions and the availability of aircraft, rather than on the risks involved.

Also, Nos 161 and 138 Squadrons had been developing the tricks of their trade since early 1942, and all RAF bomber crews were trained in night flying.

Yet according to Persico, who was given unrestricted access to OSS files, the Americans succeeded in infiltrating *three* times more agents into Germany from England than the British. This remarkable claim does justice neither to his country's wartime allies nor to his own otherwise excellent research, and cannot be allowed to go unchallenged.

Without any access to SIS files, and with only limited information from the archives of the now defunct SOE, I have been able to establish that the Hudsons alone dropped 62 agents into Germany. As most of the 200 or so American-trained agents went in by land routes across the German frontiers it is difficult to see how Persico arrived at his figures of three times more.

A possible explanation is that he was unable to obtain the full information from this side of the Atlantic. Successive British governments have had a mania for holding on to secrets long after the need for secrecy has passed.

No 161 Squadron's Stirlings, and those of No 138 Squadron, are also known to have dropped another 33 agents, most of them into Germany, in the last five war months of 1945.

There is no way of knowing how many of the agents dropped by the RAF were working for OSS; undoubtedly some of them were, but not enough to justify the claim that American-trained agents carried out the bulk of clandestine operations in Germany.

In addition to those British agents dropped by parachute, there were undoubtedly some who were infiltrated by the direct land routes from Switzerland and Holland. There is every reason to believe, therefore, that the British effort was at least equal to the American in spite of an early reluctance to set up German underground networks.

The actual value of this effort is another matter again, and one more difficult to establish.

Terence Helfer and his crew dropped ten of the 62 agents sent to Germany by Hudson. Their first attempt was on 31 December when two agents were dropped 'blind' in an operation code-named *Alder*. Helfer reported later that the ground detail of the target area had been clearly identified before the agents jumped.

American fliers, unfamiliar with clandestine operations, were not always so careful. The OSS estimated that at one time nearly half of their agents were being dropped up to twenty miles from their targets. On one occasion two agents were dropped smack in the middle of a Waffen SS Division deployed near Karlsruhe.

Dense cloud, heavy concentration of flak, and a lack of liaison between crews and agents contributed to these failures. There was also the fact that with the exception of German-speaking Belgians, the agents were for the most part Germans, and to many an American a *kraut* was a *kraut* no matter whose side he was on. So did it matter particularly if he was dropped a little off target? It was his own country, wasn't it? He would soon be able to orientate himself.

It was not so much that the British were better at the job; just better motivated. To the RAF crews the war had been a personal thing for five years. They had been fighting on their own doorstep while the Americans were far from home and their own country had never been threatened.

The weather in the winter of 1944–45 was the worst of the century and as a result the activities of the secret squadrons were seriously curtailed.

In November, only six Hudson operations could be attempted and only three of them were successful, with Ferris, Webb and Ibbott dropping a total of five agents into Germany.

In December, the weather over Britain would have permitted flying, but over the routes to the target areas low-lying cloud formations blotted out pinpoints so that only two operations were successful out of five attempted.

Both of them were on New Year's Eve. Helfer, with his experienced crew, dropped two agents in what he described as 'excellent visibility'. Morris was in N-for-Nan with a crew he had built into a team since gaining his commission and converting from Halifaxes the previous spring: Pilot Officer Durrell, Warrant Officer Street and Warrant Officer Dunseith. They also dropped two agents safely, although they slid down the chute at what would appear to be the perilously low altitude of 600 feet.

There was the added complication that month of the Battle of the Bulge. In what was Hitler's desperate last throw, two Panzer armies under von Rundstedt broke through the American line in the Ardennes on 16 December in an abortive attempt to reach the

Channel ports. While the atrocious weather negated the superiority of Allied air power, it also slowed the German advance to a crawl and gave the Americans time to recover. But for the four weeks in which the front line was fluid, most airborne operations planned by the intelligence agencies had to be postponed.

In the New Year the situation became even worse, with snow and freezing conditions causing the squadron to be ineffective throughout January.

'The worst (month) on record,' was how Alan Boxer described it.

All Stirling operations were scrubbed and attempts by Helfer and Webb to drop agents from Hudsons were called off at the last minute because of low cloud. It was in this month that the last *Ascension* operations were carried out by the Hudsons with a total of three successes out of seven attempts. N-for-Nan, which had flown the first *Ascensions* back in October 1943, was able to log two of the last successes.

It was in this unpromising start to the last year of the war that Boxer came to the end of his tour as the commanding officer of No 161 Squadron and was posted to Bomber Command headquarters for the next step in what was to be an illustrious career.

During his ten months at Tempsford the squadron had reached its peak of efficiency. In 53 pick-up operations by Lysander and Hudson a total of 145 agents had been flown into Europe and 162 passengers had been brought back. He had flown five of the 15 Hudson pick-ups, bringing his personal tally to 25 agents into France and 19 passengers back. And, of course, many more agents had been parachuted into the field during this period by the squadron's Halifaxes and Stirlings, as well as 84 dropped by Hudsons.

These successes had been achieved at a cost to the Lysander flight of two pilots killed and four aircraft destroyed on actual operations. The Hudson losses were more serious: three destroyed on operations and one crashed in training, with the deaths of 16 aircrew.

Significantly, none of the destroyed aircraft were lost while making the actual pick-up on the field. They were all shot down on their way to or from their targets; an indication that Hugh Verity's training manual was of top quality.

Weather conditions remained bad during the early part of February, but a slight improvement later in the month enabled the Hudsons to attempt 20 dropping operations over Germany and Denmark. Eleven were successful and a total of 22 agents were parachuted behind the German lines.

On St Valentine's Day – the squadron's third anniversary – there was a ridiculous and unnecessary casualty. Flying Officer E. Timperley was returning to Tempsford after a training flight in a Stirling when he was buzzed by an American Mustang of the No 383 Fighter Squadron USAAF. The American pilot made a dummy attack over the village of Potton and struck the tail of the cumbersome bomber. The fighter pilot and all seven of the Stirling crew were killed.

The anniversary celebrations had a subdued air that week, but with more than a thousand officers and men of two squadrons based at Tempsford, little time was spent in mourning their loss and there were packed houses for two ENSA shows, *Piccadilly Revels* and *Passed to You*.

When Boxer departed from the squadron office with a DSO, a DFC and an air vice-marshal's baton in his knapsack, he was succeeded as the CO by a newly-promoted wing commander, George Watson. He was a pre-war regular who had come up through the ranks with a DFM to his credit, and a distinguished record with No 161's sister squadron.

Only three months earlier he had carried out an outstanding operation to supply arms to *Milorg*, the military organisation which was the backbone of resistance in Norway. He had flown a No 138 Squadron Halifax through 800 miles of dense cloud, dropping six eagerly-awaited arms containers right on target in a reception area at Flekkefjord, marked by only two faint pinpoints of light.

He brought to his duties with No 161 Squadron the same qualities of leadership-by-example as his predecessors: Mouse Fielden, Charles Pick Pickard, Bob Hodges and Alan Boxer.

Four weeks later he was dead.

On 21 February he went out to familiarise himself with the Hudsons in K-for-King, piloted by Olly Oliver, a relatively inexperienced flight lieutenant who had only two droping operations to his credit with the squadron, none of them over Germany. His first was to Holland. The second was to Denmark when the agent he dropped over Jutland became a personal assistant to one of the senior Danish resistance leaders and was eventually awarded the MBE.

Watson decided to go with him on his first attempt to penetrate the defences over Germany. The navigator was Flight Lieutenant O.M. Morgan, a Canadian, and the gunner was Flying Officer J.M. Hartman. The wireless operator was Dick Jarman, the Australian who had taken Ray Escreet's place on the flight to Gex with Helfer, on what was the squadron's last pick-up operation. He had just been promoted to flight lieutenant. It is not known if they ever reached their target. The aircraft failed to return and there is no file on their Operation *Croc* in SOE archives.

It was the second loss of a Hudson and a crew in the five months since the beginning of operations to put agents into Germany.

The destruction of the Hudson Flight was now only a month away.

On the night K-for-King went missing, Helfer and his crew were out in M-for-Mike on a double operation code-named *Carham Postbox Panting*. The squadron records claim that two agents were dropped into Germany at 2203. They were followed into the night air a little later by a shower of propaganda leaflets over Islingen and Lauterbach to mislead German ground forces about the real nature of the mission being carried out by the aircraft heard overhead.

A further two agents were then said to have been dropped at separate targets in the vicinity of the first. But according to SOE records only one agent was dropped, so the other three were probably working for SIS. The SOE agent was a non-commissioned officer in the German Army who had been captured during the fighting in France.

During the standard interrogation by field intelligence officers it was established that he held violent anti-Nazi views. After more careful screening in an attempt to establish how much of his antipathy to the Nazis was genuine, and how much was a natural desire to ingratiate himself with his captors, he was offered the chance of volunteering to be parachuted back into Germany to carry out sabotage operations.

The NCO, who was to be flown to Germany by Helfer, passed all security and training tests satisfactorily, and was able to convince SOE training officers of his loyalty. The key test, the one which could never be carried out on training courses, was always a question mark next to the name of any potential German agent: Would he be willing and able to kill other Germans?

Baker Street had to take the chance. The big day came and *Carham*, as he was code-named, was driven to Tempsford in a car with blacked-out windows and without so much as a quick drink in the mess he was bundled into M-for-Mike with three other men, their blackened faces all indistinguishable in the pale moonlight.

After a flight lasting about four hours he was warned to stand by as Helfer pressed a button on his control panel to switch on a red warning light. Escreet stood over him watching, and when the light went green he tapped the German on the shoulder and he plummeted away into the night.

He was dropped into the Geissen area, twenty miles north of Frankfurt-am-Main, with orders to organise and carry out sabotage operations in the rear of German units facing an impending attack across the Rhine by Patton's Third Army.

It will never be known what happened to him; whether he was a plausible rogue or an unsung hero. He may have been killed, or he may have made his way back to his home town or village, to fade into civilian anonymity. His incomplete file in the Foreign Office does not relate what, if anything, he ever accomplished.

On the night after this drop Helfer took off on his second operation of the month, but shortly after take-off Harry Johnson called out from the navigator's position to say Gee had broken down and they had to return. Gee was the navigational aid which picked up radio pulses transmitted from ground stations. These enabled navigators to calculate where they were no matter how bad the weather. Skilled navigators, and Johnson certainly ranked among them, were able to produce a 'fix' within a minute of picking up a transmission.

It took another day for the Gee equipment to be put right, and another two days for the weather to improve before they could go out again in M-for-Mike. This time they were again carrying four agents to be dropped at two different locations, ten miles apart. The first two, code-named *Montford* and *Everybody*, were dispatched safely over Hersbruck, just outside Nuremberg.

But the bad weather deteriorated further and Helfer was unable to pick out the pinpoint for the second operation. The two agents, codenamed *Vasco* and *Telegraph*, were brought back to Tempsford. It was on this flight that Escreet celebrated the achievement of completing 1,000 flying hours.

Three nights later, on 28 February, the crew went out again and dropped the two men in the neighbourhood of Hochstadt village, also near Nuremberg.

Montford and *Everybody* are reported to have made radio contact with London soon after landing. They were able to pass on snippets of information about troop reinforcements heading north to block Montgomery's 21st Army Group, and west to meet the Americans under Bradley. They also organised small groups of resistance which pin-pricked the German rear by cutting telephone wires, blowing up sections of railway line, and generally making a nuisance of themselves.

The second pair, *Vasco* and *Telegraph*, infiltrated the foreign labour force conscripted from France, Poland and other conquered nations. Their mission was to organise strikes and carry out minor industrial sabotage. The sabotage operations were of a nature which subsequent investigations would be unlikely to detect as actual sabotage.

Fan belts on machines would snap, engines would overheat, nuts and bolts would come loose. Again, just pin-pricks.

But they managed to cause maddening delays to production at a time when the Germans were fighting for the first time on their own soil, and when every delay meant slower delivery to fighting men at the front. And they in turn, the soldiers and airmen, became as bitter as any combatants in defeat when they suspect the civilians at their backs are not pulling their weight.

The morale value of these pin-prick operations is incalculable..

Bob Ferris, like Helfer, also carried out three successful dropping operations over Germany during February. All of them were flown in N-for-Nan with his crew of Penhale, Hutton and Traill. The first was probably an SIS operation and was code-named *Acacia*. Although it was reported a success with three agents dropping safely, the same operation was carried out by a different crew a month later.

They dropped another three agents the following night, on 22 February. They were Germans trained by SOE and their job was to destroy the double track railway line from Sigmaringen and Hattingen, and the line from Sigmaringen to Tottlingen, to bring all traffic to a halt. Tragically they failed. One man was captured after being wounded in a skirmish with a patrol, but the other two escaped to reach Switzerland and were eventually able to get back to London.

On 28 February Ferris dropped a German recruit into a locality just north of Hassfurt where he had claimed during a prisoner-of-war interrogation there was a strong anti-Nazi element which would be prepared to sabotage the German war effort. He volunteered to organise them and was as good as his word. He assembled a small team of resisters and they made their way to the east where they carried out successful attacks on certain targets specified by SOE in the Halle area, not far from Leipzig. They then headed south to make their escape over the frontier into Switzerland.

Chris Ragan and his crew – Warrant Officer F.E. Gray, Flight Sergeant P Bradley, and Flight Sergeant C.A. Thomas – flew two successful sorties into Germany during the month. It was the young

Canadian flying officer's first active duty with the Hudsons since the previous August. Flying a new Hudson L-for-Love, which replaced the one in which Reg Wilkinson had been killed, Ragan went out on 22 February to drop a wireless operator code-named *Imala* and a group organiser, *Bolingbrook*.

They were both Belgians and their instructions were to infiltrate and organise resistance among the Belgian workers who had been deported by the Germans into the Darmstadt-Mannheim area in the Rhine Valley. Their mission was a failure. They were captured soon after landing, although *Imala* managed to escape and make contact with advancing American patrols.

On his second sortie, Ragan dropped three agents of German nationality just west of the Weissenbach area. He reported heavy cloud over the target, but managed to find his way through a gap which opened up just as he was about to give up hope. Two of the men had been briefed to sabotage the rail link between Aschaffenburg and Gemunden, and the third was to attempt to derail trains running between Gelnhausen and Schluechtern.

SOE never heard from them again.

March came at last and with it the end of the foul winter. At Tempsford the signs of spring appeared in the hedgerows; in Germany the Reich was crumbling and victory really *was* in the air and no one doubted that this time the war would be over well before next Christmas.

The new squadron CO, posted in to replace George Watson, was Wing Commander Mickey Brogan, who had the DFC awarded after a bombing tour. On 4 March he went out in a Stirling on an operation to Denmark and failed to return. He had been in command of the squadron for less than a fortnight and many of the men on the station never even learned his name.

Len Ratcliff, now a wing commander with a DSO and a DFC, was a natural choice for the command of No 161. He had left Tempsford the previous April for a spell in the Air Ministry, and had returned to plan all operations for the two secret squadrons.

He knew all there was to know about the job and if anyone was going to keep the squadron on its toes during the critical operations over Germany, he was the man with all the right qualifications.

The Stirlings of 'B' Flight had a remarkable success rate for his first month of command, completing 53 of the 65 sorties attempted, most of them container drops to supply scattered resistance units just behind the German lines.

But the price was high. Two other aircraft and their seven-man crews, in addition to Brogan's, failed to return.

The Hudsons of 'A' Flight, carrying out their more specialised role of putting agents into the field, were able to complete only seven of the 17 operations attempted. Five agents were dropped into Germany, two into Denmark, one into Holland, and one was dropped by Harold Ibbott in the first Hudson operation to Norway.

But again the price was high . . .

Two attempts were made early in March at one particular operation. The fact that they had to be aborted was to have a fateful significance for Terence Helfer and the three men who had flown with him during all the perils of pick-up operations during the previous year.

The first attempt at Operation *Express Benedict Leader* was made by Chris Ragan.

He flew to within forty miles of the target deep inside Germany before he was forced to turn back because of the weather.

On the following night of 3 March a second attempt was made by Ronald Morris, who by now had been promoted another step to flying officer. But again, heavy clouds made it impossible for him to locate the target with any degree of accuracy. The high standards demanded of the squadron fliers when they had 'Joes' in their care gave him no option but to head back for home.

The three agents, all Belgians, very young and extremely brave, were told it would not be possible to make another attempt until later that month.

The first successful operations for March were carried out on the night of the 2nd when Ibbott dropped two agents into Germany, and Helfer one over Barneveld, some twenty miles from the south shore of the Zuider Zee.

Two nights later Helfer and his crew flew P-for-Peter to drop two agents over Denmark. By one of those coincidences which make fate appear to be the work of some malign hand it was on the same night Brogan went to his death, just as his predecessor had done on the night of another Helfer operation the previous month.

Operations to Denmark came under the umbrella codename of *Tablejam*. Because of its proximity and relatively easy access to neutral Sweden, Denmark had been a beehive of intelligence activity since the unopposed German invasion in 1940.

In many ways it was a phoney occupation. The Danes, unlike the Poles and to some degree the French, were regarded as a Germanic people with good Aryan blood. It was not until the Germans began to suffer from increasing sabotage operations carried out by an underground movement fostered by SOE and supplied by the RAF that Denmark began to feel the full weight of the jackboot in the summer of 1943.

. It was then that Hitler decided the softly, softly policy of moderation was not being appreciated, and orders were given to the Army to cleanse the nation of its impure Jews and Communists.

This led to one of the greatest rescue operations of the war.

The underground, aided by ordinary people and in some cases by sympathetic German troops, managed to get most of the country's 7,000 Jews away to the safety of Sweden. Only a few, perhaps 300, were arrested and transported to concentration camps in Germany.

One of the two agents dropped by Helfer on 4 March had been involved in that latter-day exodus. At the outbreak of war this young man had become active in the production and distribution of illegal, anti-Nazi newspapers as a member of a students' organisation in Copenhagen.

By 1943 he had extended the scope of his activities to include smuggling agents and information between Denmark and Sweden in small fishing boats. He was well-placed when the time came to play an important part in ferrying the Jews across the narrow stretch of water between Zeeland and Sweden.

However, in the December of that year one of his boats ran foul of a German sea patrol and he had to flee to Sweden himself to avoid the Gestapo. While there he contacted the British Legation and arrangements were made to send him to England where he was promptly taken in hand by SOE.

He returned to Denmark in Helfer's Hudson as a lieutenant with an emergency commission in the British Army. He was eventually awarded a Mention in Despatches for his work in organising resistance groups. The agent who travelled back with him on that same flight had been a law student at Copenhagen when the Germans marched in. By 1941 he was organising groups of militant young men who found sabotage operations a more satisfying method of resistance than the mere distribution of anti-Nazi newspapers.

Although he was a good co-ordinator of the various underground factions, he was found to be lacking in technical ability. The study of musty legal documents was hardly a suitable preparation for making bombs from plastic explosives. Consequently he was sent to England to improve his 'education'. After passing with honours through the various SOE training colleges he was also given an emergency commission before being taken to Tempsford to climb aboard P-for-Peter.

He was parachuted to a reception party in Zeeland and as Helfer turned for home one of his crew reported seeing a green flare, signifying all had gone according to plan. From Zeeland, the unknown 'Joe' was transferred to Jutland as the SOE liaison officer with the local resistance organisation.

Within two weeks he had formed an organisation of his own, comprising five couriers, a bodyguard and a secretary, all of them with previous underground experience. He set up a depot for small arms and organised communications to link up with other units by a system of couriers and secret letter boxes.

SOE headquarters staff were impressed by his efficiency and reported glowingly on the tact and courage he displayed in carrying out his duties. Much of the 'highly satisfactory' liaison between Jutland and England has been attributed in a secret report* to the work he carried out. He, too, was awarded a Mention in Despatches when the war ended.

At Tempsford, there was a lull in operations during the second and third weeks of the month, although the day-to-day business of running an air base continued unabated with arrangements being made to transfer No 138 Squadron to Tuddenham. Its role as a clandestine unit was at an end and the crews left to be re-trained for Main Force bombing operations.

No 161 remained at Tempsford, but all the paper work needed to keep the squadron flying was transferred from No 3 (Bomber) Group to No 38 (Fighter) Group for administrative purposes. As there was no work in prospect for the Lysanders, the two remaining pilots, Flying Officers Alexander and Cruickshank, were sent to Andover to learn how to fly helicopters.

Everyone knew the war could not last much longer. In anticipation of the event a flight sergeant 'liberated' a quantity of the foreign currency doled out to aircrew as part of their survival kit in the event of being shot-down over enemy territory. He was caught red-handed and his court of inquiry documents were just a small part of the air force 'bumf' flying in all directions, in quintuplicate formation, from desk to desk.

No one was quite sure what the squadron would be doing next,

* SOE archives.

but the latrine grapevine was insisting that routine transport duties would take the place of secret operations so far as the Hudsons were concerned.

The WAAF contingent – there were around 300 girls in blue on the station by now – made plans for celebrating the third anniversary of their section's arrival at Tempsford. They settled for a 'gala dance' and tea, complete with a birthday cake.

Orders were passed down from the station office to the effect that all airmen and airwomen should take part in a scheme to keep fit by doing physical exercises 'While-you-Work'.

The *Daily Express* 'Brains Trust' visited the station to give a performance in one of the hangars, and a show was put on by the Dramatic Club from the nearby village of Cardington.

Their play was called . . . *A Murder Has Been Arranged*.

A week later thirteen crews were briefed for operations on a single night. Superstition played no part in RAF planning. It was a Tuesday, 20 March. Eight Stirlings and the entire Hudson flight of five aircraft were to cross the enemy lines, each on a different mission.

Helfer was the first to take off in N-for-Nan, shortly before seven o'clock in the evening. He was followed two hours later by Ferris in O-for-Oboe. In the next hour all the Stirlings took off followed by another two Hudsons: P-for-Peter flown by Webb and J-for-Jig flown by Morris. L-for-Love was the 'tail-end Charlie', taking off two hours before midnight with Ragan at the controls.

Then the waiting began.

It was well after midnight when the sound of an aircraft's engines were heard. It was a Stirling. Then another, and another, until by half-past four in the morning all eight were safely home.

But only two Hudsons came back.

'Buster' Webb was first. He had dropped a German agent code-named *Colehill* at a district called Steinhudermeer in the Berlin area. As Webb was running the gauntlet home, *Colehill* was lying low in an area he had known since childhood. It is now known that he caught a train to Berlin the following evening and quickly formed a group which printed anti-Hitler placards and posted them around the city during air raid alarms.

They also altered the texts of pro-Nazi slogans chalked up on walls as part of a propaganda campaign designed to lower morale. More effectively, *Colehill*'s group also carried out successful operations on the railways by jamming points. They derailed one locomotive and six wagons containing coal and oil at Weissensee. In another operation at Gesundrunnen station they derailed one train and caused a collision with another train coming from the opposite direction, effectively blocking the line.

Colehill's luck ran out on 23 April when he strayed into the Russian lines. He was arrested and kept in various prison camps until mid-July when he was discharged with a number of sick inmates.

It was nearly two hours after Webb's return before the second Hudson arrived back at Tempsford. It was brought back by Ronald Morris who had dropped one agent in a repetition of the *Acacia* operation flown by Bob Ferris the month before.

But where was Ferris now? And Chris Ragan and Terence Helfer?

Wing Commander Ratcliff, his eyes red-rimmed with fatigue, waited up long after the aircraft could have been expected to get back safely, hoping against hope to receive telephone calls which would tell him the three Hudsons had diverted to other bases.

The calls never came, and as dawn broke three entries were made in red ink in the squadron's Operations Record Book.

Several days were to pass before he could put together the full horror of what happened that night. Ragan was shot down and killed over Germany. His crew, Bradley, Gray and Thomas, died with him. They never reached their destination and there is no record of their mission, *Walnut*, in SOE archives.

Ferris and his all-Canadian crew of Traill, Penhale and Hutton dropped their solitary SOE agent east of the Allied bridgehead over the Rhine at Remagen. His instructions were to blow up the main railway line between Betzdorf and Wissen. It was a vital link which had to be cut quickly. The Germans were using it to rush supplies and reinforcements to stem an expected Allied offensive, which actually began the next day.

He parachuted safely out of Ferris's Hudson, but the cord which attached a supply container to his leg broke during his exit and disappeared into the night. Without explosives he was unable to carry out his mission, so he began making his way towards the American lines as O-for-Oboe headed back for home.

It never got there.

Ferris was over France when he was shot down and killed with his crew.

N-for-Nan, meanwhile, was on the way back from *Express Benedict Leader*, the operation with three Belgian officers which had been twice attempted and aborted at the beginning of the month.

The Hudson's cockpit showing pilot's instrument panel. A practical passageway to starboard led past the pilot to the navigator's position forward.

An unusual rear view of a Tempsford Hudson showing the clear field of fire from the dorsal turret over the twin tail fins. Flying Officer Len Smith (peaked cap) flew 21 *Ascension* operations to make direct radio-phone contact with agents in the field, in this and other squadron Hudsons. Also shown here are the sergeant mechanic Sam Hollis (*centre, standing*) and the rest of Smith's regular crew: Flight Sergeant William 'Jock' Hunter, navigator (*seated*), Flight Sergeant Joe Wilford, wireless operator (*left*) and Flight Sergeant Ken Morgan, gunner (*right*). Morgan was later killed on operations on a Halifax but the rest all survived the war.

The Hudson's bomb racks.

*

About 0045 hours, March 21, 1945: The crew were cold and tired. Terence Helfer had been at the controls for nearly six hours and there were still 300 miles to go.

Harry Johnson had been crouched over the charts on his navigator's table for much of that time, while Ray Escreet and Tommy Thompson had been searching the skies unceasingly for the warning glow of a nightfighter's exhaust or the suspicion of a fleeting silhouette against the clouds. The three Belgians just sat there with nothing to do, their mission called off yet again.

Below, in a cottage at Maulesmühle, 34-year-old Madame Marguerite Daman-Uilbert lay sleeping in a room next to her two children. She was awakened by the noise of gunfire. The war, she thought. The war has come back.

A few hundred miles to the west another woman lay asleep . . .

. . . She came out of the nightmare with a start of fear, and in that half-world between sleep and wakefulness she could still hear Terry's voice calling out to her.

It's a dream, she thought, just a dream. But she sat up, trembling in the narrow iron cot, her nightdress damp with perspiration, and was soothed by the familiar night sounds of the base.

She knew it must be well after midnight, and she wondered if Terry had gone out on ops that night. It was the moon period, but the weather was terrible. Then she remembered her dream and she knew deep down in the recesses of her subconscious that he was in danger.

Section Officer Jean Helfer was the WAAF head of administration at Bourn, the Cambridgeshire base for a Pathfinder squadron. She had wangled a compassionate posting there because it was only a few miles from Tempsford and she would be able to spend more time with the man she had married fifteen months earlier. She felt like an old married woman now, although they had never shared a home together.

Jean was 18 when she left grammar school at Dover to become a trainee in the beauty and hairdressing section of Bentall's, the famous departmental store at Kingston-upon-Thames. She loathed it, but jobs for girls were hard to find in the 'thirties.

When the war came two years later she volunteered for the Wrens with her younger sister Cynthia, but the Royal Navy was choosy and told them to go away and learn some useful skills. Like typing.

Undeterred, Jean tried the WAAF and this time she was accepted. A year later she was commissioned – Officer Number 2588 – at just about the time a man she had yet to meet was sitting in a dinghy in the North Sea, waiting to be rescued.

They finally came together at Newmarket where Terry Helfer had been posted for target-towing duties and she was the WAAF(G) in charge of about three hundred airwomen. She and her assistant, Blew-Jones – it was a hyphenated name but everyone called her 'Blue' – were the only women in an officers' mess of about a hundred men, and consequently very much in demand at parties and dances.

They were tragic but heady days. It was the autumn of 1943 by then and Britain's bomber force was flying around 5,000 sorties a month, and faces which had become familiar to her over the breakfast table would be there one day and gone forever the next.

Very few of those boys from her first squadron were left when the war was drawing to a close.

She and Terry got on well together from the start. They were a popular couple. When they went out on their first 'secret' date to the cinema on Newmarket's High Street, the entire flight had turned up to fill the rows front and behind.

They had a lot in common. Her father, a regimental sergeant-major in the 5th Dragoon Guards, had died when she was young; Terry had lost both his parents at an early age and was brought up by his sister Carol.

He was Jean's first real romance. There had been a brief pre-war engagement to a journalist on the *Kent Messenger*, but he was in RAF Intelligence now and they had drifted apart. There was no time for long engagements in wartime, although Terry had insisted on getting her an emerald ring to go with the one-guinea gold wedding band which was all the Government would allow wartime brides to buy.

The wedding at Caxton Hall had been a rush job. She had not expected a white wedding, but she wished she had been able to wear a dress instead of having to make do with her uniform. All the boys from the flight had been there and it had been all very much a conveyor belt business: Terry's flight commander was married in the morning; she and Terry in the afternoon.

Still, it had saved the cost of two receptions. After an overnight stay at a Mayfair hotel, they honeymooned at Bramley Grange, the luxury hotel at Guildford where Lord Nuffield had left a standing instruction that all aircrew bills should be sent to him.

The days had sped by and the war had been far away as they toured the countryside in a trap pulled by a horse, known to hundreds of RAF brides, called 'John Brown'.

When Terry was posted to the secret squadron two months later, she was posted to Little Staughton, some ten miles away, and their married life took on a curious pattern:

There were long leaves spent with Carol at the home in Torquay where she had gone to escape the London blitz, weekend passes at Bramley Grange, and the occasional night together during the weekdays at a village halfway between Tempsford and Little Staughton.

They stayed there at the White Horse, an ancient inn with sloping, uneven floors, where the boys would often join them for a drink and a sing-song, back in those wild days of 1944. Now so many of them were no more than young faces grinning out from a wedding photograph which was already beginning to fade.

'Sugar' had gone and so, too, had poor, dear Bunney. And old 'Crafty' Binns, who had so often walked her home from the mess, had survived the Hudson operations only to be killed in a Stirling.

Ronnie Morris was still flying, and that attractive Canadian, Bob Ferris. Were they out on this awful March night? And where was Terry now, the man among a hundred others who had swept her off her feet because he had been able to make her laugh in her brittle administration world of casualty returns.

Jean Helfer, née Harris, was a level-headed young woman, not given to superstitious fears, and when she awoke from a dream and heard Terry's voice calling out to her, she dismissed it for what it was: a dream. She had cried enough for the young men who had not come back to cry now for a husband who was probably tucked up safely in bed. So she went back to sleep, only vaguely uneasy. The telephone call came the next day.

13

The plan was simple. The only difficulty would be dropping the agents in the right spot, deep in the heart of Germany, at a time when the country was in chaos and every stranger a potential terrorist.

The three men chosen for the job were young, but very experienced in their trade of clandestine warfare.

They were all nineteen years old and students when war was declared. Guy Corbisier, who came from a wealthy family in the shipping industry, was at the Lycée Française in Antwerp.

Jean Morel was at the college of Sainte-Marie in Brussels.

Léon de Winter was about to take his entrance examination to become a cadet at Belgium's military academy.

When the Germans occupied their country in 1940 they resolved, independently, to escape to England. De Winter travelled down one of the early escape lines, probably the one set up by his countrywoman Andrée de Jongh. But soon after crossing the Pyrenees he ran into trouble and spent many long, frustrating months in the concentration camp at Miranda de Ebro before he was able to make his way to freedom.

It was at the camp that he met Morel, who had walked into Spain with two Belgian newspaper workers by way of the classic route through L'Iraty only to bump into Franco's police just as he was congratulating himself on reaching safety.

Corbisier managed to get as far as Pamplona before the Spanish caught up with him, but he was not as lucky as his two compatriots. The police hurriedly bundled him into a van and drove him back to the border where he was handed over to the Vichy authorities and put into a French prison.

He did not stay there for long. With the help of sympathetic Frenchmen he made his escape across the Pyrenees yet again, this time making contact with the British end of the escape line.

Like Morel and de Winter he reported in London to the Belgian Government-in-exile where he, too, volunteered for special missions with the *Service de Renseignement et d'Action* (SRA), which co-operated closely with the British under the watchful eye of SOE.

They were among a total of about 250 highly-trained *agents parachutistes* who were trained by the British and dropped back into

Belgium to organise resistance. About 150 of them died in action or captivity.

By the summer of 1944 the trio of ex-students were primed and ready to go on three different missions. De Winter went into the field shortly before D-Day to rejoin a *réseau* with which he had been working in the early days, and Corbisier was dropped at Gembloux to organise active resistance groups south of Brussels in the area where another dictator had met his Waterloo.

Morel was dropped further west at Leuze and was in action within minutes of landing. The Germans had known he was coming and an ambush was prepared at the reception area. With gunfire blazing all around them, Morel and a companion called Kelson, managed to slip through the net, and by creeping half-submerged along the bed of a stream they were able to put tracker dogs off their scent to make good their escape.

Later, the speed of the Allied advance made them all redundant. Their war in Belgium was virtually over, but not their hatred of Nazism. While all about them their countrymen were cheering the liberation and settling down to the unreal days of peace, they never for one moment hesitated or wavered from the course they had set back in 1940.

It was not enough that the Germans should be driven out of Belgium; they had to be beaten decisively, once and for all, so that Belgium would never again be forced to submit to the oppressor from across the Rhine.

So they opted to continue the fight instead of returning to their homes and families. As far as the Belgian Government was concerned, they were sent on indefinite leave on 30 November 1944, and how they spent that leave was entirely their own affair.

The Belgian bureaucracy, as much sticklers for protocol as any other bureaucracy the world over, chose not to know officially that their nationals may be working for a friendly foreign power.

So at a time when SOE was desperately scratching around for recruits capable of working in Germany, Corbisier, Morel and de Winter appeared at Baker Street to offer their services. Their qualifications were excellent. They had experience of work in the field and were motiviated by ideals rather than by the still worthy, but more dangerous spirit of adventure.

Adventurers were in it for the money and the thrills, and might take unnecessary risks. Idealists were more likely to be guided by a sense of purpose and put their mission before personal gratification.

On the debit side they were all Walloons – French-speaking Belgians – but as such they could still pass themselves off as sympathetic to the German cause if they were ever in a tight corner. After all, there *were* Walloons and Flemings fighting side-by-side with the Germans as part of an SS Division on the Russian Front.

So they took their indefinite leave in England, and were packed off back to school for a rigorous session of SOE training. They learned about life in wartime Germany, about the black-out, the black market, and how to use their ration cards. They were brought up to date on the versions of war news being fed to the Germans through Goebbels' propaganda machine, and they were instructed to memorise the latest jokes and the names of cult figures on the stage, in films and on radio.

After six weeks of study more intensive than anything they had experienced at their pre-war colleges, they passed all their finals and were told to report to an office in London for their final briefing.

On 13 February 1945, some 800 British bombers pulverised the beautiful and ancient German city of Dresden.

The Americans followed up the next day and the day after, creating firestorms of such intensity in an already devastated wasteland that thousands of bodies were never recovered.

A fourth and final raid was carried out on 2 March as Corbisier, de Winter and Morel were heading east in a Hudson flown by Chris Ragan. The plan was to drop them in the countryside where they would be able to mingle with the shattered survivors fleeing from the city and the oncoming Red Army.

They were carrying papers which identified them as conscripted workers in the German's foreign labour force in Dresden. It was not anticipated that they would have any problems. The Germans were believed to be demoralised by the bombing and in all likelihood their highly efficient administrative machine would have broken down with all the records and documents lost or destroyed.

The three Belgians, all with temporary commissions as lieutenants on the British Army payroll in case they should be overrun by the Russians, were to infiltrate the columns of refugees streaming westwards. They were equipped with a radio to send reports back to London, and with explosives to blow vital bridges and railway lines to add to the confusion in the enemy rear.

Quite simply, their orders were to cause the maximum chaos in an already chaotic situation. If at the same time they were able to send back any intelligence on troop movements by the Germans – and possibly by the Russians? – then so much the better.

But when Dresden was bombed for that fourth time and the three agents were finally on their way by Hudson, Chris Ragan was forced to abort within forty miles of the blazing city because of the weather. A second attempt by Ronnie Morris the following night was also abandoned and the Belgians were taken back to London to await more favourable conditions.

On 20 March they were driven to Tempsford in the same staff car with blacked out windows. Once again they went through the routine at the ramshackle building called Gilbraltar Farm. Their pockets were checked for incriminating evidence like British coins and cigarettes, then they were helped into their bulky flying suits and strapped into their parachute harnesses.

The staff car took them the remaining few hundred yards where the bulky outline of a Hudson could be seen against the early evening sky.

There they met the crew: Flight Lieutenant Helfer, with Thompson, Escreet and Johnson by now all promoted to the rank of flying officer. There were no introductions. Corbisier had assumed his field name of *Benedict*, Morel was *Express* and de Winter, obscurely, was *Leader* although Corbisier had actually been selected to command the team.

For the sacrifice they were to make that night, all three of them were to be awarded posthumously the Croix de Guerre with Palm, and become in death Chevaliers of the Order of Leopold.

There was just a brief moment when the three young Belgians and the four RAF officers stood together on the tarmac in the twilight of that Tuesday on the eve of the first day of spring.

Then, with casual farewells to the ground crew, all seven climbed aboard the Hudson N-for-Nan.

*

About 0045 hours, March 21, 1945: The parish priest of Hupperdange was about to go to bed when he heard the sound of engines. He listened anxiously for a moment, then relaxed. It was an aeroplane, not tanks. It had been a bad time for the village. They had brought out the flags for the victory celebrations, then just before Christmas the Germans had come back and their American liberators had gone as suddenly as they had arrived with their candy and chewing gum, and once more the streets had swarmed with the field-grey of the Wehrmacht.

Then just as suddenly the Germans had retreated once more, destroying everything in their way, and when the Americans came back they told the villagers that this time it would be for good. What became known as the Battle of the Bulge was over and there would be no more fighting in war-weary Luxembourg.

There was only a blackness in the forests of the Ardennes and a silvery glint of the River Oûr as N-for-Nan roared on through the night. They had tried, pushing themselves and their aircraft to the limits of endurance, but the weather had beaten them and now it was back to Blighty and breakfast.

Below them but unseen, the Allied armies were massing at their jumping off positions for the start of the spring offensive . . . a woman slept in a cottage next to her children . . . a priest listened for the sounds of war . . .

. . . It was during his last leave after Christmas that Ray Escreet told his mother: 'It's hard to believe, but twenty years after all this is over men will be walking on the moon.'

He was wrong by no more than a few years, but in any case it was only a figure of speech to illustrate his disgust at the technological marvels of which man was capable in the air, while still making a mess of things on the ground.

He had been kept waiting for several hours to catch the train taking him home on leave. It was then, too, that he allowed some of the tensions of clandestine operations to break through the casual manner he affected to allay the fears of his parents.

'When this war is over,' he said, 'I'm going to tell you something about the moon. I'll tell you stories that'll make your hair stand on end. I'm sick and tired of moonlight. There's no romance in it, I'm beginning to hate it.'

They had no idea what he was talking about, although his father guessed. He remembered how it had been in the other war, when men had cowered in holes in the ground to avoid the light of the moon and flares.

Ray's leave soon came to an end and after seven days with his family he set off with Ruth, his fiancée, to visit her mother in Somerset before returning to Tempsford. They left at six in the morning. Janet Escreet watched them from her usual place at the front bedroom window. Frank Escreet had left home earlier to begin his day's work at the fruit and vegetable market.

He caught sight of them fleetingly on a bus going through Paragon Square on the way to Hull railway station, and he waved as they passed.

The bus had gone before he could notice if they had waved back.

Harry Johnson was more than just a little upset. After all the work he had done on it, and all the money he had spent, and still the thing refused to go.

This time it had broken down at Grantham. It was his pride and joy; a Ford Seven replica of the one acquired by Tommy Thompson after 'Scotty' had been killed. But at least Tommy's did not keep breaking down although it *did* need to be kicked into life on these cold mornings.

Now he would have to wait until the moon period ended before he could hitch a lift back to Grantham to pick it up. Edith was right. He was too much of a dreamer to know anything about the mechanics of a complicated bit of machinery like a car.

His sister, meanwhile, was feeling uneasy. Harry had seemed different on his last leave. Friends had called for the weekend, and the boys had spent their time playing billiards and snooker on a battered old table they had set up in the back room.

He had been even quieter than usual, and on the day before he was due to return to Tempsford he had spent a restless night in the room next to hers, tossing and turning, and occasionally murmuring inaudible words in his fitful sleep.

She knew how much her younger brother hated the war.

Tommy Thompson had a lot to think about. He was going to be a father. He had not wanted children until the war was over, because he could still remember the mental and physical collapse of a girl married to one of his close friends. She had not been able to love or care for the child born shortly after her husband had been killed in action.

He had hated the thought of that happening to Olive. But a child was on the way nevertheless. They had talked about it on his last weekend pass as they wandered with arms around each other through the beautiful pinewoods of Woburn Sands.

'If it's a girl I want her to be called Anne,' he said, 'and I don't care if you put an "e" on the end or not. Anne! It's a wizard name.'

He knew there was to be another operation that night. A long one, probably into Germany. At breakfast Olive had given him shredded wheat and she had been unable to understand his laughter until he told her they fed horses with stuff that looked just the same back home on the farm in Waipiro Bay.

As he was leaving home for the half-hour drive to Tempsford she asked if he wanted to take a clean pair of socks. He thought about it for a moment.

'No,' he replied, 'these will do.'

And as he stepped out into the road he squared away his cap at the regulation angle instead of settling it at the usual rakish tilt over one eye, and she looked at him oddly as he turned away.

He had never done that before. He looked so serious, so different.

Terence Helfer knew it was going to be a rough operation. The weather would be bad over the target, but there was no chance of it being scrubbed for a third time as long as there was a chance of it being successful.

He wondered if Jean would ring. She always did during the moon period, at about seven in the evening. If she did tonight it would be too late, he would be already on his way.

They had not seen each other for several days now, not since shortly after the beginning of the month when they had dropped two 'Joes' over Denmark on their last operation. This time it would be to Germany, for the sixth time. He had been there before on routine bombing operations in the old days, and he knew just how rough it could be.

That all seemed in the dim and distant past now, before he met Jean at Newmarket – at a church parade, of all places. He was in charge of a contingent of aircrew at the time, marching them in their usual slovenly fashion down the High Street, followed by a well-drilled WAAF unit who were stepping out briskly with their arms snapping up to shoulder level in the approved military style.

Even in their uniforms, with flat shoes and drab stockings of blue lisle, they were a smart looking lot and always drew admiring glances from civilians as they went by.

As the marching files reached a steep hill, the airmen lengthened their shambling stride and just allowed gravity to take them down. What Helfer was not aware of at the time was the plight of the women behind. His men should have shortened their stride for the hill, to keep the formation in order.

Instead, there was chaos at the back, with the WAAFs having to break into a trot to keep up.

When they reached the church he was approached by the section-officer in charge and told in no uncertain terms that his men were thoughtless, beastly and had no idea how to march.

But both of them knew that aircrew were notoriously ill-disposed to the disciplines of the barrack square. No one who had flown over Germany need ever be intimidated by drill sergeants.

Helfer and the young WAAF section-officer sat together during the church service and when it was over, their difference was forgotten, and they marched their parties back to base, this time in step. A love affair was born.

Now they were married and he was about to go out on another op. He left the mess with his crew, without knowing if she had tried to call him.

She had, but the switchboard was jammed by calls from other wives and sweethearts.

*

About 0045 hours, 21 March 1945: As the priest listened to the fading drone of the aircraft engines he heard another sound, sharp and imperative, and he recognised it as a burst of machine-gun fire. Then another burst, and another, staccato in the night air, and as he rushed to the window he saw a bright glow in the sky, and just as quickly it had gone and there was silence . . .

. . . It was all over in seconds. Pieces of molten metal exploded through the cabin, and a gout of flame mushroomed through the floor from ruptured fuel lines.

The world turned crazily as the aircraft sloped down at a steep angle, hurtling out of control with metalwork crumpling and disintegrating. There was a rush of cold air on his blistering face as an escape hatch above his head flew open. He reached up to lever himself out, and as the slipstream snatched at him he remembered to reach for the ripcord before he blacked out with pain and shock.

Several minutes after those three bursts of gunfire the priest's doorbell rang. A tall man in a tattered uniform stood outside.

'Help me, please,' he said. 'I am an RAF officer . . .

. . . The bodies were found by a detachment of Belgian soldiers bivouacking in the Maulesmühle area. They were shown the way by a woman who had heard the aircraft come down.

'The engines were very loud and then there was a noise like an explosion,' Madame Daman-Uilbert told them, and she pointed the way to a footpath which would take them up the hillside.

The men had died in their aircraft. It was still smouldering, the metal too hot to touch. At first the soldiers thought there were only four of them, but a little later it was established that there had been six. They were buried in temporary graves next to the wreckage and the soldiers moved on.

In a house at Hupperdange a few miles away a man was lying on a mattress, covered by a blanket. Father Michel Majerus, the parish priest, brought him yet another cup of coffee, but he was still unable to hold it. His hands were burned, and there was a particularly deep wound on his right wrist where red hot metal had burned down to the bone.

His face was a mass of burned skin around the eyes, forcing his eyelids tightly shut so that he thought for a time he was going blind.

The priest kept apologising for his reluctance to open the door. 'My sister, *monsieur*, she thought you were a German,' he explained. 'She was afraid it was a German trap.'

The injured man tried to get up. 'Please,' he said, 'you must find the others, my comrades.'

Father Majerus soothed him, pressing him back gently on the pillow and knowing the lie even as he spoke it. 'I do not think your aeroplane crashed, *monsieur*. There was no explosion. I cannot see any fire.'

'Are you sure?'

'I am sure.'

After dressing the survivor's burns with a bandage made from the only linen they had, his sister spooned generously again into the meagre supply of coffee missed by the Germans who had looted the area during their retreat a few weeks earlier.

'How did you fall?' he asked.

'I don't know,' the man replied. 'Suddenly there was an explosion. The plane was on fire. I was burning all over.'

He became silent again then suddenly exclaimed, 'My parachute. Is my parachute burned?'

During his exit from the aircraft the pack containing his parachute harness had caught fire, but the flames had gone out before reaching the silken canopy, and it had brought him down safely although he could remember none of it.

He remembered finding himself by a roadway and how he had staggered along it until he came to a cottage with a light in the window. He knocked, but the people inside refused to come to the door. Then he spotted a barn and managed to prise open a heavy door, only to shut it hurriedly when a dog began barking.

With his strength fading fast he continued along the road until he saw what appeared to be a small church, and next to it a house with steps leading up to the front door.

He walked up the steps and rang the bell, not quite believing the incongruous situation was real. Here he was, in the dead of night, wearing torn flying gear and feeling he was on fire all over, ringing a stranger's doorbell as if he were paying a normal visit.

In spite of his burned hands and blurred eyesight he was able to draw a rough diagram of the road he had taken to the priest's house, and Father Majerus went out later and found a flying helmet where the injured man said he had left it. A parachute was lying in folds nearby. As there was neither a telephone nor a car in the village, a messenger was sent to Clervaux, where the forward elements of an American infantry division were resting before their push to the Rhine.

The officer in charge sent a party out to investigate at daybreak, but when they stepped inside the priest's house all they could see in the darkened room was a prone figure lying on a mattress on the floor, with what appeared to be jackboots protruding from the blankets.

One of the GI's exclaimed angrily and viciously kicked the wounded man in the ribs. Then they left, clattering down the front steps pursued by the horrified priest and his sister.

'He is English, he is an English officer,' they shouted.

The soldiers stopped and went back to investigate, and amid a babble of apologies and profanities, they lifted him gently into their jeep and delivered him to a mobile field hospital at Clervaux.

Even then his ordeal was not quite over. By now completely unable to see and able to move one arm only with difficulty, he was borne along in the rear of the American advance. Through the pain and fatigue he could not help thinking he was in as much danger as he had ever been in five years of war; more so on one occasion when the hospital unit blundered into a minefield.

Eventually the infantry reached the small German town of Trier on the east bank of the River Mosel, and to his intense relief he heard the clipped and unmistakable accent of a British liaison officer. He was safe at last and soon he would be going home.

Two weeks after she was told he had been posted missing and believed killed in action, Jean Helfer received a second telephone call.

Her husband was alive.

Epilogue

Terence Helfer was never to forget his ordeal. He did not attempt to contact the relatives of his dead friends as there was nothing he could say to them. By the time he had recovered from his injuries the war was about to end and he could not bring himself to re-open the wounds of others.

What could he tell them? That the men they loved had died trapped in a burning aircraft and he had been unable to help them?

There was Janet Escreet, living in hope for weeks that her son had escaped and was in a prisoner-of-war camp, and her husband Frank who knew the truth but did not want to believe it . . .

Edith Johnson, haunted by the memory of her gentle brother's last restless night at home . . .

And Olive Thompson, who was soon to give birth to a daughter and, remembering, was to call her Anne . . .

Helfer owed his life to his habitual practice of using his parachute as a cushion while flying, in the manner of fighter pilots. Thompson, crammed in the perspex bubble of his gun turret would certainly not have been wearing his.

Nor would Escreet and Johnson. They were too bulky for comfortable movement. But Corbisier, de Winter and Morel would have been wearing theirs, and the fact that none of them managed to get out of the aircraft indicates that they were killed or incapacitated when the plane was hit.

Helfer remembers only the burst of firing, an explosion, the disintegration of the controls which burned through his wrists, and his exit through the escape hatch when everything around him was falling apart.

That N-for-Nan should have been shot down when the war was all but over is but one tragedy among millions. There will always be someone who is the last man to die, and first or last it is all the same to the dead.

The real tragedy is the strong possibility that Helfer was shot down by an American interceptor. They were active in the area at the time because of the impending offensive, and a solitary aircraft crossing the zone would immediately be a suspected 'bandit'.

The Americans were not familiar with the Hudson and the only other twin-engine aircraft still in use by the Allies were the Wellingtons which flew with the bomber streams; and then only occasionally since 1943.

But the Luftwaffe's Messerschmitt 110 and Junkers 88 both had twin engines and were used in a nightfighter role. And like the Hudson, the Messerschmitt also had a distinctive twin tailplane. It would have been easy to make a mistake.

Helfer himself prefers to believe his attacker was a German, and certainly the method used bore all the hallmarks of the Luftwaffe. Many of their nightfighters were equipped with *schräge musik*, a pair of upward-sloping cannon which enabled the pilots to creep up on a bomber's blind side from below and rip its belly open from close range. It was a classic mode of attack which the bombers had no defence against.

But German or American, it makes little difference now; the nightfighters of any nationality were just part of the hazards facing Hudson crews in their lonely sorties across the night skies of Western Europe.

When Helfer returned to the squadron the following month it was to find many of the old faces gone. It was of little consolation to receive an immediate award of the DFC. In recommending him for the award Wing Commander Len Ratcliff wrote: 'In spite of this most unpleasant experience, Flight Lieutenant Helfer remains keen on operational flying.'

The station commander, Group Captain Palmer, added: '. . . (he) has shown great determination to carry out the most hazardous missions.'

He and his crew were responsible for putting 35 agents into enemy territory, and the question of whether their eventual sacrifice was worth it is as irrelevant as the answer. There was a war on and the Hudson crews had a job to do, and while their individual efforts in the closing stages of the war may have been no more than pin-pricks, final victory was possible only because there were enough men and women who believed it was all worth while.

In the end the beast of Nazism was bled to death by those pin-pricks.

After the disaster of the night of 21 March the Hudson flight was crippled, but not defeated. Eleven more operational sorties were made to Germany and one to Holland during April. Most of them were flown by Harold Ibbott, who won a DFC, Ronald Morris, who was awarded a Flying Cross by the Dutch, and a replacement pilot from Canada called J.L. Nicholson.

Buster Webb had an engine failure on his way back from one operation in P-for-Peter. His crew of Watson-Smyth, Smith and Gough all bailed out and landed safely. Webb stayed at the controls and crash-landed at Dorking, receiving only a slight injury.

By the end of the month the remaining two Hudsons had put another 23 agents into Germany, and two into Holland, the last operational sortie of the war being flown by Flying Officer Nicholson on 24 April.

The war ended on 8 May. But not the dying. Ten days after the German surrender, when 'A' Flight was carrying out a peacetime role of ferrying prisoners-of-war back to England, a replacement crew with a flying officer called Hawkins was detailed to fly a Hudson to Luneberg. He arrived to find only two men there awaiting transport home.

He was diverted to Brussels to pick up another batch when the aircraft displayed the landing characteristic which all Hudson pilots had learned to respect during those hazardous pick-ups in the moonlit fields of France.

Hawkins hit the runway too hard and the aircraft bounced badly, flying level for a short time before rearing up steeply, then falling back in a tail slide before stalling and nosediving onto the tarmac. The Hudson burst into flames. There were no survivors.

No 161 Squadron was disbanded a few weeks later.

What then did it achieve, this 'Most Secret' unit whose Broken Shackle emblem and motto – 'Liberate' – symbolised the fight against tyranny? When the peace was only a few weeks old, Eisenhower wrote to Colin Gubbins, Director of SOE:

> ... I consider that the disruption of enemy rail communications, the harassing of German road moves, and the continual and increasing strain placed on the German war economy and internal security services throughout Occupied Europe by the organised forces of resistance, played a very considerable part in our complete and final victory.

Without the unstinting efforts of the secret squadrons, that resistance would have been without teeth or muscle. The Hudsons' part in that effort was considerable. There were no more than six aircraft available at the flight's disposal at any one time, and a flying strength of about thirty men.

But their pick-up operations were vital in that they were able to carry more passengers than the Lysanders in a single operation . . .